GREAT DAYS OUT 1998

GREAT DAYS OUT 1998

A calendar of exciting events
in Britain in 1998

BFP BOOKS London

British Library Cataloguing in Publication Data:

A catalogue record for this book is available from the British Library

ISBN 0-907297-46-3

Published by BFP Books, Focus House, 497 Green Lanes, London N13 4BP.
Printed by Biddles Ltd, Guildford, Surrey.

Contents

Introduction

Great Days Out 1998 provides a comprehensive selection of the many interesting and entertaining events taking place throughout Britain in the coming year. It includes information on over 800 individual events, covering the widest possible range of enthusiasms, but the emphasis is on visual excitement and "Things to see". Thus most of these events will appeal not only to people who are specifically interested in those subjects, but to anyone looking for a "great day out" – a day during which you can see many interesting and exciting things, whether it be top sporting action or the natural beauties of the flower show.

The events are listed in twelve monthly sections from January to December. Each gives the date(s), the official title of the event, the venue, and a short description of what can be seen at the event.

All of the events and dates given here were confirmed by the organisers at the time of going to press. Those few whose dates were still only provisional at that time are marked with an asterisk (*). However, it is always possible that due to unforeseen circumstances events may be cancelled or rescheduled. Similarly, opening or start times may also be unconfirmed or subject to change at short notice. It is therefore always advisable that such details be checked with the organisers nearer to the date of the event.

Every entry includes a contact name and address and/or telephone number to assist in obtaining further information. However, these are busy people and we would ask readers not to bother organisers with minor inquiries about matters that may easily be ascertained at the event itself.

A considerable number of these events are free or held in public spaces where a fee is not applicable (N/A). For the others admission charges are given where possible, but often these are not firmly set until nearer the time of the event, in which case they are "TBA" (To Be Announced). Where fees for the previous year's event are known, these are provided as a guide (i.e. 1997 guide: £5 adults; £2 children).

At the back of the book there is not only a standard general index, but also a regional index to assist you in finding events in your own region or in areas which you may be planning to visit.

We hope this guide will help you to enjoy many Great Days Out!

January

1 Jan
THE LONDON PARADE
A two-and-a-quarter mile route in Westminster, starting at Parliament Square, along Whitehall, round Trafalgar Square, along Piccadilly, ending at Berkeley Square.
The largest and most colourful street event of its kind in the world, witnessed by around a million spectators.
Things to see: Parade headed by the The Lord Mayor of Westminster. 8000 performers from all over the USA, Europe and the UK entertain the crowds. Award-winning marching bands, dancers, cheerleaders, clowns and spectacular floats and super-giant balloons are all on display.
Contact: Mark Phillips, Press & Publicity, London Parade Ltd, Research House, Fraser Road, Perivale, Middlesex UB6 7AQ. Tel: 0181-566 8586.
Admission: Free. **Times**: 12 noon - 3pm approx.

1 Jan
NEW YEAR'S DAY BOYS & MENS BA'
Through the streets of Kirkwall, Orkney.
A centuries-old game of mass street football.
Things to see: Mass street football played between Up-the-Gates (Uppies) and Down-the-Gates (Doonies). Goals are the site of an old castle and the waters of the harbour. Upwards of 200 men take part and each side attempts to take the ba' (ball) to its own goal. The ba' can be carried, kicked or smuggled – there are no rules and games can last for hours.
Contact: J D M Robertson, Shore Street, Kirkwall, Orkney. Tel: 01856 872961.
Admission: N/A. **Times**: Boys ba' thrown up at 10.30am, and the Mens ba' thrown up at 1pm.

1 Jan
NEW YEAR'S DAY TREASURE TRAIL
Leeds Castle, Maidstone, Kent.
Treasure hunt.
Things to see: Intriguing clues lead the visitor all round the Castle grounds. An invigorating, entertaining and informative way to start the New Year. Super prizes also on offer.
Contact: Leeds Castle, Maidstone, Kent ME17 1PL. Tel: 01622 765400.
Admission: £6.50 adults; £5 students/OAPs. Free admission for accompanied children. **Times**: 10am - 2pm.

1-4 Jan
HOLIDAY ACTITIVIES
The National Waterways Museum, Llanthony Warehouse, Gloucester Docks.
Fun activities.
Things to see: Special fun activities for all the family included in admission price. Up to 40 stationary engines on display and working, within the Museum.
Contact: Mary Mills, Media/PR, National Waterways Museum, Llanthony Warehouse, Gloucester Docks, Gloucester GL1 2EH. Tel: 01452 318054.
Admission: £4.50 adults; £3.50 children/OAPs. **Times**: 10am - 5pm approx.

3-4 Jan
DEVON COUNTY ANTIQUES FAIR
Westpoint Exhibition Centre, Clyst St Mary, Exeter, Devon.
Major antiques fair.

Things to see: Beautiful antiques and collectables among the estimated one million items on offer. 500 stands in one hall. Plus free lectures, seminars and exhibitions.
Contact: Val Dennis, Devon Counties Antiques Fairs, The Glebe House, Nymet Tracey, Crediton, Devon EX17 6DB. Tel: 01363 82571.
Admission: £3.50 adults; children free. **Times**: Sat: 10am - 5pm. Sun: 10am - 5pm.

3-4 Jan
SHOW JUMPING
Towerlands, Panfield Road, Braintree, Essex.
Show jumping event.
Things to see: Junior Affiliated show jumping.
Contact: The Secretary, Towerlands Equestrian Centre, Panfield Road, Braintree, Essex. Tel: 01376 326802.
Admission: Free. **Times**: From 9.30am.

3-11 Jan
EMBASSY WORLD PROFESSIONAL DARTS CHAMPIONSHIP
Lakeside Country Club, Wharf Road, Frimley Green, Nr Camberley, Surrey GU16 6PT.
Top international darts championship.
Things to see: Top darts players, darts action, presentations, etc. All matches on stage.
Contact: Olly Croft, British Darts Organisation, 2 Pages Lane, Muswell Hill, London N10 1PS. Tel: 0181-883 5544. Fax: 0181-883 0109.
Admission: Varies from £2 to £7. **Times**: Variable, check with the organisers.

6 Jan
ANCIENT GAME OF HAXEY HOOD
Haxey Village, South Yorkshire.
Traditional event.
Things to see: A game similar to rugby played between the pubs of two villages. The ancient rules are firmly adhered to.
Contact: Mr P Coggon, Beau-Monde, Fields Road, Haxey, Doncaster DN9 2LN. Tel: 01427 752845.
Admission: N/A. **Times**: From 11am.

6 Jan-1 Feb
HOLIDAY ON ICE - 'THE BROADWAY SHOW'
Brighton Centre, Brighton, East Sussex.
Spectacular ice show for all the family.
Things to see: Ice skating, comedy, music.
Contact: Box Office, Brighton Centre, Brighton, East Sussex BN1 2GR. Tel: 01273 202881.
Admission: Various. **Times**: Various.

9 Jan
SCALLOWAY FIRE FESTIVAL
Scalloway, Shetland.
Traditional procession.
Things to see: Procession and burning galley, followed by squad acts in several halls.
Contact: Mrs E Gilbertson, 1 Blydoit Park, Scalloway, Shetland. Tel: 01595 880345.
Admission: £5 - £6. **Times**: From 7pm.

9-18 Jan
LONDON INTERNATIONAL BOAT SHOW
Earl's Court Exhibition Centre, London.
One of the UK's largest public events and the world's best known boat show.

Things to see: A large selection of boats and other craft covering all aspects of the leisure marine industry. Over 650 exhibitors.
Contact: National Boat Shows Ltd, Meadlake Place, Thorpe Lea Road, Egham, Surrey TW20 8HE. Tel: 01784 473377.
Admission: £9 adults (each adult admission can include two children under 16 free). **Times**: Show open from 10am - 7pm daily except Sun 12 Jan: 10am - 6pm.

10 Jan
BURNING OF THE CLAVIE
Various venues, Burghead, Moray.
Ancient custom.
Things to see: Half a barrel of whisky filled with tar and wood is lit and paraded around the village to drive out evil spirits.
Contact:. Aberdeen & Grampian Tourist Board, Area Office, 17 High St, Elgin, Moray IV30 1EG. Tel: 01343 543388.
Admission: N/A. **Times**: TBA.

10 Jan
OXONIAN CYCLING CLUB CYCLOCROSS RACES
Great Haseley Village Hall, Great Haseley, Nr Wheatley, Oxon.
Three cyclo-cross races for under 12s, under 16s and over 16s.
Things to see: Cyclists racing in riding positions, in bunches, individually and running with their bikes on their shoulders up slopes. The course is very open around fields and woodland with good vantage points.
Contact: John Vallis, 11 Turnberry Close, Bicester, Oxon OX6 7YQ. Tel: 01869 247145.
Admission: Free. **Times**: 10.45am for under 12s; 11am under 16s; 12 noon over 16s.

Dates can change, events can be cancelled – Please check with the organisers before setting out!

10-11 Jan
AVOCET CRUISES
Starting and finishing at Exmouth Docks, Exmouth, Devon.
Boat trips taking birdwatchers up the Exe Estuary in winter to see the variety of waterfowl.
Things to see: The Exe Estuary is an internationally important site for birds. Avocet Cruises are a unique opportunity to see more than 50 species, many at close quarters, including the famous wintering avocets. As well as the waders and wildfowl, there is the chance of seaduck at the mouth of the estuary and raptors, such as peregrine falcon, flying over the boat.
Contact: RSPB, 10 Richmond Road, Exeter, Devon EX4 4JA. Tel: 01392 432691. Tickets available from Astbury Travel, 65 Magdalen Road, Exeter EX2 4TA. Tel: 01392 53215.
Admission: £9.50 adults; £5 children (limited availability) **Times**: 10 Jan: 11am. 11 Jan: 12 noon. Cruises last 3-4 hours.

10-25 Jan
LONDON INTERNATIONAL MIME FESTIVAL
South Bank Centre - Institute of Contemporary Arts - BAC, London.
Twenty companies presenting work representing the best international theatre.
Things to see: Circus, acrobatics, mime, masks, object/animation theatre, performance art. Shows for everyone and every taste.
Contact: Mime Festival Information Line. Tel: 0171-637 5661.
Admission: £6-£12. **Times**: Start usually 7 or 8pm, lasting for one hour.

11 Jan
CAMBRIDGESHIRE HARRIERS POINT TO POINT
Cottenham Racecourse, Cottenham, Cambridge.
Point to point racing.
Things to see: Usually seven or eight races. Point-to-pointers (racehorses), stands, caterers, etc.
Contact: Mr M Gingell or Mrs C Tebbs, c/o Horningsea Manor, Horningsea, Cambridge CB5 9JE. Tel: 01223 860291.
Admission: £10 per car with two occupants; £15 with three; £20 with four or more. **Times**: 12 noon - 3.30pm approx (TBA).

16-18 Jan
SHOW JUMPING
Towerlands, Panfield Road, Braintree, Essex.
Show jumping event.
Things to see: Senior Affiliated show jumping with top riders.
Contact: The Secretary, Towerlands Equestrian Centre, Panfield Road, Braintree, Essex. Tel: 01376 326802.
Admission: Free. **Times**: From 9.30am.

17 Jan
COCA-COLA INTERNATIONAL CROSS COUNTRY
Barnett Demensne, Belfast.
International cross country race. Part of the IAAF World Cross Challenge.
Things to see: Top class international runners from both the home countries and further afield. Also Junior, Veterans and Open races.
Contact: John Allen, Northern Ireland Amateur Athletic Federation, Athletics House (Mary Peters Track), Old Coach Road, Belfast BT9 5PR. Tel: 01232 602707.
Admission: TBA. **Times**: 11.50am: commencing with Junior, Veterans, and Open races. 1.30pm: Women's International. 2.20pm: Mens International. Last race 3pm. All times provisional.

17 Jan
NORTH NORFOLK HARRIERS POINT-TO-POINT RACES
Higham, Nr Ipswich, Suffolk.
Point to point steeplechase races.
Things to see: Six to seven races, bookmakers and the Tote, trade stands.
Contact: Mrs Tina Hayward, (Secretary), Heydon, Norwich, Norfolk NR11 6RE. Tel: 0378 755168.
Admission: £15 per car. **Times**: First race 12 noon. Last race 3.25pm approx.

17-18 Jan
SLED DOG RALLY
Kielder Forest, Northumberland.
Sled dog racing.
Things to see: Sled dog teams competing in "wilderness" countryside (hopefully, in snow conditions).
Contact: Penny Evans, 3 High St, Lamport, Northampton NN6 9HB (enclose sae with enquiries). Tel: 01604 686281.
Admission: N/A. **Times**: 10am - 3pm approx.

18 Jan
NATIONAL BASKETBALL CUP FINALS
Sheffield Arena, Sheffield.
National basketball finals.
Things to see: Top basketball teams in action.
Contact: Christine O'Donovan, Events Unit, Leader House, Surrey Street, Sheffield S1 2LH. Tel: 0114 203 9387.
Admission: TBA. **Times**: TBA.

22 Jan
DRESSAGE AT TOWERLANDS
Towerlands, Panfield Road, Braintree, Essex.
Dressage event.
Things to see: Unaffiliated dressage.
Contact: The Secretary, Towerlands Equestrian Centre, Panfield Road, Braintree, Essex. Tel: 01376 326802.
Admission: Free. **Times**: From 9.30am.

23 Jan
HADDO BURNS SUPPER
Haddo House Hall, near Tarves, Aberdeenshire.
Traditional Burns Supper.
Things to see: Piping in of haggis, address to haggis, Highland dancers and singers.
Contact: Haddo House Hall, Aberdeenshire AB41 0ER. Tel: 01651 851770. Ticket Office: 01650 851111.
Admission: £15 including supper. **Times**: From 7.30pm.

24-25 Jan
AVOCET CRUISES
Starting and finishing at Exmouth Docks, Exmouth, Devon.
Boat trips taking birdwatchers up the Exe Estuary in winter to see the variety of waterfowl.
Things to see: The Exe Estuary is an internationally important site for birds. Avocet Cruises are a unique opportunity to see more than 50 species, many at close quarters, including the famous wintering avocets. As well as the waders and wildfowl, there is the chance of seaduck at the mouth of the estuary and raptors, such as peregrine falcon, flying over the boat.
Contact: RSPB, 10 Richmond Road, Exeter, Devon EX4 4JA. Tel: 01392 432691. Tickets available from Astbury Travel, 65 Magdalen Road, Exeter EX2 4TA. Tel: 01392 53215.
Admission: £9.50 adults; £5 children (limited availability) **Times**: 24 Jan: 9.30am. 25 Jan: 10.30am. Cruises last 3-4 hours.

24-25 Jan
SLED DOG RALLY
Aviemore, Scotland.
Sled dog racing.
Things to see: Sled dog teams competing in "wilderness" countryside (hopefully, in snow conditions).
Contact: Penny Evans, 3 High St, Lamport, Northampton NN6 9HB (enclose sae with enquiries). Tel: 01604 686281.
Admission: N/A. **Times**: 10am - 3pm approx.

25 Jan
CHARLES I COMMEMORATION
St James's Palace/Horseguards/Whitehall.
Commemoration of execution of Charles I in 1649.
Things to see: 500 costumed members of The English Civil War Society marching to the place of execution to lay a wreath.
Contact: Mr Taylor, The English Civil War Society, 70 Hailgate, Howden, North Humberside DN14 7ST. Tel: 01430 430695.
Admission: N/A. **Times**: Form-up at 11am. Wreath laid at Banqueting House 12 noon.

26 Jan*
WEST PERCY & MILVAIN POINT TO POINT
Ratcheugh Farm, Denwick, Alnwick.
Point to point horse racing.
Things to see: Quality hunt racing.
Contact: Mr R M Landale or Trish Punton, 18-20 Glendale Rd, Wooler, Northumberland NE71 6DW. Tel: 01668 281611.
Admission: £10. £15 per car. **Times**: 1pm - 4.30pm approx.

28 Jan
UP HELLY AA
Lerwick, Shetland Isles.
Viking fire festival.
Things to see: Torchlight procession followed by traditional burning of a Viking longship.
Contact: Mr Stanley Manson, 49 King Harald Street, Lerwick, Shetland. Tel: 01595 693782.
Admission: N/A. **Times**: 9pm - 9pm.

29 Jan-1 Feb
ROAD RACING & SUPERBIKE SHOW
Alexandra Palace, Wood Green, North

London.
London's premier motor cycle show.
Things to see: Displays of racing motor cycles, superbikes and associated products.
Contact: Anita Hancock, Shire PR & Marketing Ltd, The White House, Little Wratting, Haverhill, Suffolk CB9 7UD. Tel: 01440 707055. Ticket Office: 01440 704774.
Admission: £8 adults; £3 children/OAPs. Early booking discount offer for advance ticket at £6 adults; £2.50 children/OAPs. **Times**: Thurs & Fri 10am - 6pm. Sat & Sun 9am - 6pm.

30 Jan-1 Feb
ENGLISH NATIONAL CHAMPIONSHIP
Dolphin Leisure Centre, Haywards Heath.
National badminton championships.
Things to see: Top badminton players in action.
Contact: Maryanne Henchy, Badminton Association of England, Bradwell Road, Loughton Lodge, Milton Keynes MK8 9LA. Tel: 01908 568822. Fax: 01908 566922.
Admission: TBA. **Times**: TBA.

30 Jan-1 Feb
HYDRO-ELECTRIC SCOTTISH NATIONAL BADMINTON CHAMPIONSHIPS
Meadowbank Sports Centre, Edinburgh.
National badminton championship of Scotland.
Things to see: All of Scotland's leading badminton players in action.
Contact: Miss Anne Smillie, Chief Executive, Scottish Badminton Union, Cockburn Centre, 40 Bogmoor Place, Glasgow G51 4TQ. Tel: 0141-445 1218.
Admission: Sat: £1.50 adults; schoolchildren/OAPs 75p. Sun: £3 adults; schoolchildren/OAPs £1.50. **Times**: Fri: evening only. Sat: 9.30am - 9.30pm. Sun: 10am semi finals, 2pm finals.

30 Jan-1 Feb
INDEPENDENT TRAVELLERS WORLD '98
London Arena, Limeharbour, London E14.
The UK's premier consumer travel exhibition dedicated to independent travel.
Things to see: Travellers fashion shows, interactive features, charity travel auction, travellers talk shop, travel writing and photography workshops.
Contact: London Arena, Limeharbour, London E14 9TH. Tel: 0171-538 8880.
Admission: TBA. **Times**: TBA.

31 Jan
DEVON COUNTY ANTIQUES FAIR
Matford Centre in the Exeter Livestock Centre, Matford Park Rd, Marsh Barton, Exeter, Devon.
Major antiques fair.
Things to see: Beautiful antiques and collectables among the many items on offer. 230 stands inside and up to 200 outside stands.
Contact: Val Dennis, Devon Counties Antiques Fairs, The Glebe House, Nymet Tracey, Crediton, Devon EX17 6DB. Tel: 01363 82571.
Admission: £2 adults; children free. **Times**: 10am - 5pm.

February

1 Feb
ANNUAL GRIMALDI SERVICE
Holy Trinity Church, Beechwood Road, Dalston, London E8.
Church service for clowns.
Things to see: Up to 90 clowns in costume attending the service, followed by a clown show in the school afterwards. A space is allocated in the church to photographers and videographers, from which good picture opportunities are possible under the direction of stewards.
Contact: Mrs A Coombs, 9 Stephan Close, London E8 4LJ. Tel: 0171-249 2373.
Admission: Free. **Times**: Service begins at 4pm, but to be sure of getting in, arrive at 3pm.

1 Feb
CHINESE NEW YEAR CELEBRATIONS
Chinatown (Gerrard Street and Leicester Square), London.
Traditional Chinese New Year celebrations.
Things to see: Traditional, colourful street festivities including procession with dragon and lion etc, to celebrate the Year of the Tiger.
Contact: Chinatown Association, 15a Gerrard Street, London W1V 7LA. Tel: 0171-734 5161.
Admission: N/A. **Times**: 11am - 6pm.

1-8 Feb
BENSON & HEDGES MASTERS
Wembley Conference Centre, Empire Way, Wembley.
Snooker tournament.
Things to see: Top level snooker featuring the world's top 16 players.
Contact: Emma Wilson, Karen Earl Ltd, 2 Ledbury Mews West, London W11 2AE. Tel: 0171-243 7113.
Admission: TBA. **Times**: TBA.

4 Feb
SHOW JUMPING
Towerlands, Panfield Road, Braintree, Essex.
Show jumping event.
Things to see: Senior Affiliated show jumping with top riders.
Contact: The Secretary, Towerlands Equestrian Centre, Panfield Road, Braintree, Essex. Tel: 01376 326802.
Admission: Free. **Times**: From 9.30am.

4 Feb
SHROVETIDE FAIR AND PANCAKE RACE
Shrovetide Fair opened on Market Square, Lichfield, Staffs. Pancake Race run along Bore Street and finishing in front of the Guildhall, Lichfield, Staffs.
The Lichfield Shrovetide 'Old Fair' held on Shrove Tuesday has been held for over 300 years on Lichfield's ancient Market Square.
Things to see: The civic procession arrives at the Market Square for noon where the Town Crier makes the proclamation to opent the Fair. The 'pan on bell' then sounds from St Mary's steeple and led by the Mayor and City Councillors, children are invited to take their traditional free ride on the fun fair. The civic party then proceed to the front ot the Guildhall to view the pancake races. Upon completion of the races, the civic party retire to the Guildhall.
Contact: Mr P Young, Town Clerk, Lich-

field City Council, City Council Offices, Guildhall, Lichfield, Staffordshire WS13 6LX. Tel: 01543 250011.
Admission: Free. **Times:** Shrovetide Fair officially opened by the Mayor at 12 noon. Pancake races commence at 12.15pm.

4-8 Feb
OUTDOORS '98
SECC, Glasgow.
The Scottish Boat, Caravan, Camping & Leisure Show.
Things to see: Roller blade rink, archery, climbing walls - all indoors and available to visitors. Together with a large selection of boats, touring caravans, camping equipment, boats, chandlery and outdoor activity holidays.
Contact: Kirsten McAlonan, PR Manager, EVENTEX, Scottish Exhibition & Conference Centre, Glasgow G3 8YW. Tel: 0141-248 3000.
Admission: £5.50 adults; £3 children/OAPs; £14 families. **Times**: Sat: 11am - 9pm. Sun: 11am - 6pm.

5-8 Feb
SPRINGFIELDS HORTICULTURAL EXHIBITION
Springfields Exhibition Centre, Camelgate, Spalding, Lincolnshire.
Indoor flower show.
Things to see: Thousands of spring flowers in landscaped settings.
Contact: Brian Willoughby, Springfields, Camelgate, Spalding, Lincolnshire PE12 6ET. Tel: 01775 724843.
Admission: £2 adults; accompanied children free. **Times**: 11am - 9pm.

6 Feb
ROYAL GUN SALUTE FOR ACCESSION DAY
The Tower of London and in Hyde Park.
Gun salutes to mark the anniversary of the Queen's Accession to the Throne.
Things to see: Royal gun salutes fired in London by the King's Troop Royal Artillery in Hyde Park at 1200 hours (41 Gun Royal Salute) and by the Honourable Artillery Company at the Tower of London at 1300 hours (62 Gun Royal Salute).
Contact: The Information Officer, Public Information Office, Headquarters London District, Chelsea Barracks, London SW1H 8RF.
Admission: Free. **Times**: See above.

7 Feb
OXFORD UNIVERSITY POINT TO POINT
Kingston Blount, Nr Oxford (one mile north of junction 6 of the M40).
Point to point race meeting.
Things to see: At least six races over fences with betting, trade stands and refreshments. The organisers recommend warm, waterproof clothes and strong footwear.
Contact: Mrs W Brown, Manor Farm, Aldbourne, Marlborough, Wiltshire SN8 2BS. Tel: 01672 540328.
Admission: £10, £12 or £20 per car. **Times**: 12 noon - 4pm.

7 Feb
BEARS ONLY FAIR
Civic Hall, Stratford-upon-Avon.
Teddy Bear fair.
Things to see: Collectors' teddy bears including limited editions and show specials, and rare antique bears. Free bear making advice centre. Teddy bear making suppliers, Mohair etc. High quality fair for serious bear-collectors, and great family day out. Free valuations from Bonhams of Chelsea.
Contact: Maddy Aldis, 11 Wesley Street, Eccles, Manchester M30 0UQ. Tel: 0161 7077625.
Admission: £3 adults; £2.50 children; £8 family. **Times**: 10.30am - 4.30pm.

7-8 Feb
AVOCET CRUISES
Starting and finishing at Exmouth Docks, Exmouth, Devon.
Boat trips taking birdwatchers up the Exe

Estuary in winter to see the variety of waterfowl.
Things to see: The Exe Estuary is an internationally important site for birds. Avocet Cruises are a unique opportunity to see more than 50 species, many at close quarters, including the famous wintering avocets. As well as the waders and wildfowl, there is the chance of seaduck at the mouth of the estuary and raptors, such as peregrine falcon, flying over the boat.
Contact: RSPB, 10 Richmond Road, Exeter, Devon EX4 4JA. Tel: 01392 432691. Tickets available from Astbury Travel, 65 Magdalen Road, Exeter EX2 4TA. Tel: 01392 53215.
Admission: £9.50 adults; £5 children (limited availability) **Times**: 7 Feb: 9.30am. 8 Feb: 11am. Cruises last 3-4 hours.

8 Feb
CAMBRIDGE DRAGHOUNDS POINT TO POINT
Cottenham Racecourse, Cottenham, Cambridge.
Point to point racing.
Things to see: Usually seven or eight races. Point-to-pointers (racehorses), stands, caterers, etc.
Contact: Mr M Gingell or Mrs C Tebbs, c/o Horningsea Manor, Horningsea, Cambridge CB5 9JE. TEl: 01223 860291.
Admission: £10 per car with two occupants. £15 with three. £20 with four or more. **Times**: TBA.

9 Feb
ST IVES FEAST CELEBRATIONS
St Ives Town Centre, Cornwall.
Annual event in St Ives.
Things to see: Mayoral procession from Guildhall to the Well at Porthmeor, returning to the Parish Church by 10.30am after a short ceremony. Hurling of the Silver Ball occurs at 10.30am when it is thrown from the wall of the Parish Church by the mayor, is caught by one of the waiting crowd of children and adults and passed from one to another on the beaches and in the streets of the town. Other events throughout the day in this picturesque seaside town.
Contact: The Town Clerk, St Ives Town Council, The Guildhall, St Ives, Cornwall. Tel: 01736 797840.
Admission: N/A. **Times**: From 9.30am approx.

13-15 Feb
SHOW JUMPING
Towerlands, Panfield Road, Braintree, Essex.
Show jumping event.
Things to see: Senior Affiliated show jumping with top riders.
Contact: The Secretary, Towerlands Equestrian Centre, Panfield Road, Braintree, Essex. Tel: 01376 326802.
Admission: Free. **Times**: From 9.30am.

14 Feb
MALLARD ROYLE HORSE/PONY SHOW
Priory E.C., Frensham, Nr Farnham, Surrey.
Horse and pony show.
Things to see: Horses and ponies being shown both indoors and outside. Also in-hand showing classes. Described as a fun "get you started for the season" show. Good bar and restaurant facilities.
Contact: Miss J V Richards, The Rose Cottage, Horseblock Hollow, Barhatch Lane, Cranleigh, Surrey GU6 7NJ. Tel: 01483 277659.
Admission: £3 per car. **Times**: 8.30am - 6pm.

14-22 Feb
JORVIK VIKING FESTIVAL
Various venues in York.
Viking festival.
Things to see: A colourful festival including Viking Warrior's torchlit procession, fireworks displays, longboat races and combat re-enactment.
Contact: Festival Co-ordinator, Jorvik Festival Office, Jorvik Viking Centre,

Coppergate, York YO1 1NT. Tel: 01904 643211.
Admission: Many outdoor events free. **Times**: Various.

14-22 Feb
NATIONAL BOAT, CARAVAN & LEISURE SHOW
National Exhibition Centre, Birmingham (Junction 4, M6).
Displays of boats, caravans, camping equipment and tourism features.
Things to see: Canal boats, motor cruisers, sports boats, inflatables, canoes, touring and motor caravans, holiday homes, tents, trailer tents, accessories, tourist boards and special features.
Contact: Birmingham Post & Mail (Exhibitions) Ltd, 28 Colmore Circus, Birmingham B4 6AX. Tel: 0121-234 5257. Fax: 0121-212 1214.
Admission: £8.50 adults; £5 children/OAPs. **Times**: Weekends 10am - 7pm, weekdays 10am - 6pm.

15 Feb
BADSWORTH POINT TO POINT
Wetherby Racecourse.
Amateur horse racing.
Things to see: Point to point racing, plus entertainment for kids.
Contact: J W Buckley, Throstle Cottage, Aketon, Pontefract, West Yorkshire WF7 6HR. Tel: 01977 706145.
Admission: TBA. **Times**: 11.30am - 4pm.

15 Feb
BOAT JUMBLE
The Historic Dockyard, Chatham, Kent.
Boat jumble.
Things to see: Thousands of block and tackle bargains, from a shackle to a complete boat.
Contact: The Historic Dockyard, Chatham, Kent ME4 4TE. Tel: 01634 812551.
Admission: £2.50 adults; children free. **Times**: 10am - 4pm.

Dates can change, events can be cancelled – Please check with the organisers before setting out!

15 Feb
OXONIAN CYCLING CLUB CYCLO-CROSS RACES
Oxford School, Glanville Road, Cowley, Oxford.
Three cyclo-cross races for under 12s, under 16s and over 16s.
Things to see: Cycle racing around a circuit over mixed terrain which also includes sections where the bike has to be carried, usually up steep slopes or over marshy ground. The course is very open around the school playing fields and woodland with good vantage points on three levels.
Contact: John Vallis, 11 Turnberry Close, Bicester, Oxon OX6 7YQ. Tel: 01869 247145.
Admission: Free. **Times**: 11.30am for under 12s; 12 noon under 16s; 1.15pm over 16s.

15 Feb
TWESELDOWN CLUB POINT-TO-POINT STEEPLECHASES
Tweseldown Racecourse, Aldershot.
All amateur steeplechase meeting.
Things to see: Point-to-point race meeting plus trade stands.
Contact: P Scouller, Bottom House, Bix, Henley, Oxon RG9 6DF. Tel: 01491 574776 home. Tel: 01734 874311 (office).
Admission: £10 (car). **Times**: 12.30pm - 4pm.

16-20 Feb
HALF TERM FUN FOR CHILDREN
Leeds Castle, Maidstone, Kent.
Event designed for children.
Things to see: Learning and fun, including behind the scenes tours and prize quizzes, are combined in an entertainment specially laid out for children. Further details TBA.

© James Clancy

Contact: Leeds Castle, Maidstone, Kent ME17 1PL. Tel: 01622 765400.
Admission: TBA. **Times**: 10am - 3pm.

18 Feb
SHOW JUMPING
Towerlands, Panfield Road, Braintree, Essex.
Show jumping event.
Things to see: Senior Affiliated show jumping with top riders.
Contact: The Secretary, Towerlands Equestrian Centre, Panfield Road, Braintree, Essex. Tel: 01376 326802.
Admission: Free. **Times**: From 9.30am.

21 Feb
ENGLAND V WALES
Rugby Football Union Ground, Twickenham, Middlesex.
Rugby Union international.
Things to see: Top rugby action; part of the Five Nations Series.
Contact: Rugby Football Union. Tel: 0181-892 8161.
Admission: TBA. **Times**: TBA.

21 Feb
SCOTLAND V FRANCE
Murrayfield, Edinburgh.
Rugby Union International.
Things to see: Top class rugby action, part of the 5 Nations series.
Contact: Scottish Rugby Union, Murrayfield, Edinburgh EH12 5PJ. Tel: 0131 346 5000. Fax: 0131346 5001.
Admission: £25; £27; £30. **Times**: 3pm.

21 Feb
UNITED SERVICES POINT TO POINT
Larkhill, Nr Salisbury.
Point to point racing.
Things to see: A full afternoon of point to point racing. Horses and trade stands.
Contact: C J Simpson, HQ SPTA, West Doon Camp, Tilshead, Nr Salisbury SP3 4TS. Tel: 01980 674740.
Admission: £12 per car. **Times**: 12.30pm - 5pm.

21-22 Feb
INTERNATIONAL CANOE EXHIBITION
National Exhibition Centre, Birmingham.
Annual exhibition.
Things to see: Demonstrations of new canoeing equipment.
Contact: P C H Ingram, c/o British Canoe Union, John Dudderidge House, Adbolton Lane, West Bridgford, Nottingham NG2 5AS. Tel: 0115 982 1100.
Admission: £8.50 adults; £5 children. **Times**: Sat: 10am - 7pm. Sun: 10am - 5.30pm.

21-22 Feb
MOTORBIKE '98
Springfields Exhibition Centre & Arena, Spalding, Lincolnshire.
Motorcycling show.
Things to see: All relevant dealerships – Suzuki, Yamaha, Triumph, BMW, Kawasaki, Honda, etc. Demonstrations, go-karts, quad bikes, road safety, trade stands, entertainment, etc.
Contact: Brian Willoughby, Springfields, Spalding, Lincolnshire PE12 6ET. Tel: 01775 724843.
Admission: £3.50 adults; £1 accompanied children; £7 family ticket. **Times**: 10am - 5pm.

24 Feb
THE GREAT SPITALFIELDS PANCAKE RACE
The Old Spitalfields Market, Brushfield St, London E1.
Traditional pancake racing.

Things to see: Teams of four race up and down the market to raise funds for charity.
Contact: Alternative Arts, 47A Brushfield Street, Spitalfields, London E1 6AA. Tel: 0171-375 0441.
Admission: Free. **Times**: From 12.30pm.

24 Feb
SHROVE TUESDAY FOOTBALL GAME
Long Street, Atherstone, Warwickshire.
Traditional street football game.
Things to see: Football is thrown out from Barclays Bank in Long Street at 3pm. Then the ball is kicked up and down the street until at 5pm it is smuggled and the winner is taken back to the Angel Inn in Church Street, Atherstone.
Contact: Mrs M Dixon, 3 Nightingale Close, Atherstone, Warwickshire CV9 3DE. Tel: 01827 716410.
Admission: N/A. **Times**: 3pm - 5pm.

28 Feb-1 Mar
ROAD BIKE SHOW
Sandown Park Exhibition Centre, Portsmouth Rd, Esher, Surrey.
Road bikes.
Things to see: Stands covering all makes and aspects of road bikes with all the latest models and accessories.
Contact:. Nationwide Exhibition (UK) Ltd, PO Box 20, Fishponds, Bristol BS16 5QU. Tel: 0117 970 1370.
Admission: TBA. **Times**: TBA.

March

5-8 Mar
CRUFTS DOG SHOW
National Exhibition Centre, Birmingham.
World's best known and largest dog show.
Things to see: Over 18,000 top pedigree dogs competing to achieve the title of "Best In Show"; obedience, agility and flyball competitions; special Kennel Club Junior Organisation events; sports and television personalities; "Discover Dogs" feature; over 200 trade stands.
Contact: Events Department, The Kennel Club, 1 Clarges Street, London W1Y 8AB. Tel: 0171-493 6651.
Admission: £8 adults; £5 children/OAPs. Tickets available in advance from The Kennel Club Ticket Hotline: 0171-518 1012. **Times**: 8.15am - 7.30pm daily.

5-8 Mar
CREATIVE STITCHES SHOW
Scottish Exhibition Centre, Glasgow.
Sewing, needlecraft & knitting show.
Things to see: Over 120 companies representing virtually every textile craft, demonstrating, advising and selling. "Quick & Easy" workshops will introduce you to new needlecraft or help you improve your current pursuit.
Contact: ICHF Ltd, Dominic House, Seaton Road, Highcliffe, Dorset. Tel: 01425 272711.
Admission: £5.90 adults; £4.90 OAPs.
Times: 9.30am - 5.30pm (Sun 5pm).

6-8 Mar
SHOW JUMPING
Towerlands, Panfield Road, Braintree, Essex.
Show jumping event.
Things to see: Senior Affiliated show jumping with top riders.
Contact: The Secretary, Towerlands Equestrian Centre, Panfield Road, Braintree, Essex. Tel: 01376 326802.
Admission: Free. **Times**: From 9.30am.

7 Mar
WALES V SCOTLAND
Wembley Stadium.
Rugby Union international.
Things to see: Top rugby action; part of the Five Nations Series.
Contact: Press Office, Welsh Rugby Union, Hodge House, St Mary St, Cardiff CF1 1DY. Tel: 01222 781700.
Admission: TBA. **Times**: Kick off 3pm.

7-8 Mar
DEVON COUNTY ANTIQUES FAIR
Westpoint Exhibition Centre, Clyst St Mary, Exeter, Devon.
Antiques fair.
Things to see: Beautiful antiques and collectables among the estimated one million items on offer. 500 stands in one hall. Plus free lectures, seminars and exhibitions.
Contact: Val Dennis, Devon Counties Antiques Fairs, The Glebe House, Nymet Tracey, Crediton, Devon EX17 6DB. Tel:

01363 82571.
Admission: £3.50 adults; children free. **Times**: Sat: 10am - 5pm. Sun: 10am - 5pm.

7-8 Mar
FRIENDS OF THOMAS THE TANK ENGINE
Midland Railway Centre, Butterley Station, Ripley, Derbyshire.
Family fun day with a Thomas the Tank Engine theme.
Things to see: A theme event based on the Thomas the Tank Engine character with locomotives decorated as Thomas's friends, with "Oswald" the talking engine plus the Fat Controller.
Contact: Alan Calladine, Midland Railway Centre, Butterley Station, Ripley, Derbyshire DE5 3QZ. Tel: 01773 747674.
Admission: £7.95 adults; £6.50 OAPs; 2 children free with every adult. **Times**: 10.30am - 4.15pm.

8 Mar
INTERNATIONAL WOMEN'S DAY SHOW
Hackney Empire, Mare St, London E8.
Annual celebration of women.
Things to see: Annual celebration of women with new and established performers from all over the country.
Contact: Alternative Arts, 47A Brushfield Street, London E1 6AA. Tel: 0171-375 0441.
Admission: Tickets from box office on Tel: 0181-985 2424. **Times**: 7.30pm.

10-14 Mar
YONEX ALL ENGLAND OPEN BADMINTON CHAMPIONSHIPS
National Indoor Arena, Birmingham.
Open badminton championships.
Things to see: Top international badminton action, plus trade stands showing the latest clothing and equipment.
Contact: Maryanne Henchy, Badminton Association of England, Bradwell Road, Loughton Lodge, Milton Keynes MK8 9LA. Tel: 01908 568822. Fax: 01908 566922.
Admission: Details from Box Office on 0121-200 2222. **Times**: 10 Mar: 6pm onwards; 11 Mar: 10am onwards; 12 Mar: 10pm onwards; 13 Mar: 6pm onwards; 14 Mar: 1pm onwards (Finals).

11 Mar
SHOW JUMPING
Towerlands, Panfield Road, Braintree, Essex.
Show jumping event.
Things to see: Senior Affiliated show jumping with top riders.
Contact: The Secretary, Towerlands Equestrian Centre, Panfield Road, Braintree, Essex. Tel: 01376 326802.
Admission: Free. **Times**: From 9.30am.

12-15 Mar
SEWING FOR PLEASURE SHOW
NEC, Birmingham.
The National Sewing & Needlecraft Show.
Things to see: 200 stands covering a wide and varied range of fabrics, embroidery, kits, knitting & sewing machines, quilting, lace making and fabric painting.
Contact: ICHF Ltd, Dominic House, Seaton Road, Highcliffe, Dorset. Tel: 01425 272711.
Admission: £8 adults; £7 OAPs. **Times**: 9.30am - 5.30pm (Sun 5pm).

13-14 Mar*
AVOCET CRUISES
Starting and finishing at Exmouth Docks, Exmouth, Devon.
Boat trips taking birdwatchers up the Exe Estuary in winter to see the variety of waterfowl.
Things to see: The Exe Estuary is an internationally important site for birds. Avocet Cruises are a unique opportunity to see more than 50 species, many at close quarters, including the famous wintering avocets. As well as the waders and wildfowl, there is the chance of seaduck at the mouth of the estuary and raptors, such as peregrine falcon, flying over the boat.

Contact: RSPB, 10 Richmond Road, Exeter, Devon EX4 4JA. Tel: 01392 432691. Tickets available from Astbury Travel, 65 Magdalen Road, Exeter EX2 4TA. Tel: 01392 53215.
Admission: £9.50 adults; £5 children (limited availability) **Times**: 13 Mar: 1.30pm. 14 Mar: 2.15pm. Cruises last 3-4 hours.

13-15 Mar
ISLE OF MAN OPEN DARTS CHAMPIONSHIPS
Summerland Leisure Complex, Douglas, Isle of Man.
Darts championships.
Things to see: Top amateur darts players in action. It is hoped that some of the top professionals will also take part. Finals take place on Sunday.
Contact: Special Events Unit, Grandstand, Douglas, Isle of Man IM2 4TB. Tel: 01624 661930.
Admission: Free. **Times**: Fri: 8am - 2am. Sat: 9am - 7pm. Sun: 9am - 5pm.

13-15 Mar
THOMAS THE TANK ENGINE
Didcot Railway Centre, Oxfordshire.
Railway fun day for children with a Thomas the Tank Engine theme.
Things to see: Thomas and friends in steam, the Fat Controller, face painting, Punch and Judy. Also story telling, refreshments and a souvenir shop.
Contact: Jeanette Howse, Didcot Railway Centre, Didcot, Oxfordshire OX11 7NJ. Tel: 01235 817200.
Admission: £6 adult; £4 children; £5 OAPs; £18 family. **Times**: 10am - 5pm.

14 Mar
CARONJOY HORSE SHOW
Priory Equestrian Centre, Frensham, Nr Farnham, Surrey.
A charity horse and pony show.
Things to see: All types of ponies, horses and riders, showing in-hand and ridden. Plus working hunter classes. Good bar and restaurant facilities.
Contact: Miss J V Richards, The Rose Cottage, Horseblock Hollow, Barhatch Lane, Cranleigh, Surrey GU6 7NJ. Tel: 01483 277659.
Admission: £6 per car. **Times**: 8.30am - 7pm.

14-15 Mar
KERNOW LAND YACHTING REGATTA
Perranporth, Cornwall.
Event from the calendar of 'Cornwall '98, The World Watersports Festival'.
Things to see: Thrills galore as Land Yachts race across the sand at speeds of up to 70 mph. Close-up viewing opportunities at one of the UKs largest gatherings.
Contact: Cornwall '98, Trevint House, Strangways Villas, Truro, Cornwall TR1 2PA. Tel: 01872 223527.
Admission: TBA. **Times**: TBA.

14-15 Mar
NATIONAL SHIRE HORSE SHOW
East of England Showground, Peterborough.
Breed show of Shire horses.
Things to see: Shire horses showing in breed classes, including Working Harness Class and Teams in Harness With Vehicle. Working Horse demonstrations. Farriery competitions.
Contact: Shire Horse Society, East of England Showground, Peterborough PE2 6XE. Tel: 01733 234451.
Admission: TBA. **Times**: TBA.

15 Mar
ENGLISH HERITAGE EVENTS PROGRAMME PUBLICATION
Venues include over 70 castles, abbeys and Roman forts throughout England.
A wide range of historical and other events. Over 500 events held per year.
Things to see: Historical re-enactments, battles, colourful uniforms and flags, music, drama and family events set against excellent backgrounds. *The 1998 English Heritage Events Diary* is due to be

published in early-Mar and includes details of all English Heritage events held throughout Apr – Oct. Send for a free copy and choose the events that look the most interesting.
Contact: English Heritage Customer Services, 429 Oxford Street, London W1R 2HD. Tel: 0171-973 3396.
Admission: Various; consult *The Diary*. **Times**: Various; consult *The Diary*.

15 Mar
HASTINGS HALF MARATHON
Hastings and St Leonards-on-Sea, East Sussex.
Mass running event around Hastings.
Things to see: 3,500 runners taking part including top internationals, on a picturesque route including historic parts of old Hastings. Plus mini run for youngsters under 17.
Contact: E Hardwick, 219 Harley Shute Road, St Leonards-on-Sea, East Sussex TN38 9JJ.
Admission: N/A. **Times**: 10.30am - 2.30pm.

15 Mar
READING HALF MARATHON
Rivermead Leisure Complex, Reading.
Half marathon, mini marathon & fun run.
Things to see: 5,000+ runners taking part in mass road race. Live bands, street entertainers, face painters, children's entertainers, sportswear traders village, celebrity guests.
Contact: Race Organiser, Reading Borough Council, PO Box 17, Civic Centre, Reading, Berkshire. Tel: 0118 9575184
Admission: N/A. **Times**: 10am - 1pm.

17 Mar
ST PATRICK'S DAY CELEBRATION
Newry Town Centre, Co Down, Northern Ireland.
National Celebration of St Patrick's Day.
Things to see: Major St Patrick's Day Parade, fun fair, traditional street music, children's entertainment, traditional dance, town centre canal events, sporting events, etc.
Contact: Catherine Donnelly, Community Services Officer, Newry-Mourne District Council, Haughey House, Greenbank Industrial Estate, Warrenpoint Rd, Newry, Co Down BT34 2QU. Tel: 01693 67226.
Admission: N/A. **Times**: 12 noon - 6pm.

19 Mar-13 Apr
THE DAILY MAIL IDEAL HOME EXHIBITION
Earl's Court, London.
Home interests show, the biggest consumer event of its kind.
Things to see: Wide range of demonstrations, spectacular exhibition stands and displays. Over 300 exhibitors, a showcase for every conceivable product and service relating to the home, inside and out. Showhouses, roomsets. Plus celebrities and special events.
Contact: Marketing Department, DMG Exhibition Group, Times House, Station Approach, Ruislip, Middlesex HA4 8NB. Tel: 01895 677677. For advance booking Tel: 0990 900090.
Admission: £10 adults; £6 children. **Times**: 10am - 8pm daily (late night Thursdays).

20 Mar
SPRING EQUINOX CEREMONY
Tower Hill Terrace (South Side), London.
Traditional Druidic ceremony.
Things to see: Processions, trumpet call, sheathing of the sword, entry of Ceridwen – "Mother Earth" – bearing cornucopia, seeds & flowers, scattering of the seeds, call of peace and address from the Chief Druid. Held in a circle; spectators are asked not to cross the processions, enter or crowd the circle.
Contact: Honorary Secretary, The Druid Order, 23 Thornsett Road, Anerley, London SE20 7XB. Tel: 0181-659 4879.
Admission: N/A. **Times:** 1200hrs GMT.

21 Mar
DEVON COUNTY ANTIQUES FAIR
Salisbury Leisure Centre, The Butts, Hulse Road, Salisbury, Wiltshire.
Antiques fair.
Things to see: Beautiful antiques and collectables among the many items on offer. 140 stands in one hall.
Contact: Val Dennis, Devon Counties Antiques Fairs, The Glebe House, Nymet Tracey, Crediton, Devon EX17 6DB. Tel: 01363 82571.
Admission: £1.50 adults; children free. **Times**: 10am - 5pm.

21 Mar
DUKE OF BUCCLEUCH'S HUNT POINT TO POINT
Friarshaugh, Kelso, Roxburghshire.
Point-to-point racing.
Things to see: Horses jumping and galloping with thrills and spills.
Contact: Mrs V Scott Watson, Easter Softlaw, Kelso, Roxburghshire. Tel: 01573 224641.
Admission: £12. **Times**: 1.30pm - 4.30pm.

21 Mar
HEAD OF THE RIVER RACE
From Mortlake to Putney, River Thames, London.
Major rowing race.
Things to see: Processional race of some 400 eight-oared crews starting off at 10-second intervals.
Contact: Mr Andrew Ruddle, 59 Berkeley Court, Oatlands, Weybridge, Surrey KT13 9HY. Tel: 01932 220401.
Admission: N/A. **Times**: From 10am.

21-22 Mar
THE LONDON CLASSIC MOTOR SHOW
Alexandra Palace, London.
Classic car show.
Things to see: Hundreds of gleaming classic cars plus autojumble, trade stands, *concours* competition, etc.
Contact: Sally Greenwood, Greenwood's Exhibitions, PO Box 49, Aylesbury, Bucks HP22 5FF. Tel: 01296 631181/632040. Fax: 01296 630394.
Admission: £7 adults; £3 children. **Times**: 10am - 6pm.

22 Mar
SCOTLAND V ENGLAND
Murrayfield, Edinburgh.
Rugby Union International.
Things to see: Top class rugby action, part of the 5 Nations series.
Contact: Scottish Rugby Union, Murrayfield, Edinburgh EH12 5PJ. Tel: 0131 346 5000. Fax: 0131346 5001.
Admission: £25; £27; £30. **Times**: 3pm.

22 Mar
PIONEER MOTORCYCLE RUN
From Epsom Downs to Madeira Drive, Brighton.
Motorcycle run.
Things to see: Large number of veteran motor cycles all pre-1915 solos, sidecars and tricycles.
Contact: William D Pile, Highdown, Gun Hill, Horam, Heathfield TN21 0JR. Tel: 01825 872336.
Admission: N/A. **Times**: 8am - 3pm approx.

23-27 Mar
ALTERNATIVE FASHION WEEK
The Old Spitalfields Market, Brushfield St, London E1.
Daily fashion shows.
Things to see: Fabulous fashion event showing creations by Britain's most innovative young designers.
Contact: Alternative Arts, 47A Brushfield Street, Spitalfields, London E1 6AA. Tel: 0171-375 0441.
Admission: Free. **Times**: From 1.15pm.

25 Mar
SHOW JUMPING
Towerlands, Panfield Road, Braintree, Essex.
Show jumping event.
Things to see: Senior Affiliated show jumping with top riders.

Contact: The Secretary, Towerlands Equestrian Centre, Panfield Road, Braintree, Essex. Tel: 01376 326802.
Admission: Free. **Times**: From 9.30am.

27 Mar
GOOD FRIDAY GIGANTIC EASTER EGG HUNT
Crealy Park, Clyst St Mary, Exeter, Devon.
An easter egg hunt aimed at children.
Things to see: Hunting the tokens throughout the park to exchange for thousands of chocolate eggs, plus prizes of chocolate bunnies! Featuring Gemini Road Show and super Gemini prizes.
Contact: Reception, Crealy Park, Sidmouth Road, Clyst St Mary, Nr Exeter, Devon EX5 1DR. Tel: 01395 233200.
Admission: £4.50 adults; £3.75 children/OAPs. **Times**: TBA.

28 Mar
ARLINGTON GROVE SHOW
Priory Equestrian Centre, Frensham, Nr Farnham, Surrey.
A charity horse and pony show.
Things to see: Horses and ponies showing in-hand and ridden. Plus working hunter classes and fun classes. Bar and restaurant facilities.
Contact: Miss J V Richards, The Rose Cottage, Horseblock Hollow, Barhatch Lane, Cranleigh, Surrey GU6 7NJ. Tel: 01483 277659.
Admission: £5 per car. **Times**: 8.30am - 6pm.

28 Mar
FITZWILLIAM POINT TO POINT
Cottenham Racecourse, Cottenham, Cambridge.
Point to point racing.
Things to see: Usually seven or eight races. Point-to-pointers (racehorses), stands, caterers, etc.
Contact: Mr M Gingell or Mrs C Tebbs, c/o Horningsea Manor, Horningsea, Cambridge CB5 9JE. TEl: 01223 860291.
Admission: £10 per car with two occupants; £15 with three; £20 with four or more. **Times**: First race 2pm.

Dates can change, events can be cancelled – Please check with the organisers before setting out!

28 Mar
LOSSIEMOUTH SPRING FLOWER SHOW
Lossiemouth Community Centre, Coulardbank Road, Lossiemouth, Moray.
Spring flower show.
Things to see: Plants, bulbs and flowers of all kinds in season, floral art, children's handiwork, alpines, etc.
Contact: Mr J Millar, 23 South Covesea Terrace, Lossiemouth IV31 6NA. Tel: 01343 813912.
Admission: TBA. **Times**: 1pm - 4.15pm.

28 Mar
THE OXFORD & CAMBRIDGE BOAT RACE
River Thames, from Putney to Mortlake.
Annual rowing race between England's two oldest and most famous universities.
Things to see: Arrive early and take up a position on one of the following bridges for the best viewpoint: Putney, Hammersmith, Barnes or Mortlake.
Contact: Lucy Cohn, Boat Race Press Office, Scope Sponsorship, Tower House, 8-14 Southampton Street, London WC2E 7HA. Tel: 0171-379 3234. Fax: 0171-465 8241.
Admission: N/A. **Times**: 2.30pm start.

28-29 Mar
BRITISH RHYTHMIC GYMNASTICS CHAMPIONSHIPS
Bletchley Leisure Centre, Milton Keynes.
Gymnastics championships.
Things to see: Competitive gymnasts working with apparatus, rope, hoop, ball, clubs and ribbon. Flash photogra-

phy not permitted.
Contact: Mrs J Warren, BAGA, Ford Hall, Lilleshall NSC, nr Newport, Shropshire TF10 9NB. Tel: 01952 677137.
Admission: £5 per day. **Times**: Sat: 2pm - 5.30pm approx (Senior Overall). Sun: 2pm - 5pm (Senior and Junior Finals).

28-29 Mar
EASTER EGG HUNTS
Crealy Park, Clyst St Mary, Exeter, Devon.
An easter egg hunt aimed at children.
Things to see: Over 15,000 chocolate eggs hidden all around the park, plus treasure hunt competitions, spring lambs, chicks and baby rabbits to cuddle.
Contact: Reception, Crealy Park, Sidmouth Road, Clyst St Mary, Nr Exeter, Devon EX5 1DR. Tel: 01395 233200.
Admission: £4.50 adults; £3.75 children/OAPs. **Times**: TBA.

29 Mar
LEIGHTON BUZZARD RAILWAY TEDDY BEARS' OUTING
Page's Park Station, Billington Road, Leighton Buzzard, Beds.
Railway event for children.
Things to see: Train rides for children with teddy bears. Plus entertainment, competitions and Bedfordshire's biggest teddy.
Contact: Mr Graham Stroud, Leighton Buzzard Railway, Page's Park Station, Billington Road, Leighton Buzzard, Beds LU7 8TN. Tel: 01525 373888.
Admission: Train fare £4.50 adults; £1 children (free with bear). Displays free. **Times**: 11am - 5pm.

April

2-4 Apr
GRAND NATIONAL MEETING
Aintree Racecourse, Liverpool.
Major horse race meeting.
Things to see: Top level horse racing, featuring the world's greatest steeplechase. The Grand National itself is run on the 4th.
Contact: Racecourse Manager, Aintree Racecourse, Liverpool L9 5AS. Tel: 0151-523 2600. Fax: 0151-530 1512.
Admission: From £9. **Times**: TBA.

4 Apr
DEVON COUNTY ANTIQUES FAIR
Matford Centre in the Exeter Livestock Centre, Matford Park Rd, Marsh Barton, Exeter, Devon.
Antiques fair.
Things to see: Beautiful antiques and collectables among the many items on offer. 230 stands inside and up to 200 outside stands.
Contact: Val Dennis, Devon Counties Antiques Fairs, The Glebe House, Nymet Tracey, Crediton, Devon EX17 6DB. Tel: 01363 82571.
Admission: £2 adults; children free. **Times**: 10am - 5pm.

4 Apr
ENGLAND V IRELAND
Rugby Football Union Ground, Twickenham, Middlesex.
Rugby Union international.
Things to see: Top rugby action; part of the Five Nations Series.
Contact: Rugby Football Union, Whitton Road, Twickenham TW1 1DZ. Tel: 0181-892 8161.
Admission: TBA. **Times**: TBA.

4 Apr
WALES V FRANCE
Wembley Stadium.
Rugby Union international.
Things to see: Top rugby action; part of the Five Nations Series.
Contact: Press Office, Welsh Rugby Union, Hodge House, St Mary St, Cardiff CF1 1DY. Tel: 01222 781700.
Admission: TBA. **Times**: Kick off 3pm.

4-5 Apr
MIDLAND HILLCLIMB CHAMPIONSHIP
Prescott Hill, Cheltenham, Glos.
Hillclimb car racing.
Things to see: Roadgoing sports cars and racing cars ascending a narrow twisting hill road at speeds of up to 110mph. Plus cars in paddock etc.
Contact: Mrs S Ward, Bugatti Owners Club, Prescott Hill, Gotherington, Glos GL52 4RD. Tel: 01242 673136.
Admission: £7 adults. **Times**: 10am - 5pm approx.

5 Apr
BOATJUMBLE
Beaulieu Abbey, Beaulieu, Brockenhurst, Hampshire.
Boatjumble at Beaulieu.
Things to see: 1,000 stalls display everything for the boating enthusiast from complete boats to hundreds of boating bits and pieces.
Contact: Stephen Munn, Marketing Manager, Beaulieu Abbey, Beaulieu, Brockenhurst, Hampshire SO42 7ZN. Tel: 01590 612345.
Admission: TBA. **Times**: From 10am.

5 Apr
A GRAND OPENING!
National Tramway Museum, Crich, Matlock, Derbyshire.
Grand opening to new exhibition.
Things to see: New for 1998! Come and see the new Horse-Tram Exhibition - inside information on the horse-tram era & its evolution.
Contact: Lesley Wyld, Marketing Manager, National Tramway Museum, Crich, Matlock, Derbyshire DE4 5DP. Tel: 01773 852565. Fax: 01773 852326.
Admission: £5.90 adults; £3 children; £5.10 OAPs; £16.20 family ticket. **Times**: 10am - 5.30pm.

10 Apr
BLANTYRE PARK SHOW
Priory Equestrian Centre, Frensham, Nr Farnham, Surrey.
A charity horse and pony show.
Things to see: All types of ponies, horses and riders, showing in-hand and ridden. Plus working hunter classes. Good bar and restaurant facilities.
Contact: Miss J V Richards, The Rose Cottage, Horseblock Hollow, Barhatch Lane, Cranleigh, Surrey GU6 7NJ. Tel: 01483 277659.
Admission: £5 per car. **Times**: 8.30am - 6pm.

10 Apr
CIRCUS SKILLS
East Riddlesden Hall, Keighley, West Yorkshire.
Easter entertainment for children.
Things to see: Circus skills, juggling, stilt walking, diablo, etc.
Contact: Liz Houseman, East Riddlesden Hall, Bradford Road, Keighley, West Yorkshire BD20 5EL.
Admission: £3.20 adult, £1.70 children; £8 family ticket. **Times**: 12 noon - 4pm.

10-13 Apr
BLACKPOOL HOCKEY FESTIVAL
Stanley Park; Rossall School; Kirkham Grammar School; Lytham High School; Blackpool.
National hockey festival.
Things to see: Men's, women's and mixed hockey action on synthetic turf pitches. 330 hockey matches in four days. 24 men's, 12 women's and 24 mixed teams.
Contact: Peter Danson, 10 Heathfield Nook Road, Buxton, Derbyshire SK17 9RX. Tel: 01298 24962.
Admission: Free. **Times**: 10am - 7pm daily.

10-13 Apr
CIRCUIT OF IRELAND MOTOR RALLY
Start and finish in Bangor, County Down.
Motor rally around Ireland.
Things to see: The longest tarmac motor rally in Britain. Various spectactor stages.
Contact: Ulster Automobile Club, 29 Shore Avenue, Holywood BT18 9HX. Tel: 01232 426262. Fax: 01232 421818.
Admission: N/A. **Times**: Contact the U.A.C.

10-13 Apr
LANCASTER MARITIME FESTIVAL
Maritime Museum, St George's Quay, and other quayside venues, Lancaster.
Annual event celebrating Lancaster's "Golden Age" as an important west-coast trading port.
Things to see: Four days of events centred around a unique gathering of the country's finest shantymen and sea songsters. Supporting events include ships-in-bottles demonstrations, nautical dramas, salty storytelling, Punch and Judy, and a costumed press gang. Over a hundred separate events – a free programme will be available a couple of weeks before the festival.
Contact: Lancaster Tourist Information Centre, 29 Castle Hill, Lancaster LA1 1YN. Tel: 01524 32878.
Admission: Depends on event – see programme. Many events free. **Times**: Various throughout each day.

10 Apr-15 May
ENFIELD FESTIVAL OF THE COUNTRYSIDE
London Borough of Enfield.
A six week festival which celebrates the countryside, countryside activities and traditional crafts of the area.
Things to see: Country shows, folk music, guided walks, exhibitions, traditional crafts.
Contact: Helen Winchester, Tourism Development Officer, PO Box 58, Enfield, Middlesex EN1 3LQ.
Admission: Some events will be charged. **Times**: Various.

10-13 Apr
EASTER FESTIVAL OF SPORT & DRAMA
Various venues on the Isle of Man.
Sports and drama.
Things to see: Along with varied drama the sports involved are: hockey, shooting, senior football, junior football, fell running/marathon, rugby, table tennis and athletics.
Contact: Special Events Unit, Grandstand, Douglas, Isle of Man IM2 4TB. Tel: 01624 661930.
Admission: TBA for drama. Free for sports events. **Times**: TBA.

10-13 Apr
EASTER WEEKEND AT HEVER CASTLE
Hever Castle, Edenbridge, Kent.
Brass bands and children's 'Easter Egg Treasure Trail' at Hever Castle.
Things to see: Brass bands entertaining visitors each day on the castle forecourt. Children competing in the 'Easter Egg Treasure Trail' around the gardens. Many other things to see such as the Castle itself (Anne Boleyn's childhood home) and award winning gardens – suitable for picnics. New water maze.
Contact: Jan Roberts or Pauline Scott, Hever Castle, Edenbridge, Kent TN8 7NG. Tel: 01732 865224.
Admission: £7 adults; £3.80 children; £6 OAPs; £17.80 family (2 adults, 2 children). **Times**: Gardens open 11am. Castle opens 12 noon. Last admission 5pm. Final exit 6pm.

10-13 Apr
JAN KJELLSTROM INTERNATIONAL FESTIVAL OF ORIENTEERING
Dolgellau, Wales.
Major international orienteering event.
Things to see: The competition final run-in, involving several thousand competitors. Information stands about the sport and equipment stands. Plus the chance to try the sport on the day on easier courses for novices – identify yourself at the enquiries tent and seek assistance.
Contact: Judith Powell, 22 The Willows, Raglan, Gwent NP5 2HB. Also: British Orienteering Federation, Riversdale, Dale Road North, Darley Dale, Matlock, Derbyshire De4 2HX. Tel: 01629 734042.
Admission: Free. **Times**: 10am - 3pm approx.

10-13 Apr
WINDSURF NATIONAL RACING CHAMPIONSHIP
Marazion, Cornwall.
Event from the calendar of 'Cornwall '98, The World Watersports Festival'.
Things to see: One of the country's premier course racing events with over 100 of the finest competitors hoping for high winds and high speeds.
Contact: Cornwall '98, Trevint House, Strangways Villas, Truro, Cornwall TR1 2PA. Tel: 01872 223527.
Admission: TBA. **Times**: TBA.

10-19 Apr
INTERNATIONAL SAND & SURF FESTIVAL '98
Gwithian, Hayle, Cornwall.
Event from the calendar of 'Cornwall '98, The World Watersports Festival'.
Things to see: High energy fusion of wave and wind disciplines. A unique combo of surfing, speedsailing and wavesailing events with some of the

world's top competitors homing in on Cornwall for awesome action in and out of the water.
Contact: Cornwall '98, Trevint House, Strangways Villas, Truro, Cornwall TR1 2PA. Tel: 01872 223527.
Admission: TBA. **Times**: TBA.

11-13 Apr
EASTER LAMBS
Cogges Manor Farm Museum, Nr Witney, Oxon.
Historic House and traditional farm animals.
Things to see: Cotswold farm buildings with farm animals including lambs over the Easter holidays. Manor house with room displays & cooking in the Victorian kitchen.
Contact: Carol Nightingale, Site Manager, Cogges Manor Farm Museum, Church Lane, Cogges, Nr Witney, Oxon OX8 6LA. Tel: 01993 772602.
Admission: £3.25 adults; £2 OAPs; £1.75 children; £9 family. **Times**: Sat/Sun: 12 noon - 5.30pm. Mon: 10.30pm - 5.30pm.

11-13 Apr
FOUR SEASONS CRAFTS SHOW
Sandown Park, Esher, Surrey.
Craft fair.
Things to see: Quality crafts created by experts from all over the country. Easter theme.
Contact: Four Seasons (Events Ltd), 23A Brockenhurst Rd, South Ascot, Berkshire SL5 9DJ. Tel: 01344 874787.
Admission: £2.50-£3.50 adults; £2-£2.50 OAPs; £1 children. **Times**: TBA.

11-13 Apr
LEEDS CASTLE CELEBRATION OF EASTER
Leeds Castle, Maidstone, Kent.
Easter activities over the Bank Holiday weekend.
Things to see: Morris dancers, maypole dancing, exhibition of kite-flying, Punch and Judy shows, egg and face painting for children.
Contact: Leeds Castle, Maidstone, Kent ME17 1PL. Tel: 01622 765400.
Admission: 1997 guide: £6.50 adults; £5 students/OAPs; £4 children; £19 family ticket (2 adults, 3 children). **Times**: 10am - 5pm.

12 Apr
EASTER BONNET PARADE
Millbuies, Nr Elgin, Scotland.
Easter bonnet parade.
Things to see: Parade and Easter bonnet competition; best egg competition; It's a Knockout competition; bands and displays.
Contact: E McGillivray, Arts Development Officer, Technical & Leisure Services Dept, High Street, Elgin IV30 1BX. Tel: 01343 563403.
Admission: Free. **Times**: 12 noon - 4.30pm.

12-13 Apr
EASTER FUN FOR CHILDREN
New Lanark Visitor Centre, Scotland.
Easter event designed for children.
Things to see: Children's treasure trail, Easter bunnies, roundabout and bouncy castle.
Contact: Annie Bell, New Lanark Conservation Trust, New Lanark, Scotland ML11 9DB. Tel: 01555 661345.
Admission: Nominal charge for treasure trail. **Times**: 12 noon - 4pm.

12-13 Apr
EASTER EGGSTRAVAGANZA
Beningbrough Hall, Shipton, Beningbrough, York.
Fun and games for children aged 3-12.
Things to see: Garden Bunny Hunt, decorated egg competition, activity sheets, easter quiz.
Contact: The National Trust, Beningbrough Hall, Shipton, Beningbrough, York YO6 1DD. Tel: 01904 470666.
Admission: TBA. **Times**: 12 noon - 4pm.

12-13 Apr
MAD HATTER'S TEA PARTY
The Historic Dockyard, Chatham, Kent.
Special event designed for children.
Things to see: Meet the Mad Hatter, watch the magic show, clown and Punch & Judy, face painting, fun and games.
Contact: The Historic Dockyard, Chatham, Kent ME4 4TE. Tel: 01634 812551.
Admission: £2.50 adults; children free.
Times: 10am - 4pm.

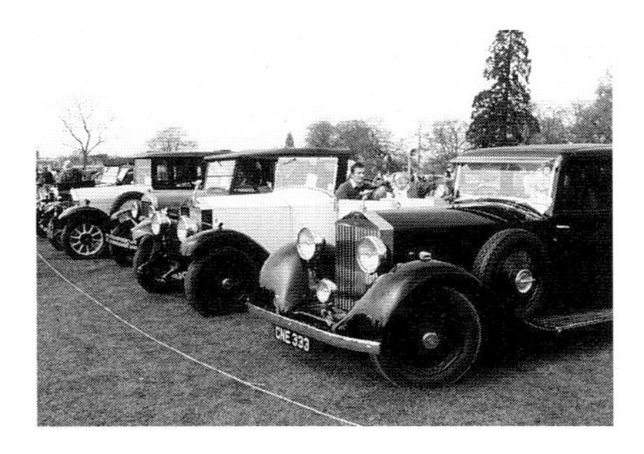

12-13 Apr
MIDLAND FESTIVAL OF TRANSPORT
Weston Park, Shifnal, Shropshire (on A5. 6 miles J12 M6).
Vintage & classic vehicle show with full attractions for all the family.
Things to see: Veteran and vintage cars, historic commercials, veteran and vintage motor cycles, classic motor bikes, sporting cars, classic cars, American cars, custom and kit cars, buses, midget coaches, vintage farm machinery, fire engines, military vehicles, stationary engines, club displays, etc.
Contact: Mr W J Chatwin, c/o Country Fairs, 9 Beechfield Rise, Lichfield, Staffs WS13 6EL. Tel: 01543 417878 or 0973 333116.
Admission: £5 adults; £2 children.
Times: 10am - 6pm.

12-13 Apr
MILL AND FARM OPEN DAYS
Worsbrough Country Park, Worsbrough Bridge, Barnsley.
Open days at Worsbrough Corn Mill and Wigfield Open Farm.
Things to see: Water powered corn milling, rare & traditional breeds of farm animals, new born lambs. Set in 200-acre Worsbrough Country Park.
Contact: Debra Bushby, Worsbrough Country Park, Off Park Road, Worsbrough Bridge, Barnsley, South Yorkshire S70 5LJ. Tel: 01226 774527.
Admission: Farm: £1.50 adults; 75p children/OAPs. Mill: 50p adults; 25p children/OAPs.**Times**: 12 noon - 5pm.

12-13 Apr
THE SAXON MARKET
West Stow Anglo-Saxon Village, West Stow Country Park, Bury St Edmunds, Suffolk.
Saxon traders, entertainers and craftspeople bring to life the reconstructed Saxon village at West Stow.
Things to see: Saxons in costume in and around the reconstructed buildings, craft demonstrations, stalls selling authentic goods of the period, moneyer striking coins, storyteller, etc.
Contact: Liz Proctor, The Visitor Centre, West Stow Country Park, Icklingham Road, West Stow, Bury St Edmunds, Suffolk IP28 6HG. Tel: 01284 728718.
Admission: £4.50 adults; £3 children/OAPs; £12.50 for family ticket (2 adults and up to 3 children). **Times**: 11am - 5pm.

12-13 Apr
STEAM UP
Coldharbour Mill, Working Wool Museum, Uffculme, Cullompton, Devon.
Steam event.
Things to see: 1910 300hp mill engine in steam, Lancashire boilers, steam pumps. Also turn-of-the-century spinning and weaving machinery. Beam engine. New world tapestry.
Contact: Miss Jill Taylor, Coldharbour Mill, Uffculme, Cullompton, Devon EX15 3EE. Tel: 01884 840960.

Admission: £5 adults; £2.50 children. **Times**: 10.30am - 5pm.

12-26 Apr
PRIMROSE WEEKS
Fairhaven Garden Trust, South Walsham (9 miles NE of Norwich on B1140).
Horticultural display.
Things to see: Wild and cultivated flowers, trees and shrubs in their various seasons. Also bird sanctuary.
Contact: Mr G E Debbage, Resident Warden, The Fairhaven Garden Trust, 2 The Woodlands, Wymers Lane, South Walsham, Norwich, Norfolk NR13 6EA. Tel: 01603 270449.
Admission: £3 adult; £2.70 OAP; £1 child. Bird sanctuary £1. **Times**: 11am - 5.30pm.

13 Apr
CIRCUS SKILLS
East Riddlesden Hall, Keighley, West Yorkshire.
Easter entertainment for children.
Things to see: Circus skills, juggling, stilt walking, diablo, etc.
Contact: Liz Houseman, East Riddlesden Hall, Bradford Road, Keighley, West Yorkshire BD20 5EL.
Admission: £3.20 adult, £1.70 children; £8 family ticket. **Times**: 12 noon - 4pm.

13 Apr
EASTER EXTRAVAGANZA
Culdrose Manor, Helston, Cornwall.
Fun and games for children.
Things to see: Free Easter eggs for all children under 12. Party in the park with entertainment, clowns, jugglers, buskers. Colourful award-winning gardens, rides and exhibitions. Outstanding opportunities for photography.
Contact: Bill Finlay, Executive Manager. Tel: 01326 573404.
Admission: TBA. 1997 guide: £5.99 adults; £4.99 children under 12; £3.99 over-55s; £17.50 family ticket **Times**: From 10am.

Dates can change, events can be cancelled – Please check with the organisers before setting out!

13 Apr
LONDON HARNESS HORSE PARADE
Battersea Park, London.
Show of working horses.
Things to see: Extremely attractive parades of working horses and ponies competing for prizes of rosettes, brass merit badges and prize cards. Events end with a grand parade. Plus a fun fair.
Contact: Tonie Gibson OBE, East of England Showground, Peterborough PE2 6XE. Tel: 01733 234451. Fax: 01733 370038.
Admission: Free. **Times**: From 9am.

13 Apr
OLD BERKS HUNT POINT TO POINT
Lockinge, Nr Wantage, Oxon.
Point to point race meeting.
Things to see: At least six races over fences, with betting, trade stands and refreshments. Excellent viewing from car park.
Contact: Mrs W Brown, Manor Farm, Aldbourne, Marlborough, Wiltshire SN8 2BG. Tel: 01672 540328.
Admission: £15; £20 per car. **Times**: 2pm - 5pm.

13 Apr
WORLD COAL CARRYING CHAMPIONSHIP
Start: The Royal Oak, Owl Lane, Ossett. Finish: The Green, Gawthorpe, Ossett, West Yorkshire.
Coal carrying races.
Things to see: Races involving men carrying a 50kg bag of coal for 1 mile; ladies carrying 20kg of coal for 1 mile.
Contact: Mrs S D Walshaw, 23 Branstone Grove, Gawthorpe, Ossett WF5 9SU. Tel:

01924 260141.
Admission: None. **Times**: 12.15pm - 1.15pm.

13-17 Apr
RYA NATIONAL YOUTH SAILING CHAMPIONSHIPS
Looe, Cornwall.
Event from the calendar of 'Cornwall '98, The World Watersports Festival'.
Things to see: Come and see Britain's potential Olympians make their mark in the year's foremost sailing event for under 19's.
Contact: Cornwall '98, Trevint House, Strangways Villas, Truro, Cornwall TR1 2PA. Tel: 01872 223527.
Admission: TBA. **Times**: TBA.

17-20 Apr
EASTER STEAMINGS
Didcot Railway Centre, Didcot, Oxfordshire.
Easter family fun with trains.
Things to see: Four days steaming with train rides, easter egg hunts on Sunday and Monday, etc.
Contact: J C Howse, Didcot Railway Centre, Didcot, Oxfordshire. Tel: 01235 817200.
Admission: £6 adult; £4 children; £5 OAPs; £18 family. **Times**: 10am - 5pm.

17-18 Apr
STAKIS CASINOS SCOTTISH GRAND NATIONAL
Ayr Racecourse, Scotland.
One of Scotland's premier horse race meetings.
Things to see: Two days of top horse racing including the Scottish Grand National on Sat.

Dates can change, events can be cancelled – Please check with the organisers before setting out!

Contact: George Steel, Sales & Promotions Manager, The Western Meeting Club, 2 Whitletts Road, Ayr KA8 0JE. Tel: 01292 264179.
Admission: TBA. 1998 guide: Grandstand Enclosure: 17 Apr £8 per day; 19 Apr £10. **Times**: TBA.

17-19 Apr
MORPETH NORTHUMBRIAN GATHERING
Morpeth, Northumberland.
Festival devoted to the language, music and heritage of Northumberland (Tweed - Tyneside).
Things to see: Border Cavalcade, street dancing (morris/rapper), crafts exhibition, song and music competitions, concerts, barn dance, dance and craft workshops, historic tours, dialect, song & music workshops, films, pageant, storytelling, etc.
Contact: J Bibby, Westgate House, Dogger Bank, Morpeth, Northumberland NE61 1RF. Tel: 01670 513308.
Admission: Varied. **Times**: 9.30am onwards.

18 Apr
ESSEX & SUFFOLK HUNT POINT TO POINT RACES
Higham Racecourse (between Ipswich & Colchester just off the A12).
Amateur horse racing over jumps.
Things to see: Horses jumping and galloping with thrills and spills.
Contact: Miss J Taylor, Water Mill, Nedging, Ipswich, Suffolk IP7 7HF. Tel: 01449 740 258.
Admission: £15 per car. **Times**: Gates open 12 noon. First race 2pm.

18 Apr
SCOTTISH BANDS CONTEST
Brunton Halls, Musselburgh.
Band event.
Things to see: Contest for all forms of bandwork – pipes/drums; bugles/trumpets; flutes. Young people preparing for and playing musical instruments, perfor-

mance and display, presentation to successful bands. Make arrangements for access to practice/tuning areas.
Contact: T Boyle Secretary for Training, The Boys' Brigade, Carronvale House, Carronvale Road, Larbert FK5 3LH. Tel: 01324 562008.
Admission: £2. **Times**: 10am - 5pm.

18-19 Apr
SOUTH OF ENGLAND HORSE TRIALS
South of England Showground, Ardingly, West Sussex.
Major equestrian event.
Things to see: Horse trials featuring novice, intermediate and advanced horses including internationals.
Contact: Mrs J Nolan, South Eastern Equestrian Services, Oatridges, Best Beech, Wadhurst, East Sussex TN5 6JL. Tel: 01892 783227.
Admission: £8 per car. **Times**: From 9am.

18-19 Apr
STEAM WEEKEND
The Tropical Bird Gardens, Rode, Nr Bath, Somerset.
Steam trains and birds.
Things to see: Visiting steam, diesel and electric locomotives on a very scenic railway route. Plus 280 varieties of birds.
Contact: Mr M D Marshall, Millbrook Cottage, The Hollow, Child Okeford, Blandford Forum, Dorset DT11 8EX. Tel: 01258 861689.
Admission: TBA. **Times**: 11am - 5pm.

18 Apr-4 May
EMBASSY WORLD SNOOKER CHAMPIONSHIP
Crucible Theatre, Sheffield.
World championship snooker.
Things to see: One of the most popular and prestigious events in the sporting calendar. The top 16 players plus 16 qualifiers competing for the title of Embassy World Champion.
Contact: Tournament Office, WPBSA, 27 Oakfield Road, Bristol BS8 2AT. Tel: 0117 974 4491.
Admission: TBA. 1997 guide: £4 - £20 depending on session/match. Visitors are advised to book tickets in advance. **Times**: Three sessions a day; starting times vary.

19 Apr*
COBWEB RUN
Amberley Museum, Arundel, West Sussex.
Vintage car and motorcycle gathering.
Things to see: Veteran cars from before the First World War, limousines and sports cars of the '20s and '30s, and post-war classics of the '40s and '50s. Motorcycles from the belt-driven era through to the much-loved Nortons, Matchless, Vincents, etc of the post-war years. In addition to the event itself visitors can enjoy all the usual museum attractions, including craftsmen at work, train rides, vintage bus rides, etc
Contact: Howard Stenning, Amberley Museum, Arundel, West Sussex BN18 9LT. Tel/fax: 01798 831370.
Admission: 1997 guide: £4.50 adults, £2.10 children, £3.50 OAPs. **Times**: 10am - 5pm.

19-20 Apr
MEDIEVAL ENTERTAINMENTS
Old Sarum Castle, Salisbury, Wiltshire.
Medieval entertainers (various groups) to tie in with Salisbury St George's Day celebrations.
Things to see: Fighting knights, dancing, children's games, etc.
Contact: Mark Selwood, Special Events Unit, Room 101, English Heritage, Keysign House, 429 Oxford Street, London W1R 2HD. Tel: 0171-973 3420. Fax: 0171-973 3430.
Admission: TBA. **Times**: TBA.

21 Apr
HOCKTIDE AT HUNGERFORD
The Town Hall and High Street, Hungerford, Berkshire.
Old custom in Hungerford.

Things to see: The Tutti (or Tything) Men visit each of the houses of the commoners to collect a "Head Penny" in recognition of the Ancient Rights. See children scrambling in the street for pennies thrown by the Tutti Men; the flower bedecked staves of the Tutti Men; the Orangeman, the Bellman and Town Crier; maypole and clog dancing in the street; the ancient (since 1362) Hocktide Court; the shoeing of the colts at the Hocktide Lunch; etc. Arrive by 8am to catch the Bellman, and 9am for the start of the tour of duty by the Tything Men, following the presentation of their staves of office.
Contact: Bruce Mayhew, Constable of the Town and Manor of Hungerford, 34 High Street, Hungerford, Berkshire RG17 0NF. Tel: 01488 682376.
Admission: N/A **Times**: 9am - 9pm.

21 Apr
ROYAL GUN SALUTE FOR THE BIRTHDAY OF HM THE QUEEN
The Tower of London and in Hyde Park.
Gun salutes to mark the Queen's birthday.
Things to see: Gun salutes are fired in London by the King's Troop Royal Artillery in Hyde Park at 1200 hours (41 Gun Royal Salute) and by the Honourable Artillery Company at the Tower of London at 1300 hours (62 Gun Royal Salute).
Contact: The Information Officer, Public Information Office, Headquarters London District, Chelsea Barracks, London SW1H 8RF.
Admission: Free. **Times**: See above.

23-26 Apr
HARROGATE SPRING FLOWER SHOW
Great Yorkshire Showground, Harrogate, North Yorkshire.
The first major national flower show of the season.
Things to see: Spectacular exhibits and plant sales by Britain's leading nurserymen. Gardening accessories for sale, top garden designers and displays by the Alpine and Daffodil Societies.
Contact: North of England Horticultural Society, 4A South Park Road, Harrogate, North Yorkshire. Tel: 01423 561049.
Admission: Thurs: £10. Fri: £9. Sat: £9. Sun: £8. Reduced rates for parties of 20 or more. **Times**: Thurs-Sat: 9.30am - 6pm. Sun: 9.30am - 4.30pm.

25-26 Apr
WISCOMBE PARK SPEED HILL CLIMB
Wiscombe Park, Southleigh, Colyton, Devon (RAC signposted).
Speed hill climb for cars.
Things to see: Racing, sports and saloon cars being driven at high speed on a narrow and tortuous tarmac track. Speeds in excess of 100mph have been recorded. Cars of great mechanical interest can be viewed static in the pits.
Contact: Dr R A Willoughby, Tudor Cottage, Sulhamstead, Reading RG7 4BP. Tel: 01734 302439.
Admission: £3 - £4. **Times**: 9am - 5.30pm.

26 Apr
AMBERLEY VETERAN CYCLE DAY
Amberley Museum, Arundel, West Sussex.
Veteran cycle rally.
Things to see: Grand assembly of veteran bicycles and tricycles from the "boneshakers" of the 1870s onwards, with many of the riders in period costume. Grand parade with commentary at 3pm. In addition to the event itself visitors can enjoy all the usual museum attractions, including craftsmen at work, train rides, vintage bus rides, etc
Contact: Howard Stenning, Amberley Museum, Arundel, West Sussex BN18 9LT. Tel/fax: 01798 831370.
Admission: 1997 guide: £5 adults, £2.50 children, £4.50 OAPs. **Times**: 10am - 5pm.

26 Apr
THE FLORA LONDON MARATHON
From Greenwich to The Mall, London.
One of the world's most prestigious marathons.
Things to see: Marathon over 26.2 miles with around 29,000 runners. The race includes some of the world's elite marathon runners at the head of the field, followed by thousands of club runners, runners raising money for charity and those in fancy dress. All set against London's best known landmarks. Access to certain areas (especially the start and finish) is restricted.
Contact: Jane Cowmeadow, Press Officer: The Flora London Marathon, PO Box 1234, London SE1 8RZ. Tel: 0171-620 4117.
Admission: N/A. **Times**: TBA.

26 Apr
PEEBLES RUGBY SEVENS
The Gytes, Peebles, Scotland.
Seven-a-side rugby tournament.
Things to see: Rugby action, plus fine views of River Tweed.
Contact: A J Hogarth, 22 Wemyss Place, Peebles, Scotland EH45 8JT. Tel: 01721 722362.
Admission: £5. **Times**: 1.30pm - 6.30pm.

26 Apr
TAPLOW HORSE SHOW
Barge Farm, Taplow, Bucks (easy access from M4, M40, M25).
Horse show plus other events.
Things to see: Show jumping, driving and trade turnouts, showing classes and displays in the Main Ring. Plus dog show and agility tests, trade stands and amusements for all.
Contact: Show Secretary, Marshmead, Taplow, Bucks SL6 0DE. Tel: 01628 603179.
Admission: Ringside cars may be booked in advance otherwise entry on gate. **Times**: 8.30am – 6pm approx.

26 Apr
THE THREE PEAKS RACE
Start/finish Horton in Ribblesdale, Nr Settle, North Yorkshire.
Fell race over Pen Y Ghent, Whernside and Ingleborough.
Things to see: A 24-mile race with runners ascending and descending steep-sided mountains. Be prepared to leave car and climb one of the peaks to obtain the best views.
Contact: Bill Wade, Meadowbank, Wath Rd, Pateley Bridge, Harrogate, North Yorkshire HG3 5LN. Tel: 01423 712000.
Admission: N/A. Car park at Horton £2.
Times: 10am start. Winners finish time 12.50pm approx.

30 Apr-4 May
SAILORS HOBBY HORSE
The streets of Minehead, Somerset.
An old tradition of Minehead.
Things to see: The Sailors Hobby Horse comes out on the eve of May Day, and for the first three days of the month dances and frolics freely around the streets. The horse's frame is made from withy sticks lashed together with tarred cord into the shape of a boat with a dome-shaped head and a painted tin face. The custom is so old that there is no accurate record of its commencement.
Contact: Mr Peter Creech, Hillcrest, 9 The Ball, Dunster, Nr Minehead, Somerset TA24 6SD. Tel: 01643 821040.
Admission: N/A (donations to charity).
Times: 30 Apr: 6pm proceeding from the Old Ship Aground, The Quay, around the town for Show Night. 1 May: from The Old Ship Aground at 5am via Higher Town to be at White Cross at 6am. During the day the horse is around the town. Then 6.30pm at the Yarn Market proceeding to Dunster Castle for 7pm and afterwards around Dunster Village. 2 May: from the Old Ship Aground at 6pm to Alcombe. 4 May: from the Old Ship Aground at 5.30pm to be at The Bootie, Wellington Square at 7.30pm.

May

1 May*
2000 GUINEAS STAKES
Rowley Mile Racecourse, Newmarket, Suffolk.
Classic horse race.
Things to see: Top level horse racing.
Contact: The Clerk of the Course, Westfield House, The Links, Newmarket, Suffolk CB8 0TG. Tel: 01638 663482.
Admission: £5/£12/£25. Children free. Half price reductions for 16-25 year olds (on proof of age). **Times**: First race 2pm.

1 May
CAMBRIDGESHIRE UNITED POINT TO POINT
Cottenham Racecourse, Cottenham, Cambridge.
Point to point racing.
Things to see: Usually six or seven races. Point-to-pointers (racehorses), stands, caterers, etc.
Contact: Mr M Gingell or Mrs C Tebbs, c/o Horningsea Manor, Horningsea, Cambridge CB5 9JE. TEl: 01223 860291.
Admission: £10 per car with 2 occupants. £15 with 3. £20 with 4 or more. **Times**: TBA (evening meeting).

Dates can change, events can be cancelled – Please check with the organisers before setting out!

1 May
KING'S LYNN MAY GARLAND PROCESSION
King's Lynn town centre (starting at the Saturday Market Place), Norfolk.
Traditional event held on the real May Day.
Things to see: A traditional celebration to welcome summer. A large double-garland of flowers, beads and ribbons, surrounding a doll, is mounted on a pole and carried about by the local morris dancers, usually accompanied by children with their own garlands. The procession is enlivened by the lusty blowing of ox-horns, and there are frequent stops in the streets and the two market places of the old town for dancing displays. The event takes place mainly in the pedestrian precinct, giving good, safe access.
Contact: David Jackson (Bagman, The King's Morris), 9 Edward Street, King's Lynn, Norfolk PE30 5QS. Tel: 01553 768930.
Admission: N/A. **Times**: 12 noon - 2pm.

1-3 May
BICTON HORSE TRIALS
Bicton Arena, East Budleigh, Devon.
Horse trials.
Things to see: Horses jumping fences over a cross country course.
Contact: A C Stevens, St Giles Cottage,

Northleigh, Colyton, Devon EX13 6BL. Tel: 01404 871296.
Admission: £5 per car to include occupants. **Times**: 8.30am - 6pm.

1-3 May
SCOTTISH NATIONAL GYMFEST
Inverness Sports Centre.
Festival of gymnastics.
Things to see: Over 1,000 gymnasts performing gymnastics and dance to music.
Contact: Gordon Scott, 17 Cradlehall Park, Inverness IV1 2BZ. Tel: 01463 791513.
Admission: TBA. **Times**: TBA.

1-4 May*
HASTINGS TRADITIONAL JACK IN THE GREEN
Hastings, East Sussex.
Festival of traditional English music and dance.
Things to see: 800 morris dancers, rapper dancers, clog dancers with English giants, traditional folk, animals and mummers. A memorable sight against the backdrop of Hastings and its castle. With barn dances, folk concerts and more. Ancient traditional Jack in the Green ceremony. Contact the organisers for programme and more information.
Contact: Keith Leech, 9 Old Humphrey Avenue, Old Town, Hastings, East Sussex.
Admission: Most events free. £5 concert admission prices. **Times**: TBA.

1-4 May
PEEL SPORTS FESTIVAL
Various locations around Peel and Castletown, Isle of Man.
Sports festival.
Things to see: A variety of sports: netball, hockey, football, rugby, pub sports.
Contact: Special Events Unit, Grandstand, Douglas, Isle of Man IM2 4TB. Tel: 01624 661930.
Admission: Free. **Times**: TBA.

1-12 May
JANE ROSS FESTIVAL
Limavady, Co Londonderry.
Fortnight of activities including Mayor's Parade.
Things to see: Visiting artists and performers, music, drama, street theatre, plus the Mayor's Parade with fancy dress, bands and floats.
Contact: Limavady Borough Council, Council Offices, 7 Connell Street, Limavady, Co Londonderry BT49 0HA. Tel: 015047 60304/22226.
Admission: Various. **Times**: TBA.

2 May
GAWTHORPE MAYPOLE MAY DAY PROCESSION
Gawthorpe, Ossett, West Yorkshire.
May Day procession.
Things to see: Procession of floats, fancy dress, marching band, jazz band, etc.
Contact: Mrs S D Walshaw, 23 Branstone Grove, Gawthorpe, Ossett WF5 9SU.
Admission: N/A. **Times**: 1.45pm - 5.15pm (followed at 6pm by maypole dancing).

2 May
MIDSHIRES SIAMESE CAT ASSOCIATIONS CHAMPIONSHIP SHOW
Town Hall, Leamington Spa, Warwicks.
Cat show.
Things to see: Top cats on show – Siamese, Balinese and household pets.
Contact: Mrs D Harper, Woodlands Farm, Bridford, Exeter, Devon EX6 7EW. Tel: 01647 252486.
Admission: £1.50 adults; 75p OAPs and children. **Times**: 1pm - 5pm.

2 May
TEDDY BEARS' PICNIC
The Green, Abinger Hammer, Nr Dorking, Surrey (on A25).
Event designed for children.
Things to see: Children and their bears. Classes for bears, Pooh sticks championship in Tillingbourne. Village fair,

© James Clancy

stalls, entertainments, games, etc. Often a celebrity judge.
Contact: Shirley Corke, Eversheds, Abinger Hammer, Dorking RH5 6QA. Tel: 01306 730868.
Admission: Free (75p to enter bear classes; each bear gets a certificate). **Times**: 2pm - 5pm.

2 May
TORCHER PARADE
Aberdeen city centre.
Torchlit student parade in aid of charity.
Things to see: The largest student parade in Europe. Torchlit parade with painted and decorated floats (all built and decorated on the day), students in fancy dress. After the parade floats are completely destroyed. Ends a fortnight which includes a variety of other fundraising events.
Contact: Carolyn Forrest, ASCC President, 50-52 College Bounds, Old Aberdeen AB24 3DS. Tel: 01224 272967. Fax: 01224 272977.
Admission: N/A but bring something for the collecting cans! **Times**: 8pm - 10pm (approx).

2-3 May
BEALE MODEL BOAT FESTIVAL
Beale Park, Lower Basildon, Reading, Berkshire.
Widely considered by modellers to be the best model boat show in the country.
Things to see: This festival makes great use of the variety of waters at Beale Park, includes demonstrations, competitions and many trade stands.
Contact: Beale Park, The Child-Beale Trust, Lower Basildon, Reading, Berkshire RG8 9NH. Tel: 0118 984 5172.
Admission: £4 adults; £3 OAPs; £2.50 children. **Times**: 10am - 6pm.

2-3 May
BRITISH HILLCLIMB CHAMPIONSHIP
Prescott Hill, Cheltenham, Glos.
Hillclimb competition.
Things to see: Roadgoing sports cars and racing cars cars ascending a narrow twisting hill road at speeds of up to 110mph. Plus cars in paddock etc.
Contact: Mrs S Ward, Bugatti Owners Club, Prescott Hill, Gotherington, Glos GL52 4RD. Tel: 01242 673136.
Admission: £7 adults. **Times**: 10am - 5pm approx.

2-3 May
DEVON COUNTY ANTIQUES FAIR
Westpoint Exhibition Centre, Clyst St Mary, Exeter, Devon.
Antiques fair.
Things to see: Beautiful antiques and collectables among the estimated one million items on offer. 500 stands in one hall. Plus free lectures, seminars and exhibitions.
Contact: Val Dennis, Devon Counties Antiques Fairs, The Glebe House, Nymet Tracey, Crediton, Devon EX17 6DB. Tel: 01363 82571.
Admission: £3.50 adults; children free. **Times**: Sat: 10am - 5pm. Sun: 10am - 5pm.

2-3 May
SOUTH WEST CUSTOM & CLASSIC BIKE SHOW
Royal Bath and West Showground, Shepton Mallet, Somerset.
Motorcycle show.
Things to see: Motorcycles, 120 stands, bike jumble, fun fair, special features.
Contact: Kim or Brad, The Showground,

Shepton Mallet, Somerset BA4 6QN. Tel: 01749 823 260.
Admission: £6 adults; £3 children/OAPs. **Times**: 9am - 6pm.

2-3 May
WORLD PILOT GIG CHAMPIONSHIPS
Isles of Scilly.
Rowing championships.
Things to see: Pilot gigs are 32x5ft craft rowed by six oarsmen with a coxswain in the open sea. This event attracts many boats and featured crews from Cornwall, Scilly, Holland and the USA. A very colourful event. Best views are from on board the launches which follow races, or on the beach between events.
Contact: Steve Watt, Tourist Information Centre, St Marys, Isles of Scilly TR21 0JY. Tel: 01720 423371. Fax: 01720 422049.
Admission: N/A. **Times**: TBA.

2-4 May
BATH ANNUAL SPRING FLOWER SHOW
Royal Victoria Park, Bath.
Flower show.
Things to see: Major horticultural show, with a large floral marquee, floral art, crafts, horticultural sundries, British food and farming exhibition, band concerts and refreshments.
Contact: Sarah Giovannini, Leisure Services, Bath & N.E. Somerset Council, Northgate House, Upper Borough Walls, Bath BA1 1RG. Tel: 01225 396021.
Admission: £4 adults; £3.50 OAPs; accompanied children under 16 free. **Times**: 10am - 6pm.

2-4 May*
THE CLASSIC & SPORTSCAR SHOW
National Exhibition Centre, Birmingham.
Largest display of classic and sports cars in the UK.
Things to see: The largest most diverse collection of classic cars under one roof. Special feature areas, classic cars on display and for sale, classic car clubs, massive autojumble, trade stands and charity car rides in amazing classic cars.
Contact: BBC Haymarket Exhibitions, 55 North Wharf Road, London W2 1LA. Tel: 0171-402 2555.
Admission: TBA. **Times**: TBA.

2-4 May
FOUR SEASONS CRAFTS SHOW
Morden Hall Park, Morden, Surrey.
Craft fair.
Things to see: Quality crafts created by experts from all over the country. Robin Hood theme.
Contact: Four Seasons (Events Ltd), 23A Brockenhurst Rd, South Ascot, Berkshire SL5 9DJ. Tel: 01344 874787.
Admission: £2.50-£3.50 adults; £2-£2.50 OAPs; £1 children. **Times**: TBA.

2-4 May
MAY DAY MUSIC & DANCE
Hever Castle, Edenbridge, Kent.
May Day festivities.
Things to see: Festivities in May Day tradition with Morris dancers and Maypole dancing in the grounds. Many other things to see such as the Castle itself (Anne Boleyn's childhood home) and award winning gardens – suitable for picnics. New water maze.
Contact: Jan Roberts or Pauline Scott, Hever Castle, Edenbridge, Kent TN8 7NG. Tel: 01732 865224.
Admission: £7 adults; £3.80 children; £6 OAPs; £17.80 family (2 adults, 2 children). **Times**: Gardens open 11am. Castle opens 12 noon. Last admission 5pm. Final exit 6pm.

2-4 May
NATIONAL HOVERCRAFT RACING CHAMPIONSHIPS
Leisure Lakes, Mere Brow, Tarleton, Preston, Lancashire.
Formula Hovercraft racing. First leg of UK Championships.
Things to see: Fast furious light sports hovercraft racing. 4 Formulas including Junior (11-16 yrs). Seek permission from

organiser to view machines in paddock, otherwise free access round course.
Contact: Rev. W G Spedding, 26 Milverton Close, Lostock, Bolton BL6 4RR. Tel: 01204 841248.
Admission: Site entry fee £5 per car. **Times**: 11am - 5.30pm.

2-4 May
NEWBURY STEAM FUNTASIA
Newbury Agricultural Showground, Chieveley, Nr Newbury, Berkshire.
Steam rally.
Things to see: Show that attracts 40 of the best steam engines in the country, with 200 vintage cars, motorcycles, commercial vehicles and stationary engines. Non-stop arena events and children's attractions with a real Victorian steam-driven fun fair.
Contact: Frank Marchington, Barren Clough Farm, Buxworth, High Peak, Derbyshire SK23 7NS. Tel: 01663 732750.
Admission: £4 adults; £2 children/OAPs; under 5s free. **Times**: 10am - 6pm.

2-4 May
PORTSMOUTH HEAVY HORSE WEEKEND
Castle Field, Southsea, Hants.
Largest UK gathering of heavy horses.
Things to see: Sat: K9 Kapers Dog Show. Sun & Mon: Heavy horses, vintage working carts and carriages, arena displays and competitions. All weekend: trade and craft stands.
Contact: Guildhall Entertainments Manager, Guildhall, Guildhall Square, Portsmouth PO1 2AB. Tel: 01705 834146.
Admission: Free. **Times**: 10am - 5pm.

2-4 May
ROCHESTER SWEEPS FESTIVAL
Rochester High Street, Kent.
England's largest May festival.
Things to see: The Rochester Sweeps Festival takes place throughout the city during the weekend. This festival is unique and celebrates a tradition where sweeps parade their "Jack-in-the-Green" (an 8ft walking bush) through the city on May Day. The "Jack-in-the-Green" awakening ceremony takes place at Blue Bell Hill, 5.32am on 1 May, followed by the May Day procession. Free entertainment in the street, Children dressed as sweeps, morris dancers, music and song.
Contact: Visitor Information Centre, 95 High Street, Rochester, Kent. Tel: 01634 843666.
Admission: N/A. **Times**: 10am - 6pm (unconfirmed).

2-4 May
SPALDING FLOWER FESTIVAL & SPRINGFIELDS COUNTRY FAIR
Springfields Gardens, Spalding, Lincs.
Flower festival, parade and country fair.
Things to see: Parade of flower floats and bands, etc (Saturday only 1pm - 4pm). Entertainments, crafts, trade displays and much more.
Contact: B Willoughby, Springfields, Spalding, Lincolnshire PE12 6ET. Tel: 01775 724843 or 713243.
Admission: £5 adults; children free. **Times**: 10am - 6pm daily.

2-4 May
WEALD OF KENT CRAFT SHOW
Penshurst Place, Nr Tonbridge, Kent.
Craft show.
Things to see: Over 170 quality traditional craftsmen demonstrating and selling hand-made British crafts. Held under marquee, it forms a perfect family day out to see rural crafts, bands and dancers, to name but a few attractions.
Contact: ICHF Ltd, Dominic House, Seaton Road, Highcliffe, Dorset. Tel: 01425 272711.
Admission: £4.50 adults; OAPs £3.50; children (under 16) £1 or free if accompanied by parent. **Times**: 10am - 6pm.

2-24 May
BRIGHTON INTERNATIONAL FESTIVAL
Various venues in Brighton.
England's largest mixed arts festival.

Things to see: Over 700 events including concerts in the Royal Pavilion, opera at the Royal Theatre, a weekend of spectacular street theatre and a colourful parade. Plus lots of free exhibitions, comedy, contemporary dance, literature festival and town tours.
Contact: Brighton Festival, 21-22 Old Steine, Brighton BN1 1EL. Tel: 01273 292950/1. Free brochure available March.
Admission: Consult brochure. **Times**: Consult brochure.

3 May*
HISTORIC COMMERCIAL VEHICLE SOCIETY LONDON TO BRIGHTON RUN
Start: TBA, (London). Route follows A23 from Streatham to finish at Madeira Drive, Brighton.
The 35th annual London to Brighton Historic Commercial Vehicle Run.
Things to see: Road run for commercial vehicles over 20 years of age. Static display until 4pm on Madeira Drive. *Concours d'elegance*. Best vantage points are en route – paddock area very busy after midday.
Contact: The Secretary, HCVS, Iden Grange, Cranbrook Road, Staplehurst, Kent TN12 0ET. Fax: 01580 893227.
Admission: Entry to paddock area by programme for non-members of Society after 2pm. **Times**: Start 7am. Arrive Madeira Drive from 10.30am.

3 May*
1000 GUINEAS STAKES
Rowley Mile Racecourse, Newmarket, Suffolk.
Classic horse race.
Things to see: Top level horse racing.
Contact: The Clerk of the Course, Newmarket Racecourses Trust, Westfield House, The Links, Newmarket, Suffolk CB8 0TG. Tel: 01638 663482.
Admission: Members, £25; grandstand & paddock, £12. Silver ring family enclosure £5. Children free in all enclosures.
Times: First race 2pm. Final race 5.15pm.

3 May
THE SPITALFIELDS DOG SHOW
The Old Spitalfields Market, Brushfield St, London E1.
Champion event "for local woofs".
Things to see: All kinds of dogs.
Contact: Alternative Arts, 47A Brushfield Street, Spitalfields, London E1 6AA. Tel: 0171-375 0441.
Admission: Free. **Times**: From 12 noon - 5pm.

3 May
SPRING PLANT FAIR
Newby Hall & Gardens, Ripon, North Yorkshire.
Approximately 25 nurseries and specialist growers invited from all over the country.
Things to see: Nurseries, specialist growers, antiquarian book stall & gardening pottery.
Contact: Mr R G Alexander, Opening Administrator, Newby Hall, Ripon, North Yorkshire HG4 5AE. Tel: 01423 322583.
Admission: TBA. **Times**: From 10am - 4.30pm.

3 May
WELSH FESTIVAL OF DRESSAGE
The Showground, Gwernesney, Usk, Gwent.
Top dressage competition.
Things to see: Horses and riders competing in arenas, showing horses at all stages of training for dressage.
Contact: Mrs J Hyett, Woodlands Farm, Caerphilly Mountain, Mid Glamorgan CF83 1NF. Tel: 01222 885697.
Admission: N/A. **Times**: 9am - 6pm.

3-4 May
LEICESTER COUNTY SHOW
Dishley Grange, Loughborough, Leics.
Agricultural show.
Things to see: Horses and ponies, cattle, sheep, goat show, show jumping, dog show, trade stands, craft fair, food hall and various other events.

Contact: Miss A Currer Briggs, Leicestershire Agricultural Society, Show Office, Dishley Grange Farm, Derby Road, Loughborough, Leicestershire LE11 0SF. Tel: 01509 646786. Fax: 01509 646787.
Admission: £5 adults; £3 children. **Times**: 8am - 5pm.

3-4 May*
LUTON HOO CLASSIC CAR SHOW
Luton Hoo, Luton, Beds.
Classic car show.
Things to see: 1,500 gleaming classic cars, plus autojumble, trade stands, live commentary, children's entertainments, *concours* competition.
Contact: Sally Greenwood, Greenwood's Exhibitions, PO Box 49, Aylesbury, Bucks HP22 5FF. Tel: 01296 631181/632040. Fax: 01296 630394.
Admission: £5 adults; £4 OAPs; £2 children. **Times**: 10am - 5pm.

3-4 May
NATIONAL KITCAR MOTOR SHOW
National Agricultural Centre, Stoneleigh, Warwickshire.
World's largest kit car show.
Things to see: Thousands of kit cars and replicas, from on the road to *concours* standard.
Contact: Mrs E Cooling, Grosvenor Exhibitions Ltd, Grosvenor House, 81 London Road, Spalding, Lincolnshire. Tel: 01775 712100.
Admission: Approx £6 adult; children £2. **Times**: 9.30am - 6pm.

3-4 May
STEAM UP
Coldharbour Mill, Working Wool Museum, Uffculme, Cullompton, Devon.
Steam event.
Things to see: 1910 300hp mill engine in steam, Lancashire boilers, steam pumps. Also turn-of-the-century spinning and weaving machinery. Beam engine. New world tapestry.
Contact: Miss Jill Taylor, Coldharbour Mill, Uffculme, Cullompton, Devon EX15 3EE. Tel: 01884 840960.
Admission: £5 adults; £2.50 children. **Times**: 10.30am - 5pm.

3-4 May
TRUCKFEST '98
East of England Showground, Peterborough.
Trucking festival.
Things to see: Celebrities, trade stands, main arena activities, fun fair, all kinds of trucks including many from America and Europe, including the latest and the best from the manufacturers. Camping available over the weekend; if caravanning book in advance.
Contact: Live Promotions Ltd, The Millstone, St Thomas Road, Spalding, Lincolnshire PE11 2XY. Tel: 01775 768661.
Admission: TBA. **Times**: 9.30am - 6pm approx.

3-4 May
WEYMOUTH INTERNATIONAL BEACH KITE FESTIVAL
Weymouth beach, Dorset.
Britain's biggest kite-flying festival.
Things to see: Over 300 kite flyers from Britain and overseas create a two-day aerial wonderland, with stunt displays, giant 100ft parafoils, fighting kites, competitions, kite workshops, musical displays, night kite flying display and free fireworks display.
Contact: Weymouth Tourist Information. Tel: 01305 785747.
Admission: Free. **Times**: 10am - 5pm. fireworks display starts 9.45pm on 4 May.

4 May
THE BELFAST MARATHON
Start/finish at Maysfield Leisure Centre, East Bridge Road, Belfast.
Major city marathon and fun run.
Things to see: Over 4,000 runners participating in a gruelling 26-mile race through the city. Includes a team relay event, fun run event and marathon walk.
Contact: Brian Morrison, Head of Com-

munity & Leisure Services, Belfast City Council, The Cecil Ward Building, 4-10 Linenhall Street, Belfast BT2 8BP. Tel: 01232 270345.
Admission: N/A. **Times**: Fun run starts at 11am; marathon and relay at 12 noon; walk at 8am.

4 May
BLANDFORD GEORGIAN FAYRE
Town Centre, Blandford Forum, Dorset.
Street fair in celebration of Blandford's Georgian heritage.
Things to see: Horse-drawn drays, rural crafts, fun fair, buskers, giants, bands, dancers, period costumes, animals. Church tours, including access to roof, Georgian architecture and permanent display of period costumes.
Contact: Nigel Port, 1 Salisbury Road, Blandford Forum, Dorset DT11 7QG. Tel: 01258 480808.
Admission: £1. Car parking free. **Times**: 10am - 6.30pm.

4 May
MAY DAY BANK HOLIDAY MARKET
Town Centre, Sandbach, Cheshire.
Traditional market, Elizabethan theme.
Things to see: Antique, bric-a-brac and charity markets, and traditional family entertainment, with a backdrop of picturesque Cheshire black & white "Magpie" buildings and Saxon Crosses.
Contact: C O'Rawe, Markets Manager, Congleton Borough Council, Council Offices, Westfield, Middlewich Rd, Sandbach, Cheshire. Tel: 01270 763231.
Admission: N/A. **Times**: 9am - 5pm.

4 May
MILL AND FARM OPEN DAYS
Worsbrough Country Park, Worsbrough Bridge, Barnsley.
Open days at Worsbrough Corn Mill and Wigfield Open Farm.
Things to see: Water-powered corn milling, rare and traditional breeds of farm animals. Set in 200 acre Worsbrough Country Park.
Contact: Debra Bushby, Worsbrough Country Park, Off Park Road, Worsbrough Bridge, Barnsley, South Yorkshire S70 5LJ. Tel: 01226 774527.
Admission: Farm: £1.50 adults; 75p children/OAPs. Mill: 50p adults; 25p children/OAPs.**Times**: 12 noon - 5pm.

4 May
NORTH SOMERSET SHOW
Ashton Court, Bristol.
Agricultural show.
Things to see: Cattle, sheep, pigs, goats, horses, rabbits, cavies, crafts, horticultural marquee, food hall, ring events, hot air balloons, trade stands etc.
Contact: Keith Pulman, Show Office, East Dundry, Bristol. Tel: 0117 9643498.
Admission: £5 adult; £2 children. Free car parking. **Times**: 8am - 7pm.

4 May
THE SOUTH OF ENGLAND TOWN CRIERS' CHAMPIONSHIP
Town Centre, Blandford Forum, Dorset.
Town criers compete for a cup.
Things to see: Approximately 20 town criers in colourful regalia and their consorts in period dress against a background of the finest example of a Georgian market town in England.
Contact: Nigel Port, 1 Salisbury Road, Blandford Forum, Dorset DT11 7QG. Tel: 01258 480808.
Admission: Free. **Times**: 1.30pm - 4pm approx.

4 May
UFFCULME SHEEP SHOW
Coldharbour Mill, Working Wool Museum, Uffculme, Cullompton, Devon.
Country show.
Things to see: Show of coloured and rare sheep breeds, with spinning and country crafts, vintage engines, etc.
Contact: Miss Jill Taylor, Coldharbour Mill, Uffculme, Cullompton, Devon EX15 3EE. Tel: 01884 840960.
Admission: £1.50 approx (not yet fixed).
Times: 10am - 4pm.

4 May
WORLD STILTON CHEESE ROLLING CHAMPIONSHIP
High Street, Stilton, Peterborough.
May celebration with cheese rolling contest.
Things to see: Traditional May Day celebrations and cheese rolling competitions. Held outside the old inns (Bell & Angel) where Stilton cheese was sold.
Contact: Mrs O K Main, 8 Caldecote Road, Stilton, Peterborough PE7 3RH. Tel: 01733 241206.
Admission: N/A. **Times**: From 9.30am onwards.

4-9 May
SCOTTISH SIX DAYS TRIAL
Fort William area.
International motorcycle event.
Things to see: Top motorcycle action in superb Highland scenery. Be prepared and bring good walking boots and wet weather gear.
Contact: Jim McColm, 28 Nelson Street, Edinburgh, Scotland. Tel/fax: 0131-552 3927.
Admission: N/A. **Times**: 7.30am - 6pm approx daily.

7-10 May
THE MITSUBISHI MOTORS BADMINTON HORSE TRIALS
Badminton, Glos.
Major international equestrian competition.
Things to see: Dressage (7-8 May), cross-country (9 May), show jumping (10 May). Walk the cross-country course for a good variety of vantage points.
Contact: Mrs Jane Tuckwell (Secretary), Badminton Horse Trials, Badminton, Glos GL9 1DF. Tel: 01454 218272.
Admission: Details and ticket application forms available from Box Office from 1 Jan at above address or tel: 01454 218375. **Times**: 8am - 6pm approx daily.

Dates can change, events can be cancelled – Please check with the organisers before setting out!

8 May
THE HELSTON FURRY DANCE
Helston, Cornwall.
An old custom in Helston.
Things to see: Various processional dances throughout the day. The streets and houses are decorated with flowers and greenery. The organisers recommend arriving on the day before to gain a layout of the town and routes of the dances.
Contact: Mr T L Oliver, 51 Coinagehall Street, Helston, Cornwall TR13 8EU.
Admission: N/A. **Times**: First dance starts at 7am.

9 May
BARBON HILL CLIMB
Barbon Manor, Barbon, Nr Kirkby Lonsdale, Cumbria.
Hill climb championship.
Things to see: Racing and sports cars competing against the clock.
Contact: Mr B G Whittaker, Hopefield House, Kentmere Road, Staveley, Nr Kendal, Cumbria LA8 9PA.
Admission: £5. Free car parking. **Times**: Practising 9.30am. Timed runs 2pm onwards.

9 May
RICHMOND MAY FAIR
Parish Church and The Green, Richmond, Surrey.
May fair.
Things to see: Maypole, May Queen's parade, Victorian carousel, Royal Ballet School dancing, children's fancy dress, quality craft fair, over 100 charity stalls, free entertainment all day.
Contact: Mrs Liz Carran, 5 Old Palace Terrace, The Green, Richmond, Surrey TW9 1NB.
Admission: Free. **Times**: 10am - 5pm.

9 May
STEYR-PUCH MANX NATIONAL RALLY
Isle of Man.
Car rally; a round of the Mintex National Rally Series.
Things to see: All-tarmac special stage car rally over closed public roads with cars travelling at high speed (including jumps). Hill and sea views provide excellent backdrop.
Contact: J E Skinner, 6 Berkeley Street, Douglas, Isle of Man IM2 3QA. Tel: 01624 626543.
Admission: N/A. **Times**: First car starts: 8.45am. First car to finish: 5.30pm.

9 May
TENNENT'S VELET CUP FINAL DAY
Murrayfield, Edinburgh.
Rugby Union Clubs Cup final.
Things to see: An entertaining festival of rugby with three cup finals; lots of fun and activities in the back pitch, for all the family.
Contact: Scottish Rugby Union, Murrayfield, Edinburgh EH12 5PJ. Tel: 0131 346 5000. Fax: 0131346 5001.
Admission: TBA. **Times**: TBA.

9 May
TETLEY BITTER CUP FINAL
RFU Twickenham, Middlesex.
Rugby knockout finals. Formerly the Pilkington Cup Final.
Things to see: Rugby – Tetley Bitter Cup Final and Tetley Bitter Shield Final.
Contact: Rugby Football Union, Rugby Road, Twickenham, Middlesex TW1 1DZ. Tel: (Ticket Information) 0181-744 3111.
Admission: TBA. 1997 guide: £20, £15, £10. Family ticket £20. **Times**: Tetley Bitter Shield kick-off 12 noon. Tetley Bitter Cup kick-off 3pm.

9-10 May
FIGHTER MEET '98
North Weald Airfield, Epping, Essex.
Show for both historic and modern fighter aircraft.
Things to see: Static and aerial displays of modern and vintage military aircraft. From World War 1 aircraft through to present day front-line jets. Mock battle scenes with real effect pyrotechnics. See modern jets flying in impressive display sequences.
Contact: Howard Webby, Fighter Meet, 2 Field End Road, Pinner, Middlesex HA5 2QL. Tel: 0181-866 9993. Fax: 0181-868 0258.
Admission: £14 adults; one child free of charge with accompanying adult, £10 for OAP and additional child. Reduced rate for advance ticket purchase. **Times**: 8am - 6pm.

9-10 May
MODEL BOAT RALLY
Steamboat Museum, Windermere, Cumbria.
Models boats.
Things to see: Model boats of of all shapes and sizes in action with the spectacular back drop of the Lakeland Fells. Also real-sized steamboats.
Contact: Bob Henson, Windermere Steamboat Museum, Rayrigg Road, Windermere, Cumbria LA23 1BN. Tel: 015394 45565.
Admission: Normal museum entry fees apply. **Times**: 10am - 5pm.

9-10 May
SPRING AUTOJUMBLE AND CLASSIC CAR SHOW
Beaulieu Abbey, Beaulieu, Brockenhurst, Hampshire.
200 classic cars and 500 stalls make this a great day out for anyone.
Things to see: Classic cars featuring vehicles of all kinds. The stalls display everything for the car enthusiast from car manuals to car models.
Contact: Stephen Munn, Marketing Manager, Beaulieu Abbey, Beaulieu, Brockenhurst, Hampshire SO42 7ZN. Tel: 01590 612345.
Admission: TBA. **Times**: From 10am.

9-10 May
STEAM SPECIAL AND VICTORIAN FAIR
The Historic Dockyard, Chatham, Kent.
Steam displays and a traditional Victorian Fair
Things to see: Experience all the fun of a traditional Victorian Fair, including a big wheel and children's rides. A host of magnificent entertainments from days gone by, including a working steam display with steam engines and steam driven machinery. Other attractions include Punch & Judy, face painting and children's games with the New Phoenix Players.
Contact: The Historic Dockyard, Chatham, Kent ME4 4TE. Tel: 01634 812551.
Admission: £2.50 adults; children free.
Times: 10am - 4pm.

10 May
COLCHESTER CLASSIC VEHICLE SHOW
Colchester Institute, Sheepen Rd, Colchester, Essex.
Over 1,000 classic vehicles of all ages.
Things to see: Classic vehicle displays, auto jumble, live music, real ale.
Contact: Show Director, Colchester Classic Vehicle Show, Colchester Institute, Sheepen Rd, Colchester, Essex. Tel: 01206 718000.
Admission: £4 adults. **Times**: 11am- 4pm.

10 May
ENGINE MUSEUM OPEN DAY
Prickwillow Engine Museum, Main Street, Prickwillow, Nr Ely, Cambridgeshire.
Museum open day.
Things to see: Old engines running, plus many other attractions.
Contact: Joan Stacey, Prickwillow Engine Trust, Main Street, Prickwillow, Nr Ely, Cambs CB7 4UN. Tel: 01353 688360.
Admission: £3 adults; £2 children/OAPs; £7 family. **Times**: Museum opens 11am - 5pm; engines run 12 noon - 5pm.

© James Clancy

10 May
COVENT GARDEN MAY FAYRE & PUPPET FESTIVAL
St Paul's Church Gardens, Bedford Street, London WC2.
Annual celebration of puppetry.
Things to see: An extensive display of puppetry, including Punch and Judy professors from all over the country.
Contact: Alternative Arts, 47A Brushfield Street, London E1 6AA. Tel: 0171-375 0441.
Admission: Free. **Times**: 10.30am-5.30pm.

10 May
PENINSULA CLASSIC FLY FISHING COMPETITION
Siblyback Lake, Nr Liskeard, Cornwall.
Event from the calendar of 'Cornwall '98, The World Watersports Festival'.
Things to see: Some of the country's most skilful fly fishing experts. Top tips, tall tales, tremendous cast.

Contact: Cornwall '98, Trevint House, Strangways Villas, Truro, Cornwall TR1 2PA. Tel: 01872 223527.
Admission: TBA. **Times**: TBA.

10 May
SOUTH SUFFOLK AGRICULTURAL SHOW
Ampton point-to-point course, Ingham, near Bury St Edmunds, Suffolk.
Major agricultural show.
Things to see: Livestock and horses of all kinds, farm machinery, plus many other attractions and amusements.
Contact: Geoff Bailes, 35 Dalham Road, Moulton, Newmarket, Suffolk CB8 8SB. Tel: 01638 750 879.
Admission: £5 adults; £3 children under 14 years. **Times**: 8.30am onwards.

10 May
STATIONARY ENGINE RALLY
The National Waterways Museum, Llanthony Warehouse, Gloucester Docks.
Engine rally.
Things to see: Up to 40 stationary engines on display and working, within the Museum.
Contact: Mary Mills, Media/PR, National Waterways Museum, Llanthony Warehouse, Gloucester Docks, Gloucester GL1 2EH. Tel: 01452 318054.
Admission: £4.50 adults; £3.50 children/OAPs. **Times**: 10am - 5pm approx.

10 May
VINTAGE VEHICLE RALLY
Almond Valley Heritage Centre, Millfield, Livingston, West Lothian.
Vehicle rally.
Things to see: A wide range of vintage vehicles on display and in action within the attractive surroundings of Livingston Mill Farm.
Contact: Elaine Dunsire, Livingston Mill Farm, Millfield, Livingston, West Lothian EH54 7AR. Tel: 01506 414957.
Admission: £2.20 adults; £1.10 children. **Times**: 10am - 5pm.

10 May
WISCOMBE PARK SPEED HILL CLIMB
Wiscombe Park, Southleigh, Colyton, Devon (RAC signposted).
Speed hill climb for cars.
Things to see: Cars being driven at high speed on a narrow and tortuous track. Cars of great mechanical interest can be viewed static in the pits.
Contact: Dr R A Willoughby, Tudor Cottage, Sulhamstead, Reading RG7 4BP. Tel: 01734 302439.
Admission: £3 - £4. **Times**: 9am - 5.30pm.

13 May
BENSON & HEDGES CELEBRITY PRO-AM
The Oxfordshire Golf Club, Thame, Oxon.
Special pro-am golf tournament to precede the Benson & Hedges International Open.
Things to see: Stars from sport and showbusiness, plus instructional exhibitions, putting competitions & spectator village.
Contact: Benson & Hedges International Open, The Oxfordshire Golf Club, Milton Common, Thame, Oxon. Ticket Hotline: 01844 278292.
Admission: Tickets start from £11. Discounts for OAPs/children. **Times**: TBA.

13-15 May
BALMORAL SHOW
Balmoral Showgrounds, Belfast BT9 6GW.
Agricultural show.
Things to see: Horses, cattle, sheep, pigs, goats, poultry, show jumping, small animals, rare breed exhibits, dog agility, cookery demonstrations, band performances, etc. Plus exhibits including agricultural and horticultural machinery and consumer goods.
Contact: Royal Ulster Agricultural Society, The King's Hall, Balmoral, Belfast, Northern Ireland. Tel: 01232 665225.
Admission: TBA. **Times**: 9.30am - 8pm.

13-17 May*
ROYAL WINDSOR HORSE SHOW
Home Park, Windsor Castle, Berkshire.
Major annual equestrian event.
Things to see: International show jumping, showing classes, dressage, international driving Grand Prix, Royal pageantry, etc. Two thousand horses in competition. Most members of the Royal Family in attendance, especially HM The Queen. Floodlit evening programme.
Contact: Miss Penelope Henderson, Secretary, Royal Windsor Horse Show, The Royal Mews, Windsor Castle, Windsor, Berkshire SL4 1NG. Tel: 01753 860633.
Admission: TBA. **Times**: TBA.

14-17 May
BENSON & HEDGES INTERNATIONAL OPEN
The Oxfordshire Golf Club, Thame, Oxon.
European Tour golf tournament.
Things to see: Top European tour professionals in competition, plus instructional exhibitions, putting competitions & spectator village.
Contact: Benson & Hedges International Open, The Oxfordshire Golf Club, Milton Common, Thame, Oxon. Ticket Hotline: 01844 278292.
Admission: Tickets start from £11. Discounts for OAPs/children. **Times**: Telephone the day before to confirm starting times.

15 May
LADIES EVENING
Aintree Racecourse, Liverpool.
Horse race meeting with half price admission for ladies.
Things to see: Top level horse racing.
Contact: Racecourse Manager, Aintree Racecourse, Liverpool L9 5AS. Tel: 0151-523 2600. Fax: 0151-530 1512.
Admission: Full price admission from £10. Ladies from £5. **Times**: 5.45pm - 8.45pm.

Dates can change, events can be cancelled – Please check with the organisers before setting out!

15-16 May
SHROPSHIRE & WEST MIDLANDS SHOW
Agricultural Showground, Shrewsbury, Shropshire.
Two-day county show.
Things to see: Livestock, horses, trade fair, horse show, countryside activities, machinery, crafts, entertainment, countryside skills, fly casting, etc.
Contact: The Agricultural Showground, Shrewsbury, Shropshire. Tel: 01743 362824.
Admission: £7 adults; £5.50 OAPs; children £4. **Times**: 8.30am - 6pm.

16 May
INTERNATIONAL NORTH WEST 200
Portstewart, Coleraine, Portrush Circuit, Northern Ireland.
9 mile motor cycle road race over public roads held on the north coast of Northern Ireland.
Things to see: Top world motor cyclists in action.
Contact: Mervyn White, 99 Edenmore Rd, Limavady, Co Londonderry, Northern Ireland BT49 0NH. Tel: 01504 863094.
Admission: None. **Times**: Start 12 noon.

16 May
THE MIDDLESEX SEVEN-A-SIDE FINALS
RFU Twickenham, Middlesex.
Seven-a-side rugby.
Things to see: A day of rugby seven-a-side competitions, featuring some of the top Union clubs in Britain.
Contact: MCRFU, 124 The Walk, Potters Bar, Hertfordshire EN6 1PS. Tel: 01707 664600.
Admission: £20. **Times**: 11.20am - 7pm.

16 May
OTLEY SHOW
The Show Ground, Bridge End, Otley, West Yorkshire.
Agricultural show.
Things to see: Livestock, show jumping, ring attractions, farriers, tug of war, animals, produce and handicrafts, craft marquee, etc.
Contact: Mrs J M Raw, Secretary, Wharfedale Agricultural Society, 15 Bridge Street, Otley, West Yorkshire LS21 1BQ. Tel: 01943 462541.
Admission: £4 adults; £2 OAPs; £1.50 children. Tickets can be purchased in advance at the following prices: £3 adults; £1.50 OAPs; £1 children. **Times**: 8.30am - 6.30pm.

16 May
PUTNEY TOWN REGATTA
River Thames, Putney, London.
Rowing regatta.
Things to see: Various rowing events. Best vantage point is the embankment at Putney.
Contact: Miss P Lambe, 36 Belvedere Court, Upper Richmond Road, Putney, London SW15 6HY. Tel: 0181-788 9151.
Admission: N/A. **Times**: 10am - 6pm.

16-17 May
BISHOP BURTON HORSE TRIALS
Bishop Burton College, Bishop Burton, Beverley, East Yorkshire.
BHS horse trials.
Things to see: Top level dressage, show jumping and cross country. Trade stands, refreshments and licensed bar.
Contact: Miss L Johnson, Secretary, Bishop Burton College, Bishop Burton, Beverley, East Yorkshire. Tel: 01964 553085.
Admission: £5 per car approx. **Times**: 9am - 5pm approx.

16-17 May
FESTIVAL OF ENGLISH FOOD AND WINE
Leeds Castle, Maidstone, Kent.
This event offers the very finest foods and wines from Kent and the South-East of England.
Things to see: A display marquee will house demonstrations covering a wide-range of culinary and wine related topics throughout the weekend. There will be opportunities to sample and purchase "Kentish Fare", much of which is prepared using traditional methods. Music and morris dancing will add to the lively atmosphere and for children there is a Punch and Judy show, complete with stolen sausages!
Contact: Leeds Castle, Maidstone, Kent ME17 1PL. Tel: 01622 765400.
Admission: TBA. 1997 guide: £6.50 adults; £5 students/OAPs; £4 children; £19 family ticket. **Times**: TBA.

16-17 May
HORSES WEEKEND
The National Waterways Museum, Gloucester Docks.
Heavy horses and waterside activity.
Things to see: Heavy horses, carts and wagons, horse care, harness-making and parades in interesting waterside location. Peter the Museum horse entertains his friends and colleagues.
Contact: Jane Savory, National Waterways Museum, Llanthony Warehouse, Gloucester Docks, Gloucester GL1 2EH. Tel: 01452 318054.
Admission: £4.50 adults; £3.50 children/OAPs; £10-£12 family tickets. **Times**: 10.30am - 5.30pm.

16-17 May
DIESEL & STEAM WEEKEND
Midland Railway Centre, Butterley Station, Ripley, Derbyshire.
Railway event.
Things to see: Train services featuring both steam and diesel power, narrow-gauge and model railways, museum, country park, farm park, etc.
Contact: Alan Calladine, Midland Railway Centre, Butterley Station, Ripley, Derbyshire DE5 3QZ. Tel: 01773 747674.
Admission: £7.95 adults; £6.50 OAPs; 2

children free with each adult. **Times**: 10.30am - 4.15pm.

16-30 May
CANDELABRA PRIMULA WEEKS
Fairhaven Garden Trust, South Walsham, Norfolk (nine miles NE of Norwich on B1140).
Floral display.
Things to see: Wild and cultivated flowers, trees and shrubs; Candelabra primulas, azaleas, rhododendrons in bloom; bird sanctuary for ornithologists.
Contact: Mr G E Debbage, Resident Warden, The Fairhaven Garden Trust, 2 The Woodlands, Wymers Lane, South Walsham, Norwich, Norfolk NR13 6EA. Tel: 01603 270449.
Admission: £3 adults; £2.70 OAPs; £1 children. Entry to bird sanctuary £1. **Times**: 11am - 5.30pm.

17 May
COMBE MILL IN STEAM
Combe Mill (just off the A4095 at Long Handborough, Oxfordshire).
Special steam day.
Things to see: An 18thC beam engine and three other steam engines in steam. Plus working museum featuring blacksmiths and wood turners. Delightful riverside picnic area.
Contact: F A Huddleston, Braemar, The Ridings, Stonesfield, Witney, Oxfordshire OX8 8EA. Tel: 01993 891785.
Admission: £2.50 adults; £1 children/OAPs. **Times**: 10am - 5pm.

17 May
FA UMBRO TROPHY FINAL
Wembley Stadium.
Football final.

Dates can change, events can be cancelled – Please check with the organisers before setting out!

Things to see: Senior cup competition for non-league teams.
Contact: Steve Clark, Competitions Secretary, Lancaster Gate, London W2 3LW. Tel: 0171-402 7151.
Admission: TBA. **Times**: 3pm kick-off.

17 May
THE GREAT PAW TREK & DOG SHOW
Longleat House, Nr Warminster, Wiltshire.
Sponsored Dog Walk and exemption Dog Show in aid of Guide Dogs for the Blind Association.
Things to see: There is a mass start from the steps of Longleat House with several hundred dogs and owners at 11am. Lord Bath is hoping to attend as well as a band and Dog display team. The walk takes in 2 mile circuit of the grounds through wood and sculpture trail.
Contact: Andrew Frostick, Treasurer, Warminster & Westbury Guide Dogs for the Blind, 25 Portway, Warminster, Wiltshire BA12 8QG. Tel/fax: 01985 216187.
Admission: Normal grounds and gardens fee to Longleat. **Times**: 10am - 4pm.

17 May
HEART OF WORCESTERSHIRE BIKE RIDE
Start/finish: Abby Sport Stadium, Birmingham Road, Redditch, Worcs.
Charity cycle ride.
Things to see: Over 400 participants cycling through 40 miles of rural scenery and small villages.
Contact: Mr M Wilkes, British Heart Foundation, 271 Bromsgrove Road, Redditch, Worcs. Tel: 01527 66262.
Admission: N/A. **Times**: Start: 7.30am - 11am. Finish: 2pm - 5pm.

17 May
SPRING PLANT FAIR
Beningbrough Hall, Shipton, Beningbrough, York.
Sale of plants grown and donated by National Trust Volunteers and Bening-

borough Hall Gardens.
Things to see: Spring plants on sale.
Contact: The National Trust, Beningbrough Hall, Shipton, Beningbrough, York YO6 1DD. Tel: 01904 470666.
Admission: Normal admission prices apply. **Times**: TBA.

17 May
VINTAGE MOTORCYCLE RALLY
Weymouth, Dorset.
Vintage motorcycle rally.
Things to see: Over 100 vintage motorcycles parading along Weymouth seafront, plus static displays.
Contact: Mr H G Bailey, Leisure & Entertainments General Manager, Pavilion Complex, The Esplanade, Weymouth, Dorset DT4 8ED. Tel: 01305 772444.
Admission: Free. **Times**: Contact the Weymouth Tourist Information Centre for event update and programme on 01305 785747.

17 May
WISCOMBE PARK SPEED HILL CLIMB
Wiscombe Park, Southleigh, Colyton, Devon (RAC signposted).
Speed hill climb for cars.
Things to see: Cars being driven at high speed on a narrow and tortuous track. Cars of great mechanical interest can be viewed static in the pits.
Contact: Dr R A Willoughby, Tudor Cottage, Sulhamstead, Reading RG7 4BP. Tel: 01734 302439.
Admission: £3 - £4. **Times**: 9am - 5.30pm.

19-22 May
CHELSEA FLOWER SHOW
Royal Hospital, Chelsea, London SW3.
The most prestigious event on the horticultural calendar.
Things to see: A combination of breathtaking floral displays and garden designs, horticultural excellence and the very latest design ideas. It attracts exhibitors and visitors from all over the world.
Contact: Royal Horticultural Society, 80 Vincent Square, London SW1P 2PE. Tel: 0171-828 1744. Tickets are strictly limited and are all sold in advance.
Admission: RHS members only on Tues & Wed; Thurs (full day) £24; after 3.30pm £14; after 5.30pm £7. Fri (full day) £21. No children or babes-in-arms admitted.
Times: Tues - Thurs, 8am - 8pm; Fri, 8am-5pm (unconfirmed).

21 May
ENGLAND VS SOUTH AFRICA
The Oval, Kennington, London.
First Texaco Trophy one-day international.
Things to see: High class international cricket.
Contact: Surrey County Cricket Club, The Oval, Kennington, London SE11 5SS.
Admission: TBA. **Times**: TBA.

22 May
OLD SHIP ROYAL ESCAPE RACE
Opposite the Old Ship Hotel, between the two piers, Brighton.
Yacht race.
Things to see: Approximately 100 yachts set off for France in this race from Brighton.
Contact: J M Davis, General Manager, Old Ship Hotel, Kings Road, Brighton BN1 1NR. Tel: 01273 329001.
Admission: N/A. **Times**: TBA. Finish in France.

22-31 May
THE HAY FESTIVAL
Hay-on-Wye, Powys, Herefordshire.
Literary celebration.
Things to see: International authors from all over the world come to Hay for the festival; readings, book signings, discussions, etc.
Contact: Coralie Rogers, Hay Festival, Hay-on-Wye HR3 5BX. Tel: 01497 821217.
Admission: TBA. **Times**: 10am onwards.

22 May - 6 Jun
ENGLISH RIVIERA DANCE FESTIVAL
Town Hall and Victoria Hotel Ballroom, Torquay, Devon.
Dance festival.
Things to see: 14 days of competitive and social dancing for children and adults in all styles: Modern Ballroom, Latin American, Disco, Rock 'n' Roll, Sequence, etc.
Contact: Philip Wylie, 73 Hoylake Crescent, Ickenham, Middlesex UB10 8JQ. Tel: 01895 632143.
Admission: Varies; group rates and season tickets available. Contact the organisers. **Times**: Some events during the day, but the majority during the evening – contact organisers for more information.

23 May*
YORK CITY COUNCIL BUSKING FESTIVAL GRAND FINALS
Parliament Street Activity Area, York.
Busking competition.
Things to see: The best street entertainers in the North performing before a celebrity panel of judges chaired by the Lord Mayor. Presentations afterwards.
Contact: Val Carter, City Centre Services Manager, Central Building, York, North Yorkshire YO1 2RH. Tel: 01904 551677.
Admission: N/A. **Times**: 1.30pm - 4.30pm.

23 May
ATHOLL HIGHLANDERS' PARADE
Blair Castle, Pitlochry, Perthshire.
Annual parade of the Atholl Highlanders.
Things to see: One-hour parade and inspection of the Atholl Highlanders and their pipe band.
Contact: Geoff G Crerar, Adminstrator, Blair Castle, Blair Atholl, Pitlochry, Perthshire PH18 5TL. Tel: 01796 481 207.
Admission: £2 per car; £5 per mini-bus, £10 per coach.**Times**: Parade from 3pm - 4pm.

23 May
ENGLAND VS SOUTH AFRICA
Old Trafford, Manchester.
Second Texaco Trophy one-day international.
Things to see: Top class international cricket.
Contact: Old Trafford Cricket Ground, Manchester. Tel: 0161 848 7021.
Admission: TBA. **Times**: TBA. No play Sunday.

23-24 May
AIR FETE '98
RAF Mildenhall, Suffolk.
Largest airshow organised by the military anywhere in the world; NATO's biggest annual public event. Hosted by the United States Air Force and, with an audience of over 300,000, the best-attended such display in Europe.
Things to see: Daily seven-hour flying programme and extensive static aircraft parks. As many as possible of the flying display aircraft and aerobatic teams are parked and operated from directly in front of the spectators whose view along the two-mile crowdline is interrupted only by the control tower complex. The exhibition hangar offers a USAF display, careers exhibits and equipment from the British Services, plus displays from the aerospace industry and from aviation, naval and military museums.
Contact: R J Hoefling, Air Fete Office,

RAF Mildenhall, Bury St Edmunds, Suffolk IP28 8NF. Newsline: Mildenhall 01638 543341.
Admission: £17 car; £5 motorcycle; coach £125, covering vehicle and all occupants. Pedestrians: £4 adults; £1 children/OAPs; children under eight years are free. In addition there are special "park and ride", coach, train and airstrip facilities. **Times**: Car parks open 7.30am; exhibition area 8.30am; flying display starts approximately 11am - 5.30pm.

23-24 May
BRITISH LANDYACHT CHAMPIONSHIP SERIES
Pembrey Country Park, Nr Llanelli, Dyfed.
Landyacht racing championships.
Things to see: Racing for classes 3 and 5 landyachts, attracting entries from the majority of clubs in Great Britain and including British National team members. Exciting action of landyachts competing on beach, gridstarts, turning at corner marks. Sails, sand and sea. Bring wet weather clothing.
Contact: Gordon Wright, Cefn Sidan Landyacht Club, 1 Meadow Street, Swansea SA1 6RZ. Tel: 01792 519608.
Admission: Entry only to Country Park to gain access to beach. **Times**: 10.30am - 4pm.

23-24 May
HERTS COUNTY SHOW
The Showground, Redbourn, Hertfordshire (Junction 9 off the M1).
County agricultural show.
Things to see: Horses and ponies, show jumping, cattle, sheep, goats, rabbits, poultry, indoor and outdoor shopping, crafts, etc.
Contact: Mr P A Bayman, Herts County Show, The Showground, Dunstable Road, Redbourn, Hertfordshire AL3 7PT. Tel: 01582 792626. Fax: 01582 794027.
Admission: £7.50 adults (£6 pre-show); £2.50 children (£2 pre-show). **Times**: 8.30am - 5.30pm.

23-24 May
NORTHERN IRELAND OPEN ICE SKATING COMPETITIONS
Dundonald International Ice Bowl, 111 Old Dundonald Road, Belfast.
Major ice skating competition.
Things to see: Top ice skaters in action. Competitors from all over the UK travel to Northern Ireland to compete in this very prestigious event in the ice skating calendar.
Contact: Jill Simpson, PR & Events Coordinator. Tel: 01232 482611.
Admission: By Programme, approx £2. **Times**: Saturday: 10am - 6pm. Sunday: 10am - 4pm.

23-24 May
SCALE RAIL 98
New Lanark Visitor Centre, Scotland.
Major model rail show.
Things to see: Model railway layouts of all types and sizes, from all over Britain.
Contact: Development Officer, New Lanark Conservation Trust, New Lanark, Scotland ML11 9DB. Tel: 01555 661345.
Admission: £2.50. **Times**: 11am - 5pm.

23-25 May
COTSWOLD CRAFT SHOW
Sudeley Castle, Winchcombe, Nr Cheltenham, Glos.
Craft show.
Things to see: Over 150 craftsmen, many demonstrating skills, including several unusual rural demonstrations – stone walling, pole lathe, flint knapper, etc.
Contact: ICHF Ltd, Dominic House, Seaton Road, Highcliffe, Dorset. Tel: 01425 272711.
Admission: £4 adults; OAPs £3; children (under 16) £1 or free if accompanied by parent. **Times**: 10am - 6pm.

23-25 May
THE DERBYSHIRE STEAM FAIR
Hartington Moor Showground (on A515

Ashbourne to Buxton Road, seven miles north of Ashbourne).
Steam fair.
Things to see: Steam engines and allied exhibits, plus old-time fairground, crafts, arena events, Punch & Judy, children's attractions, trade stands, arena events.
Contact: Frank Marchington, Barren Clough Farm, Buxworth, High Peak, Derbyshire SK23 7NS. Tel: 01663 732750.
Admission: £4 adults; £2 children/OAPs. **Times**: 10am - 6pm.

23-25 May
ENDON WELL DRESSING
Endon Village on the A53 between Hanley & Leek.
Annual well dressing festival.
Things to see: Two decorated wells, church service, flower festival, crowning of the queen, various field entertainments, fun fair, etc.
Contact: Mr W B Thomas, 21 High View Road, Endon, Stoke-on-Trent, Staffordshire ST9 9HT. Tel: 01782 504085.
Admission: £1 adults; 50p children. **Times**: From 1.30pm daily.

23-25 May
MERRIE ENGLAND WEEKEND
Hever Castle, Edenbridge, Kent.
Medieval pastimes on display.
Things to see: Archery demonstrations, medieval stalls, music and dance. Many other things to see such as the Castle itself (Anne Boleyn's childhood home) and award winning gardens – suitable for picnics. New water maze.
Contact: Jan Roberts or Pauline Scott, Hever Castle, Edenbridge, Kent TN8 7NG. Tel: 01732 865224.
Admission: £7 adults; £3.80 children; £6 OAPs; £17.80 family (2 adults, 2 children). **Times**: Gardens open 11am. Castle opens 12 noon. Last admission 5pm. Final exit 6pm.

23-25 May
FOUR SEASONS CRAFTS SHOW
Norbury Park, Leatherhead, Surrey.
Craft fair.
Things to see: Quality crafts created by experts from all over the country. Robin Hood theme.
Contact: Four Seasons (Events Ltd), 23A Brockenhurst Rd, South Ascot, Berkshire SL5 9DJ. Tel: 01344 874787.
Admission: £2.50-£3.50 adults; £2-£2.50 OAPs; £1 children. **Times**: TBA.

23-26 May
LUTON JUNIOR TENNIS TOURNAMENT
Luton Regional Sports Centre, St Thomas Road, Stopsley, Luton.
LTA approved junior ratings tournament.
Things to see: Tennis tournament involving players of county/regional ability, all under 18 years old.
Contact: Luton Borough Council, Leisure & Cultural Services Department, Art Division (Promotions), 146 Old Bedford Road, Luton, LU2 7HH. Tel: 01582 876083.
Admission: Free. **Times**: 9.30am daily.

23-27 May
CHESTER GREEN WELL DRESSINGS
Junction of Marcus Street and Old Chester Road, Chester Green, Derby.
Traditional well dressing.
Things to see: Two wells are dressed, usually with religious pictures. The dressings are well attended by scores of visitors, press etc.
Contact: Derek Palmer, 2 Aylesbury Avenue, Chaddesden, Derby. Tel: 01332 673210.
Admission: Free. **Times**: Construction of dressings start on 20 May in the Mansfield Street Chapel. These are subsequently erected on 23 May and dismantled on 27 May.

23-30 May
THE FESTIVAL OF DOVER
Dover, Kent.
Annual community and arts festival.
Things to see: An exciting programme of

events and activities within the theme 'Coastal Landscapes'. Featuring street theatre, concerts, open air spectaculars, fireworks displays, walks, talks, workshops and lots more!
Contact: Lisa Webb, Arts Development Officer, Dover District Council, White Cliffs Business Park, Dover, Kent CT16 3PD. Tel: 01304 872058.
Admission: TBA. **Times**: TBA.

23-31 May
CONISTON WATER FESTIVAL
In and around Coniston, Cumbria.
Ten day event designed to highlight the various waterborne and shore-based activities that can be enjoyed on and around Coniston Water.
Things to see: Sailing, fishing, canoeing, country dancing, fell running, bowling, football, etc.
Contact: Ian Stancliffe, Campbell House, Coniston, Cumbria LA21 8EF. Tel: 015394 41707.
Admission: N/A. **Times**: Various.

23-31 May
DOWNY DUCKLING DAYS
The Wildfowl & Wetlands Trust, Martin Mere.
Duckery tours.
Things to see: Opportunity to see young birds hatching out. Young ducklings, goslings and cygnets in the grounds. Plus quizzes and displays.
Contact: Mrs E Beesley, Martin Mere, The Wildfowl & Wetlands Trust, Burscough, Ormskirk, Lancs L40 0TA. Tel: 01704 895181.
Admission: £4.50 adults; £3.50 OAPs; £2.75 children. Concessions for groups. **Times**: 9.30am - 5.30pm.

23-31 May
FRIENDS OF THOMAS THE TANK ENGINE
Midland Railway Centre, Butterley Station, Ripley, Derbyshire.
Family fun day with Thomas the Tank Engine theme.
Things to see: A theme event based on the Thomas the Tank Engine character with locomotives decorated as Thomas's friends, "Oswald" the talking engine, plus the Fat Controller.
Contact: Alan Calladine, Midland Railway Centre, Butterley Station, Ripley, Derbyshire DE5 3QZ. Tel: 01773 747674.
Admission: TBA. **Times**: 10.30am - 4.15pm.

24 May
BLAIR CASTLE HIGHLAND GAMES
Blair Castle, Pitlochry, Perthshire.
Annual Highland Games at Blair Castle.
Things to see: March-on by Atholl Highlanders, traditional Highland Games events including Tossing the Caber, tug of war, etc. Trade Stands, stalls and refreshments.
Contact: Geoff G Crerar, Adminstrator, Blair Castle, Blair Atholl, Pitlochry, Perthshire PH18 5TL. Tel: 01796 481 207.
Admission: £2 per car; £5 per mini-bus, £10 per coach.**Times**: TBA.

24 May
DORSET TOUR
Weymouth Pavilion/Loomoor Country Park, Weymouth, Dorset.
Vintage and classic vehicle run.
Things to see: Over 150 vintage and classic vehicles in action followed by static display at the tour showground. Plus car displays, children's rides, stalls and competitions.
Contact: Weymouth Tourist Information, 01305 785747.
Admission: Free. **Times**: Rally start at 9am, finish at 1pm - 2pm at the Pavilion. Events at Loomoor Park 11am - 5pm.

24 May
EAGLE HORSE SHOW
Beale Park, Lower Basildon, Reading, Berkshire.
A large local show with a wide range of classes.
Things to see: Mostly show jumping.
Contact: Beale Park, The Child-Beale

Trust, Lower Basildon, Reading, Berkshire RG8 9NH. Tel: 0118 984 5172.
Admission: Free. **Times**: 8am - 5pm.

24 May
ENGLAND VS SOUTH AFRICA
Headingley, Leeds.
Third Texaco Trophy one-day international.
Things to see: Top class international cricket.
Contact: Headingley Cricket Ground, St Michaels Lane, Leeds, West Yorkshire LS6 3BU.
Admission: TBA. **Times**: TBA.

24 May
SCOTTISH OUTDOOR CUP FINALS
Peffermill, Edinburgh.
Hockey tournament.
Things to see: Hockey skills in club outdoor Cup competitions (men and women).
Contact: Lesley Giblin, Scottish Hockey Union, 48 Pleasance, Edinburgh EH8 9TJ. Tel: 0131-650 8170.
Admission: TBA. **Times**: 10am - 5pm.

24 May
WELSH NSPCC IT'S A KNOCKOUT CHAMPIONSHIPS & SHOW 1998
Peoples Park, Llanelli, Dyfed.
Touring production of "It's A Knockout" for adults and children.
Things to see: Competitors engaging in "Knock Out" games, celebrities, children's characters, etc. Full supporting show with fun fair, amusements, etc.
Contact: Mrs E Field, The White House, Llanfoist, Abergavenny, Gwent NP7 9LR. Tel/fax: 01873 855552.
Admission: £3 adults; £1 children/OAPs. **Times**: 10am - 6pm.

24 May
WEYMOUTH OYSTER FESTIVAL
Weymouth Olde Harbour, Weymouth, Dorset.
Traditional harbourside festival for all the family.
Things to see: Oysters galore and much more – oyster trials, street entertainment, fancy dress, shire horses, fairground attractions, side-shows and competitions.
Contact: Weymouth Tourist Information, 01305 785747.
Admission: Free. **Times**: 10am - 5pm.

24-25 May
BATTLE MEDIEVAL FAIR & FESTIVAL OF FOOD
The Abbey Green (area immediately in front of Battle Abbey), Battle, East Sussex.
Fair with traders and stallholders in medieval costume.
Things to see: Jugglers, jesters, street musicians, peddlers, maypole dancers. At the same time English Heritage are expected to stage a major event inside the Abbey.
Contact: Mr Colin Smith, 39 High St, Battle, East Sussex TN33 0EL. Tel: 01424 774447.
Admission: Free. **Times**: 10am - 5pm.

24-25 May
GREAT YORKSHIRE KIT CAR SHOW
Great Yorkshire Showground, Harrogate, Yorkshire.
Kit car show.
Things to see: Thousands of kit cars and replicas, from on the road to *concours* standard.
Contact: Mrs E Cooling, Grosvenor Exhibitions Ltd, Grosvenor House, 81 London Road, Spalding, Lincolnshire. Tel: 01775 712100.
Admission: Approx £6 adult; children £2. **Times**: 9.30am - 6pm.

24-25 May
MANBY WHEELS '98
Manby Showground, Manby, Nr Louth, Lincolnshire.
All action motorsport event with fun for all the family.
Things to see: A variety of motorsport competitions plus many "have-a-go" events including rides in tanks, rally cars,

4x4s, quads, pilots and karts. Plus many trade stands, craft fair and childrens entertainment. Celebrity appearance on Monday 26 May.
Contact: Graham Rolfe, Viking Events Ltd, The Old Wheatsheaf, Starlode Drove, West Pinchbeck, Spalding, Lincolnshire PE11 3TD.
Admission: £5 adults; £2 children/OAPs; under-5s free. **Times**: From 10am daily.

24-25 May
MILL AND FARM OPEN DAYS
Worsbrough Country Park, Worsbrough Bridge, Barnsley.
Open days at Worsbrough Corn Mill and Wigfield Open Farm.
Things to see: Water-powered corn milling, bread baking demonstrations, hand and machine sheep shearing, rare and traditional breeds of farm animals, craft fair, etc.
Contact: Debra Bushby, Worsbrough Country Park, Off Park Road, Worsbrough Bridge, Barnsley, South Yorkshire S70 5LJ. Tel: 01226 774527.
Admission: Farm: £1.50 adults; 75p children/OAPs. Mill: 50p adults; 25p children/OAPs. **Times**: 12 noon - 5pm.

24-25 May
PENSHURST PLACE CLASSIC MOTOR SHOW
Penshurst Place, Tonbridge, Kent.
Classic car show.
Things to see: 1,200 gleaming classic cars plus autojumble, trade stands, live commentary, children's entertainments and *concours* competition.
Contact: Sally Greenwood, Greenwood's Exhibitions, PO Box 49, Aylesbury, Bucks HP22 5FF. Tel: 01296 631181/632040. Fax: 01296 630394.
Admission: £4.50 adults; £3 OAPs; £2 children. **Times**: 10am - 5pm.

24-25 May
PETERBOROUGH CLASSIC CAR SHOW MOTOR SHOW
Elton Hall, Peterborough, Cambs.
Classic car show.
Things to see: 1,000 gleaming classic cars plus autojumble, trade stands, live commentary, children's entertainments and *concours* competition.
Contact: Sally Greenwood, Greenwood's Exhibitions, PO Box 49, Aylesbury, Bucks HP22 5FF. Tel: 01296 631181/632040. Fax: 01296 630394.
Admission: £4 adults; £3 OAPs; £2 children. **Times**: 10am - 5pm.

24-25 May
THE ROMAN ARMY
Old Sarum Castle, Salisbury, Wiltshire.
Award winning Roman re-enactment group.
Things to see: Catapults, cavalrymen.
Contact: Mark Selwood, Special Events Unit, Room 101, English Heritage, Keysign House, 429 Oxford Street, London W1R 2HD. Tel: 0171-973 3420. Fax: 0171-973 3430.
Admission: TBA. **Times**: TBA.

24-25 May
SOUTHEND AIRSHOW
Western Esplanade, Southend-on-Sea.
Air show.
Things to see: A magnificent air display featuring all that's best in civil and military aviation. Recommended vantage point is Cliff Gardens, which gives panoramic views of aircraft against the backdrop of the Thames Estuary.
Contact: Special Events, Southend Borough Council, PO Box 6, Southend-on-Sea SS2 6ER. Tel: 01702 390333 or 01702 215166.
Admission: Free. **Times**: 10am - 6pm.

24-25 May
SPRING HOLIDAY STEAMDAYS
Didcot Railway Centre, Didcot, Oxfordshire.
Steam trains.
Things to see: Great Western Railway engines in steam for train rides and demonstrations, plus guided tours, signal box open, etc.

Contact: Ms J Howse, Didcot Railway Centre, Didcot, Oxfordshire OX11 7NJ. Tel: 01235 817200.
Admission: £6 adult; £4 children; £5 over-60s; £18 family. **Times**: 10am - 5pm.

24-25 May
STEAM UP
Coldharbour Mill, Working Wool Museum, Uffculme, Cullompton, Devon.
Steam event.
Things to see: 1910 300hp mill engine in steam, Lancashire boilers, steam pumps. Also turn-of-the-century spinning and weaving machinery. Beam engine. New world tapestry.
Contact: Miss Jill Taylor, Coldharbour Mill, Uffculme, Cullompton, Devon EX15 3EE. Tel: 01884 840960.
Admission: £5 adults; £2.50 children. **Times**: 10.30am - 5pm.

24-31 May
PARK WEEK
West Stow Country Park and Anglo-Saxon Village, Bury St Edmunds, Suffolk.
Countryside activities for all the family in the beautiful and very varied country park and Anglo-Saxon village.
Things to see: Different levels of guided walks in park; family environmental activities; costumed craftspeople in the village - and more.
Contact: Liz Proctor, The Visitor Centre, West Stow Country Park, Icklingham Road, West Stow, Bury St Edmunds, Suffolk IP28 6HG. Tel: 01284 728718.
Admission: To park, free. To Village (provisional): £4.50 adults; £3 children/OAPs; £12.50 families (2 adults and up to 3 children).

25 May
CALDICOT CARNIVAL
Caldicot Castle & Country Park, Caldicot, Gwent.
Annual carnival held in medieval castle grounds.
Things to see: Carnival procession through town centre, ending at the Castle Country Park where there will be numerous trade/charity stalls and entertaining field events in this delightful setting.
Contact: Mr V J T Edwards, Caldicot Town Council, Council Office, Sandy Lane, Caldicot, Gwent NP6 4NA. Tel: 01291 420441.
Admission: N/A. **Times**: 1.30pm approx.

25 May
LUTON CARNIVAL
Luton Town Centre, & Wardown Park, New Bedford Road.
Street carnival.
Things to see: Street carnival with live entertainment, stalls and very colourful procession. Procession route is published in advance.
Contact: Luton Borough Council, Leisure & Cultural Services Department, Art Division (Promotions), 146 Old Bedford Road, Luton, LU2 7HH. Tel: 01582 876052.
Admission: N/A. **Times**: Street/fair event 12 noon - 7pm; procession 2.30pm - 4.30pm approx.

25 May
NORTHUMBERLAND COUNTY SHOW
Tynedale Park, Corbridge, Northumberland.
Agricultural show.
Things to see: Show jumping, ring entertainments, truck show, sheep, cattle, goats, rabbits, dogs, heavy horses, ponies, etc.
Contact: Secretary: Mrs K Walton, Woodside, Allensgreen, Bardon Mill, Hexham, Northumberland. Tel: 01434 344443.
Admission: £5 adults; £3 OAPs; Children free. Parking free. **Times**: 8.30am - 6pm.

25 May
SURREY COUNTY SHOW
Stoke Park, Guildford, Surrey.
Agricultural show.
Things to see: Horses and livestock, plus

over 200 shops and trade stands.
Contact: Juliet Lance, 45 Bridge Street, Godalming, Surrey GU7 1HL. Tel: 01483 414651. Fax: 01483 425697.
Admission: £8 adults; £4.50 OAPs; £3 children. **Times**: 8.30am - approx 7pm.

25 May
TETBURY WOOLSACK DAY
Tetbury, Glos.
Woolsack races.
Things to see: Racers carrying 60lb woolsacks up 1 in 4 hill (open entry - for the brave). Plus street fair, market, street entertainers, village fete, Punch & Judy, Morris Dancing, handbell ringers, majorettes, etc.
Contact: Chairman: A A Stowell, Kimberley, Northfield Rd, Tetbury, Glos. Tel: 01666 502629.
Admission: £2 parking all day includes official programme. **Times**: 10am - 5pm.

25 May
A YESTERDAY MAYDAY
National Tramway Museum, Crich, Matlock, Derbyshire.
Mayday event.
Things to see: The way it was - try your hand at whip 'n top, hoops and more old fashioned games around a Maypole.
Contact: Lesley Wyld, Marketing Manager, National Tramway Museum, Crich, Matlock, Derbyshire DE4 5DP. Tel: 01773 852565. Fax: 01773 852326.
Admission: £5.90 adults; £3 children; £5.10 OAPs; £16.20 family ticket. **Times**: 10am - 5.30pm.

25-29 May
HALF TERM FUN FOR CHILDREN
Leeds Castle, Maidstone, Kent.
Event designed for children.
Things to see: Learning and fun, different activities each half-term. Further details TBA.
Contact: Leeds Castle, Maidstone, Kent ME17 1PL. Tel: 01622 765400.
Admission: TBA. **Times**: TBA.

27-28 May
STAFFORDSHIRE COUNTY SHOW
County Showground, Stafford.
Major agricultural show.
Things to see: Full main ring programme and 50 acres of entertainment. Livestock, machinery, floral decorations, equestrian displays, dogs, poultry, motor cycle displays, etc.
Contact: Mr R C Williams, Secretary, County Showground, Stafford ST18 0BD. Tel: 01785 258060.
Admission: £8. **Times**: 8am - 7pm.

27-28 May
SUFFOLK SHOW
Ipswich, Suffolk.
Agricultural show.
Things to see: Over 700 hundred trade stands, craft marquee, flower show, food hall, dog show. More than 500 livestock classes and international show jumping. A wide variety of ring events and much more.
Contact: Miss Jodie Tomlinson, Tradestand officer, The Showground, Bucklesham Road, Ipswich IP3 8UH. Tel: 01473 726847.
Admission: TBA. **Times**: 7.30am onwards.

27-30 May
THE ROYAL BATH & WEST OF ENGLAND SHOW
Royal Bath and West Showground, Shepton Mallet, Somerset.
An agricultural event for the whole family.
Things to see: Main ring events, over a thousand trade stands, judging of farm animals, rural craft displays, flower displays, conservation area, displays of the best food & wine in the West.
Contact: The Secretary, The Royal Bath and West of England Society, The Showground, Shepton Mallet, Somerset BA4 6QN. Tel: 01749 822 200. Fax: 01749 823169.
Admission: TBA. **Times**: 9am - 6pm.

28-31 May
THE DICKENS FESTIVAL
Rochester, Kent.
Celebration of Charles Dickens and his work.
Things to see: An excellent opportunity to see Dickens characters come to life and to witness live re-enactments of many famous scenes from his novels. Also Dickens Spectacular fireworks Display.
Contact: Visitor Information Centre, 95 High Street, Rochester, Kent. Tel: 01634 843666.
Admission: N/A. **Times**: TBA; approx 10am - 6pm.

29 May
CASTLETON ANCIENT GARLAND CEREMONY
Begins at The Peak Hotel car park; finish at The Market Place. Castleton, Hope Valley, Derbyshire.
Very old pagan fertility rite – a ceremony/procession that also commemorates the restoration of Charles II on Oak Apple Day.
Things to see: King on horseback, wearing beehive-shaped flower headdress, accompanied by his lady, both in Stuart costume. Also girls dancing in white flower-bedecked dresses and band playing the Garland tune. The ceremony takes the form of a procession but stops from time to time allowing spectators the opportunity to take good photos.
Contact: Secretary: Mrs V A Turner, The Walk, Buxton Road, Castleton, Hope Valley, S33 8WP. Tel: 01433 620571.
Admission: N/A. **Times**: 6.30pm - 8.30/9pm approx.

29 May
ROBERT DOVER'S COTSWOLD OLIMPICK GAMES
Dover's Hill, Nr Chipping Campden, Gloucestershire.
Olimpick games dating from 1612.
Things to see: Opening ceremony, bands, traditional games and entertainments on Dover's Hill, ending with fireworks and bonfire, and a torchlight procession into Chipping Campden.
Contact: Dr F Burns, 51 Ridge Road, Kingswinford, West Midlands DY6 9RE. Tel: 01384 274041.
Admission: £3. **Times**: 7.30pm.

29-30 May
BALLYMENA SHOW
Showgrounds, Warden Street, Ballymena, Co Antrim.
Agricultural show.
Things to see: Showing of horses, ponies, cattle, sheep, pigs, poultry, dogs, etc. Horse and pony jumping, harness events. Other special attractions such as cars, motorcycles, etc.
Contact: Mrs M Watterson, Show Office, Warden Street, Ballymena, Co Antrim BT43 7DR. Tel/fax: 01266 652666.
Admission: TBA. **Times**: Fri: 2pm - 9pm. Sat: 9am - 6pm.

29-31 May
CREATIVE STITCHES & PASTIMES SHOW
Inspiration, ideas and supplies for a more creative lifestyle.
Sewing, needlecraft & knitting show.
Things to see: Over 120 companies representing virtually every type of craft, demonstrating, advising and selling. "Quick & Easy" workshops to introduce you to new crafts or help you improve your current pursuit.
Contact: ICHF Ltd, Dominic House, Seaton Road, Highcliffe, Dorset. Tel: 01425 272711.
Admission: £5.20 adults; £4.20 OAPs. **Times**: 9.30am - 5.30pm (Sun 5pm).

30 May
ABERLOUR INVERARAY CASTLE HORSE TRIALS
Glen Shira, Inveraray.
The only British Horse Trials Association one day event in the Western Highlands.
Things to see: Dressage, show jumping and cross-country.
Contact: Mrs Macpherson, The Old

Manse, Strachur, Argyll PA27 8DF. Tel: 01369 860247.
Admission: £5 per full car. **Times**: 9am - 4.45pm.

30 May
DEVON COUNTY ANTIQUES FAIR
Matford Centre in the Exeter Livestock Centre, Matford Park Rd, Marsh Barton, Exeter, Devon.
Antiques fair.
Things to see: Beautiful antiques and collectables among the many items on offer. 430 stands in all.
Contact: Val Dennis, Devon Counties Antiques Fairs, The Glebe House, Nymet Tracey, Crediton, Devon EX17 6DB. Tel: 01363 82571.
Admission: £2 adults; children free. **Times**: 10am - 5pm.

30 May
TEES REGATTA
River Tees upstream of the newly built Tees Barrage, Stockton-on-Tees.
First class rowing.
Things to see: Classes of rowing for all standards of oarsmen. This event takes place on a purpose built, three-lane, 1000m course on the River Tees.
Contact: Graham Reeves, Events Development Officer, Stockton-on-Tees Borough Council, PO Box 116, Gloucester House, 72 Church Road, Stockton-on-Tees TS18 1YB. Tel: 01642 393939 ext 3911.
Admission: Free. **Times**: TBA.

30 May
TROOPING THE COLOUR – THE MAJOR GENERAL'S REVIEW
Horse Guards, Whitehall, London SW1.
First rehearsal for this colourful event.
Things to see: Rehearsal for The Queen's Birthday Parade (usually referred to as Trooping The Colour). A complete parade. Hand-held cameras are permitted in the seated area; video cameras are not encouraged.
Contact: HQ Household Division, Horse Guards, London SW1. Tel: 0171-414 2497. General enquiries Tel: 0891 505 453.
Admission: Allocated by ballot. Applicants must write between 1 Jan - 28 Feb to HQ Household Division, enclosing sae. Tickets are free for this event. **Times**: Ticket holders must be seated by 10am. Event finishes at 12.15pm approx.

3 0-31 May
CLASSIC CAR MEETING
Prescott Hill, Cheltenham, Glos.
Hillclimb competition.
Things to see: Classic cars cars ascending a narrow twisting hill road at speeds of up to 100mph. Plus cars in paddock etc.
Contact: Mrs S Ward, Bugatti Owners Club, Prescott Hill, Gotherington, Glos GL52 4RD. Tel: 01242 673136.
Admission: £7 adults. **Times**: 10am - 5pm approx.

30-31 May
CHESHIRE CLASSIC CAR SPECTACULAR & GIANT AUTOJUMBLE
Tatton Park, Knutsford, Cheshire (Junction 19 off the M6, Junction 7 off the M56).
Classic cars on display.
Things to see: Over 2,000 classic cars and 90+ car clubs at this show, plus an autojumble. 50th anniversary of Jaguar's XK sportscars, marked by huge display of Jaguar sportscars, including E-types, XJS cars and XK120s, 140s and 150s.
Contact: Stuart Holmes, Bridge House, Park Road, Stretford M32 8RB. Tel: 0161-864 2906.
Admission: £5 adults; children free. **Times**: 9am - 5pm.

30-31 May
TINKERS PARK TRACTION ENGINE RALLY
Tinkers Park, Hadlow Down, Nr Uckfield, East Sussex.
Steam rally.
Things to see: Steam traction engines, fair organs, narrow gauge railway, fairground, arena events and many cate-

gories of vintage vehicles.
Contact: Peter Haining, Horns Lodge, Meres Lane, Cross In Hand, Heathfield TN21 0TY.
Admission: £4 (£3.50 Saturday) adults; £1 children. **Times**: 11am - 5pm.

31 May
THE LATIN AMERICAN FIESTA DA CULTURA
Victoria Embankment Gardens, Villiers Street, London WC2.
Music/dance festival.
Things to see: Music and dancing from South America.
Contact: Alternative Arts, 47A Brushfield Street, Spitalfields, London E1 6AA. Tel: 0171-375 0441.
Admission: Free. **Times**: 2pm - 8pm.

31 May
THE NORWICH UNION RAC CLASSIC CAR RUN
Finish at Silverstone Racing Circuit, from nine starting points around the country.
Classic car run.
Things to see: National touring assembly of road cars manufactured between 1 January 1905 and 31 December 1977.
Contact: Mrs B Judson, Norwich Union RAC Classic Car Run, RAC Motorsports Association Ltd, Motorsports House, Riverside Park, Colnbrook, Slough, Berkshire SL3 0HG. Tel: 01753 681736.
Admission: For Silverstone contact the circuit. **Times**: 8am - 9am from start points.

June

1 Jun
MIDLAND COUNTIES SHOW
The Racecourse, Wood Lane, Uttoxeter, Staffordshire.
Horse show.
Things to see: Horses of all breeds including Arabs, Shetlands, Welsh ponies, etc. Also showjumping, side saddle, trade stands, crafts and general entertainment.
Contact: Miss M Liddington, Melrose, 32 Atherstone Road, Measham, Swadlincole, Derby DE12 7EG. Tel: 01530 271169.
Admission: £2 adults; £1 children. **Times**: 8.30am - 6.30pm approx.

1-12 Jun
TT FESTIVAL FORTNIGHT
TT mountain course, Isle of Man.
Recognised as the greatest motorcycle races in the world.
Things to see: An eight race meeting with solo classes from 125cc to 750cc and sidecars. Senior race day is 12 Jun.
Contact: Department of Tourism, Douglas, Isle of Man. Tel: 01624 686766.
Admission: From £6 on grandstand. **Times**: TBA.

2 Jun
ROYAL GUN SALUTE FOR CORONATION DAY
The Tower of London and in Hyde Park.
Gun salutes to mark the anniversary of the Queen's Coronation.
Things to see: Gun salutes fired in London by the King's Troop Royal Artillery in Hyde Park at 1200 hours (41 Gun Royal Salute) and by the Honourable Artillery Company at the Tower of London at 1300 hours (62 Gun Royal Salute).
Contact: The Information Officer, Public Information Office, Headquarters London District, Chelsea Barracks, London SW1H 8RF.
Admission: Free. **Times**: See above.

Dates can change, events can be cancelled – Please check with the organisers before setting out!

3-4 Jun
BEATING RETREAT BY THE MASSED BANDS OF THE HOUSEHOLD DIVISION
Horse Guards Parade, Whitehall, London SW1.
Floodlit marching display.
Things to see: A spectacular marching and musical display by the massed bands, pipes and drums of the Household Division. By floodlight.
Contact: Tickets available from 1 March. Contact: Household Division, Funds Office, Headquarters London District, Horse Guards, Whitehall, London SW1A 2AY. Tel: 0171-414 2271.
Admission: TBA. **Times**: Parade commences at 9.30pm.

4-6 Jun
RSAC SCOTTISH RALLY
Start and finish: Dumfries, Scotland.
International motor rally.
Things to see: International motor rallying. A round of the British and Scottish championships which attracts many leading European drivers.
Contact: Jonathan Lord, The Royal Scottish Automobile Club (Motor Sport) Ltd,

11 Blythswood Square, Glasgow G2 4AG. Tel: 0141-204 4999.
Admission: N/A. **Times**: TBA.

4-6 Jun
ROYAL CORNWALL SHOW
The Royal Cornwall Showground, Wadebridge, Cornwall.
Major agricultural show.
Things to see: Hundreds of trade exhibits and thousands of livestock, dogs, etc. Huge flower show, countryside conservation area, steam fair and more.
Contact: Mr C P Riddle, Secretary, Royal Cornwall Agricultural Association, The Royal Cornwall Showground, Wadebridge, Cornwall PL27 7JE. Tel: 01208 812183. Fax: 01208 812713.
Admission: TBA. **Times**: 8.30am - 7.30pm (static exhibits close at 6.30pm).

5-6 Jun
EPSOM SUMMER MEETING
Epsom Racecourse, Epsom Downs, Surrey.
Classic horse racing event, including the Derby, the premier classic horse race in the world.
Things to see: Top class horse racing. Derby Day is on the 6th; the Coronation Cup and the Oaks on the 5th. Plus the Derby Fair at Tattenham Corner, and the Derby Market, with a top class programme of pre and post race entertainment.
Contact: Miss Joanne Dillon, United Racecourses Ltd, Sandown Racecourse, Esher, Surrey KT10 9AJ. Tel: 01372 470047.
Admission: TBA. **Times**: Opens 11am approx.

5-7 Jun
WESSEX FLOWER & CRAFT SHOW
Wilton House, Wilton, Nr Salisbury, Wiltshire.
Flower and craft show.
Things to see: Traditional craftsmen making and selling hand-made British crafts. Plus music, dance and other attractions.
Contact: ICHF Ltd, Dominic House, Seaton Road, Highcliffe, Dorset. Tel: 01425 272711.
Admission: £5 adults' OAPs £4. **Times**: 10am - 6pm.

6 Jun
BARBON HILL CLIMB
Barbon Manor, Barbon, Nr Kirkby Lonsdale, Cumbria.
Hill climb championship.
Things to see: Racing and sports cars competing against the clock.
Contact: Mr B G Whittaker, Hopefield House, Kentmere Road, Staveley, Nr Kendal, Cumbria LA8 9PA.
Admission: £5. Free car parking. **Times**: Practising 9.30am. Timed runs 2pm onwards.

6 Jun
LIVERPOOL LORD MAYOR'S PARADE
Liverpool city centre.
Parade through city centre.
Things to see: Parade of vehicles, marching bands, the Lord Mayor's coach, Beauty Queen, Prince and Princess.
Contact: Osmar Media & Marketing, 377A Smithdown Road, Liverpool L15 3JJ. Tel: 0151-734 2851. Fax: 0151-734 3122.
Admission: N/A. **Times**: Start approx 3pm. Finish 4.30pm.

6 Jun
MAYOR'S PARADE
City Centre, Derry, N.Ireland.
Parade through city centre.
Things to see: A colourful parade of floats, bands, vintage cars and sideshows with Samba bands and street entertainers bringing a touch of Rio to the city.
Contact: Nuala McGee, Festivals Officer, Recreation & Leisure Department, Council Offices, 98 Strand Road, Derry BT48 7NN Tel: 01504 365151 ext 6668.
Admission: Free. **Times**: 2pm – 5pm.

6 Jun
TROOPING THE COLOUR – THE COLONEL'S REVIEW
Horse Guards, Whitehall, London SW1.
Horse Guards on parade.
Things to see: The rehearsal for The Queen's Birthday Parade – a complete parade in its own right.
Contact: HQ Household Division, Horse Guards, London SW1. Tel: 0171-414 2497. General enquiries on Tel: 0891 505 453.
Admission: Tickets allocated by ballot. Applicants write to the above address enclosing sae between 1 Jan - 28 Feb for seated tickets. **Times**: To be seated by 10am. Performance ends at 12.15pm approx.

6-7 Jun
LEEDS CASTLE BALLOON & VINTAGE CAR FIESTA
Leeds Castle, Maidstone, Kent.
Hot air ballooning event.
Things to see: A spectacular event with up to thirty (often fun-shaped) balloons rising into the sky above the battlements of Leeds Castle.
Contact: Leeds Castle, Maidstone, Kent ME17 1PL. Tel: 01622 765400. Fax: 01622 735616.
Admission: TBA. **Times**: From 6am.

6-7 Jun
OPEN DANCE FESTIVAL
Victoria Embankment Gardens, Villiers Street, London WC2.
Dance festival.
Things to see: All forms of classical, contemporary and traditional dance performed by over 50 different groups.
Contact: Alternative Arts, 47A Brushfield Street, Spitalfields, London E1 6AA. Tel: 0171-375 0441.
Admission: Free. **Times**: 12 noon - 8pm.

Dates can change, events can be cancelled – Please check with the organisers before setting out!

6-7 Jun
RAINBOW CRAFT FAIR
Newby Hall & Gardens, Ripon, North Yorkshire.
200 top quality crafts people from throughout Britain.
Things to see: Crafts people demonstrating skills and goods on sale to public.
Contact: Mr R G Alexander, Opening Administrator, Newby Hall, Ripon, North Yorkshire HG4 5AE. Tel: 01423 322583.
Admission: TBA. **Times**: From 10am - 5.30pm.

6-7 Jun
UK MASTERS
Lilleshall National Sports Centre, Nr Newport, Shropshire.
Top archery competition.
Things to see: The best archers in Great Britain competing in a beautiful tree-encircled archery field. Bring wet gear – the event has been wet one in three years!
Contact: Mr J S Middleton, Grand National Archery Society, 7th Street, Stoneleigh, Warwickshire CV8 2LG. Tel: 01203 696631.
Admission: Free. **Times**: 10am - 4pm.

6-7 Jun
BIGGIN HILL INTERNATIONAL AIR FAIR
Biggin Hill Airport, Kent.
One of the world's finest flying displays at the famous Battle of Britain fighter base.
Things to see: A spectacular five-hour flying display – military, civilian, old and new. Static aircraft park, exhibition, funfair, etc. Patrons enclosure with marquee, grandstand, seating and uninterrupted view.
Contact: Air Displays International, Biggin Hill Airport, Biggin Hill, Kent TN16 3BN. Tel: 01959 540959.
Admission: TBA. **Times:** 9am - 6pm.

6-7 Jun
MODEL RAILWAY EXHIBITION
East Anglian Railway Museum, Chappel Station, Colchester, Essex.
Railway layouts of all gauges.
Things to see: A wide selection of railway layouts of all gauges, plus a number of traders selling new and secondhand items. In addition the Museum's miniature steam railway will be in operation and there will also be a service of diesel-hauled standard gauge trains, so there will be plenty of rides all day.
Contact: Mr Steve Mew, Chappel & Wakes Colne Station, Colchester, Essex CO6 2DS. Tel: 01206 242524.
Admission: £2.50. **Times**: 10am - 5pm.

6-14 Jun
ASHFORD IN THE WATER WELL DRESSING WEEK
Ashford in the Water, Nr Bakewell, Derbyshire.
Well dressing festival.
Things to see: Well dressings are large pictures, each one made with thousands of flower petals pressed on to clay. Six wells are dressed, then blessed with a procession round the wells. All in a beautiful village setting.
Contact: Mrs D Daybell, Baslow Road, Ashford in the Water, Bakewell, Derbyshire DE45 1QA. Tel: 01629 812111.
Admission: N/A. **Times**: 7 Jun: Church service at 3pm followed by procession to bless the wells at approx 3.30pm.

7 Jun
CARRICK LOWLAND GATHERING
Victory Park, Girvan, Ayrshire.
Lowland games.
Things to see: Pipe band competition and Lowland games.
Contact: Mr Ian Fitzsimmons, 15 Smith Crescent, Girvan, Ayrshire KA26 0DU. Tel: 01465 712667.
Admission: Free. **Times**: 10.30am - 5.30pm.

Dates can change, events can be cancelled – Please check with the organisers before setting out!

7 Jun
CHILTERN RIDING CLUB SHOW
Beale Park, Lower Basildon, Reading, Berkshire.
A local show with a wide range of classes.
Things to see: Mostly show jumping.
Contact: Beale Park, The Child-Beale Trust, Lower Basildon, Reading, Berkshire RG8 9NH. Tel: 0118 984 5172.
Admission: Free. **Times**: 8am - 5pm.

7 Jun
LONDON TO BRIGHTON CLASSIC CAR RUN
Start point Route 1: Syon Park, Brentford, Middx. Check Point 1: Polesden Lacey, Surrey. Check Point 2: Amberley Museum, Arundel, Sussex. Start point Route 2: Crystal Palace, London. Check Point 1: Penshurst Place, Kent. Check Point 2: Bentley Wildfowl & Motor Museum in Halland. Finish: Madeira Drive, Brighton.
Classic car run.
Things to see: Road run for approximately 600 classic cars. Stopping points en route (as stated above) are not confirmed and need to be checked with the organisers.
Contact: Sally Greenwood, Greenwood's Exhibitions, PO Box 49, Aylesbury, Bucks HP22 5FF. Tel: 01296 631181/632040. Fax: 01296 630394.
Admission: TBA. **Times**: Cars leave Syon Park and Crystal Palace at 8.30am. First cars arrive in Brighton around 12 noon.

7 Jun
TRAM-JAM-BOREE!
National Tramway Museum, Crich, Matlock, Derbyshire.
Tramcars in operation.

Things to see: Busy and bustling streets - always a vintage tram in sight to give a taste of a long-gone rush-hour that lasts all day!
Contact: Lesley Wyld, Marketing Manager, National Tramway Museum, Crich, Matlock, Derbyshire DE4 5DP. Tel: 01773 852565. Fax: 01773 852326.
Admission: £5.90 adults; £3 children; £5.10 OAPs; £16.20 family ticket. **Times**: 10am - 5.30pm.

7 Jun*
SIR WILLIAM LYONS COMMEMORATIVE RUN
Start: Town Hall Square, Stockport. Finish: Middle Walk, Blackpool.
Jaguar car rally.
Things to see: Rally for Jaguar cars from Stockport to Blackpool stopping at Jaguar dealerships on route. Driving tests and *concours* at finish at Blackpool. Cars drive along Blackpool's Golden Mile to the finish and display area.
Contact: Alan Hewitt, JDC Area 18, 41 Broadstone Hall Road North, Heaton Chapel, Stockport SK4 5LA. Tel: 0161-292 0718.
Admission: N/A. **Times**: Start 8am, presentations 4.30pm.

7 Jun
SUMMER HEAVY HORSE SPECTACULAR
Weald and Downland Open Air Museum, Singleton, Chichester, West Sussex.
Heavy horse and farming display.
Things to see: Working teams of heavy horses, plus wagons and farm equipment on display and in use.
Contact: C Zeuner, Weald and Downland Open Air Museum, Singleton, Chichester, West Sussex PO18 0EU. Tel: 01243 811348.
Admission: TBA. 1997 guide: £4.90 adults; £2.30 children; family ticket £12 (2 adults, 2 children). **Times**: 10.30am - 4pm.

8-14 Jun
THE DFS CLASSIC
Edgbaston Priory Club, Sir Harry's Road, Edgbaston, Birmingham.
International tennis event.
Things to see: Top women's tennis action.
Contact: Tickets and information from Birmingham Convention & Visitor Bureau Ticket Shop on 0121-605 7000.
Admission: TBA. **Times**: Play commences 11.30am.

9-14 Jun
WORLD POWER BOAT CHAMPIONSHIPS
Falmouth, Cornwall.
Event from the calendar of 'Cornwall '98, The World Watersports Festival'.
Things to see: A host of the meanest 4 and 6 litre Grand Prix Power Boats from around the globe will be going flat out in this full-throttle championship.
Contact: Cornwall '98, Trevint House, Strangways Villas, Truro, Cornwall TR1 2PA. Tel: 01872 223527.
Admission: TBA. **Times**: TBA.

10 Jun
ROYAL GUN SALUTE FOR THE BIRTHDAY OF HRH THE DUKE OF EDINBURGH
The Tower of London and in Hyde Park.
Gun salutes.
Things to see: Gun salutes are fired in London by the King's Troop Royal Artillery in Hyde Park at 1200 hours (41 Gun Royal Salute) and by the Hon-

ourable Artillery Company at the Tower of London at 1300 hours (62 Gun Royal Salute).
Contact: The Information Officer, Public Information Office, Headquarters London District, Chelsea Barracks, London SW1H 8RF.
Admission: Free. **Times**: See above.

10-14 Jun
BBC GARDENERS WORLD LIVE SHOW
National Exhibition Centre, Birmingham.
National flower and garden show.
Things to see: Breathtaking displays in the RHS Floral Marquee, gardens in the open or the spectacular indoor garden displays. TV and radio gardening personalities on hand daily to answer questions and give practical advice and demonstrations around the show.
Contact: BBC Haymarket Exhibitions, 60 Waldegrave Road, Teddington TW11 8LG. Tel: 0171-402 2555. Royal Horticultural Society, 80 Vincent Square, London SW1P 2PE. Tel: 0171-828 1744.
Admission: TBA. 1997 guide: £11 adults (£7.50 after 3pm); £5 children; Under-5s free. **Times**: TBA.

11 Jun
LANARK LANIMER DAY
Main streets of Lanark, Scotland.
Traditional processions etc.
Things to see: Riding of the marches, tableaux and pageantry, bands, procession and crowning of the Lanimer Queen. Beating of Retreat and Mini Tattoo at Lanark Cross.
Contact: L W Reid CA, Hon Secretary, 25 Bloomgate, Lanark ML11 9ET. Tel: 01555 663251.
Admission: N/A. **Times**: 8.30am - 7pm.

Dates can change, events can be cancelled – Please check with the organisers before setting out!

11 Jun
MUSIC IN THE AIR
Middle Wallop, Stockbridge, Hants.
A repeat of 1997's successful open air concert.
Things to see: Concert by the London Philharmonic Youth Orchestra with synchronised flying displays.
Contact: Janet Houlton, Press & PR Officer, Museum of Army Flying, Middle Wallop, Stockbridge, Hants SO20 8DY. Tel: 01980 674421. Fax: 01264 781694.
Admission: TBA. **Times**: TBA.

11-14 Jun
BRAMHAM INTERNATIONAL HORSE TRIALS
Bramham Park, Wetherby, West Yorkshire.
International horse trials.
Things to see: Horses and top level showjumping, plus a country fair.
Contact: Gail Dale, The Estate Office, Bramham Park, Wetherby, West Yorkshire LS23 6ND. Tel: 01937 844265.
Admission: TBA 1997 guide: £5 - £8.. **Times**: 9am - 6pm.

12 Jun
THE SELKIRK COMMON RIDING
Royal Burgh of Selkirk.
Riding of the Burgh Marches.
Things to see: Cavalcade of horses with 500 – 600 riders. Pageant of casting the colours in the Town Market Place.
Contact: Jack Cruickshank, Selkirk Common Riding, Heatherlieburn, Selkirk TD7 5AL. Tel: 01750 21344. Fax: 01750 21844.
Admission: N/A. **Times**: Start at 5.30am.

13 Jun*
ENGINE MUSEUM OPEN DAY
Prickwillow Engine Museum, Main Street, Prickwillow, Nr Ely, Cambridgeshire.
Museum open day.
Things to see: Old engines running, plus many other attractions.
Contact: Joan Stacey, Prickwillow Engine Trust, Main Street, Prickwillow, Nr Ely,

Cambs CB7 4UN. Tel: 01353 688360.
Admission: £3 adults; £2 children/OAPs; £7 family. **Times**: Museum opens 11am - 5pm; engines run 12noon - 5pm.

13 Jun
MAN VERSUS HORSE VERSUS BIKE MARATHON
Llanwrtyd Wells, Powys.
Race between men, horses and mountain bikes.
Things to see: 22-mile marathon in which teams of runners, horses and mountain bikes compete on the same course in mountainous terrain.
Contact: Gordon Green, The Neuadd Arms Hotel, The Square, Lllanwrtyd Wells, Powys. Tel: 01591 610236.
Admission: TBA. **Times**: TBA.

13 Jun
ROYAL GUN SALUTE TO MARK THE QUEEN'S OFFICIAL BIRTHDAY
The Tower of London and in Hyde Park.
Gun salutes to mark the Queen's Official Birthday.
Things to see: Gun salutes fired in London by the King's Troop Royal Artillery in Hyde Park at 1200 hours (41 Gun Royal Salute) and by the Honourable Artillery Company at the Tower of London at 1300 hours (62 Gun Royal Salute).
Contact: The Information Officer, Public Information Office, Headquarters London District, Chelsea Barracks, London SW1H 8RF.
Admission: Free. **Times**: See above.

13 Jun
TROOPING THE COLOUR – THE QUEEN'S BIRTHDAY PARADE
Horse Guards Parade, Whitehall, London SW1.
Royal parade.
Things to see: Royal pageantry as the parade of Guards and Royals make their way along The Mall towards Horse Guards (essential to arrive early morning to gain good position). The Queen and other Royals return to Buckingham Palace and usually appear on the balcony for an RAF fly-past at around 1pm.
Contact: HQ Household Division, Horse Guards, London SW1. Tel: 0171-414 2497.
Admission: Apply in writing for tickets between 1 Jan - 28 Feb. Tickets allocated by ballot and likely to cost £12.50. As applications for this event are heavily oversubscribed, it may be worth asking to be included in the two other ballots for the dress rehearsals held on the two preceeding Saturdays. **Times**: Ticket holders to be seated by 10am.

13-14 Jun
AMERICAN INDIAN WEEKEND
American Museum, Claverton Manor, Bath.
Celebration of American Indian culture.
Things to see: Displays of traditional North American Indian dances in full costume, plus a special exhibition of clothing and crafts.
Contact: Miss Susan Carter, The American Museum, Claverton Manor, Bath, Avon BA2 7BD. Tel: 01225 460503.
Admission: 1997 guide: £2.50 adults; £1.25 children. **Times**: 1pm - 6pm.

13-14 Jun
MOVE IT - MIME FESTIVAL
Victoria Embankment Gardens, Villiers Street, London WC2.
Mime festival.
Things to see: Modern mime artists in a programme devised to show a variety of forms of mime and physical theatre.
Contact: Alternative Arts, 47A Brushfield Street, Spitalfields, London E1 6AA. Tel: 0171-375 0441.
Admission: Free. **Times**: 2pm - 6pm.

13-14 Jun
MIDDLE WALLOP INTERNATIONAL AIR SHOW
Middle Wallop, Stockbridge, Hants.
6 hour flying display each day.
Things to see: The latest jets to the old favourites such as Austers, Tiger Moths etc. Unique massed helicopter approach

(up to 100 helicopters advance on the audience at the low hover).
Contact: Janet Houlton, Press & PR Officer, Museum of Army Flying, Middle Wallop, Stockbridge, Hants SO20 8JB. Tel: 01980 674421. Fax: 01264 781694.
Admission: £6 adults; £3 children/OAPs.
Times: TBA.

13-14 Jun
EAST ANGLIAN DAILY TIMES COUNTRY FAIR
Melford Hall Park, Long Melford, Sudbury, Suffolk.
Country fair.
Things to see: Heavy horses, vintage farm machinery, steam engines, fire engines, classic cars, craft marquee, antiques, gun dog scurry, trade stands, children's corner, ring attractions, animal displays, etc.
Contact: Sandy Basham, 26 Third Avenue, Glemsford, Sudbury, Suffolk CO10 7QJ. Tel: 01787 280941.
Admission: £4 adults; £2 children. Advance tickets £3 adults; £1.50 children.
Times: 10am - 5.30pm.

13-14 Jun
MODEL RAILWAY EXHIBITION
The Historic Dockyard, Chatham, Kent.
Event for families as well as enthusiasts.
Things to see: A world in miniature with over two dozen superb layouts and exhibits from all over England. Also specialist traders and demonstrations.
Contact: The Historic Dockyard, Chatham, Kent ME4 4TE. Tel: 01634 812551.
Admission: £2.50 adults; children free.
Times: 10am - 4pm.

13-14 Jun
PARHAM STEAM RALLY AND FAMILY SHOW
Parham House on the A283 between Storrington and Pulborough, W. Sussex.
Vintage vehicle rally and family show.
Things to see: Steam engines and other

vintage vehicles.
Contact: Phil Read, Old Mill Steam Fair, 17 Old Mill Square, Storrington, West Sussex RH20 4NQ. Tel: 01903 743939.
Admission: £6 adults; OAPs £4; child £4; under-5s free. **Times**: 9am - 5pm.

13-14 Jun
SOUTHEND WATER FESTIVAL
Southend Seafront and Pier, Essex.
Water festival.
Things to see: Offshore power boat racing, skiff racing, yacht racing for the Town Cup, dragon boat racing, Pier Head visit by a tall ship (to be confirmed).
Contact: Lisa Tidder, Special Events, Southend Borough Council, PO Box 6, Southend-on-Sea SS2 6ER. Tel: 01702 215166/5169.
Admission: N/A. **Times**: 11am - 4pm.

13-20 Jun
THE DIRECT LINE INSURANCE INTERNATIONAL LADIES TENNIS CHAMPIONSHIPS
International Lawn Tennis Centre, Devonshire Park, Eastbourne, East Sussex.
Women's international tennis event.
Things to see: Top international tennis players in action.
Contact: Mike Marchant, Events Manager, Tourism & Leisure Department, College Road, Eastbourne, East Sussex BN21 4JJ. Tel: 01323 415442.
Admission: Ticket prices and bookings

from Central Box Office, Devonshire Park Centre, The Winter Garden, Compton Street, Eastbourne BN21 4BD. Tel: 01323 412000. **Times**: TBA.

14 Jun
FORFAR HIGHLAND GAMES
Lochside Park, Forfar, Scotland.
Highland Games.
Things to see: Running, cycling, heavy events (including Scottish Caber Tossing Championship), tug of war, Highland dancing, solo piping and pipe band.
Contact: Mrs E Webster, 5 Jeanfield Crescent, Forfar DD8 1JR. Tel: 01307 465605.
Admission: £2.50 adult; £1 children/OAPs. **Times**: Starts 12.30pm.

14 Jun
FUN & GAMES IN THE GARDEN
Beningbrough Hall, Shipton, Beningbrough, York.
Fun and games for children aged 3-12.
Things to see: Family activities, games, competitions and entertainment.
Contact: The National Trust, Beningbrough Hall, Shipton, Beningbrough, York YO6 1DD. Tel: 01904 470666.
Admission: TBA. **Times**: 12 noon - 4pm.

14 Jun
MANCHESTER TO BLACKPOOL VETERAN VINTAGE CAR RUN
Start at Granada TV Studios, Manchester outside the Rovers Return. Visiting Astley Park, Chorley; rest stop at Police HQ at Hutton, Nr Preston; finish at North Shore, Blackpool.
A road event for cars produced prior to 1945, oldest 1896.
Things to see: 100+ veteran, Edwardian and vintage cars. Watch the local press for route and timings. Travel along the route to leapfrog the cars.
Contact: Christopher David Lee, 3 Keith Avenue, Great Sankey, Warrington WA5 3NZ. Tel: 01925 791922.
Admission: Free. **Times**: From 8.30am Manchester; 11.30am Police HQ, Hutton; 12 noon Wrea Green, Nr Kirkham; finish 12.30pm - 3pm North Shore, Blackpool. 3pm for parade along Blackpool Promenade.

14 Jun
A MANE EVENT!
National Tramway Museum, Crich, Matlock, Derbyshire.
Horse-trams in operation.
Things to see: One of only two chances this year to 'trot the tracks' in one of the museums venerable horse-trams!
Contact: Lesley Wyld, Marketing Manager, National Tramway Museum, Crich, Matlock, Derbyshire DE4 5DP. Tel: 01773 852565. Fax: 01773 852326.
Admission: £5.90 adults; £3 children; £5.10 OAPs; £16.20 family ticket. **Times**: 10am - 5.30pm.

14 Jun
BROUGH CUMBRIA HOUND & TERRIER SHOW
Brough, Cumbria.
Country dog show.
Things to see: Foxhounds, beagles, working terriers, gun dog classes, childrens pets class. Also show for shepherd's crooks and walking sticks. Plus dry-stone walling competition.
Contact: Harold Thompson, 4 Bongate, Appleby, Cumbria CA16 6UE. Tel: 017683 51921.
Admission: £2. **Times**: 12 noon - 6pm.

14 Jun
LAMMERMUIR HORSE SHOW
Ayton Castle, Eyemouth, Berwickshire.
Horse show in aid of charity.
Things to see: Various classes for ridden horses, ponies, Arabs, side-saddle, showjumping, roads and tracks (which means access to woods etc. in and around the castle grounds).
Contact: Ms B Stenhouse, Lammermuir Horse Show, Kilburn House, Wetherbyres, Eyemouth, Berwickshire TD14 5SE. Tel: 01890 751161.
Admission: £2 per car. **Times**: 9am - 4pm.

14 Jun
VINTAGE VEHICLE GALA
King George V Playing Field, Uppermill, Nr Oldham.
Vintage vehicle rally and gala.
Things to see: Cars, motorcycles, stationary engines, etc. on the field and beforehand at Tanner Bros, Greenfield. And on the run – a tour of the Saddleworth villages.
Contact: Saddleworth Museum, High Street, Uppermill, Oldham OL3 6HS. Tel: 01457 874093/870336.
Admission: Small admission charge to field. **Times**: Run is at 11am. On field from 11am - 4pm approx.

14 Jun
LUTON FESTIVAL OF TRANSPORT
Stockwood Country Park, Luton.
Vintage & classic vehicle rally.
Things to see: Old vehicles on display, plus autojumble and varied entertainment.
Contact: Luton Borough Council, Leisure & Cultural Services Department, Arts Division (Promotions), 146 Old Bedford Road, Luton LU2 7HA. Tel: 01582 876083.
Admission: £2 approx. **Times**: 10am - 5pm.

14 Jun-5 Jul
GREAT ANNUAL RE-CREATION OF TUDOR LIFE
Kentwell Hall, Long Melford, Suffolk.
Re-creation of everyday life in the year 1600.
Things to see: 250-300 'Tudors' in costume, authentically being gentry, cooks, soldiers, bakers, coppicers, basketmakers, brewers, stewards, ostlers, smiths, carpenters, etc.

Dates can change, events can be cancelled – Please check with the organisers before setting out!

Contact: The Office, Kentwell Hall, Long Melford, Suffolk CO10 9BA. Tel: 01787 310207. Info Line: 0891 517475 (calls at 50p per min).
Admission: £11 adults; £7.25 children; £9.50 OAPs. Groups over 20 people get a 20 per cent discount, but must be booked in advance. **Times**: 11am - 5pm.

15-20 Jun
NOTTINGHAM OPEN
City of Nottingham Tennis Centre, University Boulevard, Nottingham.
Men's international tennis event.
Things to see: Top international tennis players in action.
Contact: Tickets and information from The Nottingham Open ticket office on 01159 482525/482626.
Admission: TBA. **Times**: Play commences 12 noon.

16 Jun
RIDING OF THE LINLITHGOW MARCHES
High Street, Linlithgow.
Traditional ceremonies to mark the town's boundaries.
Things to see: Procession along Main Street with Provost and Bailies, guests, floats and decorated vehicles with up to eight bands.
Contact: Roy W Redwood MBE, 123 Main Street, Winchburgh, Broxburn, West Lothian EH52 6QP. Tel: 01506 890124.
Admission: N/A. **Times**: First procession 5am. Main procession 11am. Final procession 5pm.

16-18 Jun
THREE COUNTIES SHOW
The Showground, Malvern, Worcestershire.
Agricultural show.
Things to see: Horse and livestock competitions, heavy horses, hot air balloons (weather permitting), main arena events (usually HM forces included, e.g. parachute jumping), military bands, vin-

tage machinery, flower show. Main arena has backdrop of Malvern Hills.
Contact: Chris Milne, The Showground, Malvern, Worcestershire WR13 6NW. Tel: 01684 584900.
Admission: TBA. **Times**: 8am - 7pm approx.

16-19 Jun
ROMAN FESTIVAL FOR SCHOOLS
The White Cliffs Experience, Market Square, Dover, Kent.
Roman festival.
Things to see: History comes alive in Roman Dubris, face painting, Roman hair styles, drama workshops, etc. Children and performers in Roman costumes.
Contact: Sally Wookey, Marketing Manager, The White Cliffs Experience, Market Square, Dover, Kent. Tel: 01304 210101.
Admission: £5.50 adults; £4.25 OAPs/students; £3.75 children. **Times**: 10am - 5pm daily.

16-19 Jun
ROYAL ASCOT
Ascot Racecourse, Berkshire.
World famous horse racing and social event.
Things to see: Top class horse racing, royalty and high fashion. One of the major events of the social calendar with members of the Royal family always in attendance.
Contact: Ascot Racecourse, Ascot, Berkshire SL5 7JN. Tel: 01344 876456.
Admission: TBA. **Times**: TBA.

18-22 Jun
ENGLAND VS SOUTH AFRICA
Lord's Cricket Ground, St John's Wood, London.
Major five-day international test match.
Things to see: Top class international cricket for over six hours a day for five days. Membership and corporate hospitality facilities contained within a first class cricketing arena.
Contact: M.C.C., Lord's Ground, London NW8 8QZ. Tel: 0171-289 8979.
Admission: 1997 guide: £20 - £35. **Times**: 10.30am - 7.30pm approx.

19 Jun
BURFORD DRAGON PROCESSION
Burford School to Burford Primary School, Burford, Oxfordshire.
Traditional procession.
Things to see: The Dragon procession proceeding from Burford School to Burford Primary School, led by the Gloucestershire Morris Men. Followed by Morris dancing. An ancient tradition dating back to the Battle of Mercia around the 8th century.
Contact: Malcolm Taylor, 109 Mayfield Close, Carterton, Oxfordshire OX18 3QS. Tel: 01993 843613.
Admission: Free. **Times**: Burford School at 6.30pm. Procession arrives at Burford Primary school at 7pm for opening of fete.

19-21 Jun
HARDEN MOSS SHEEPDOG TRIALS
Greenfield Road, Holmfirth, Huddersfield, West Yorkshire.
Sheepdog trials.
Things to see: Sheepdogs in action, plus a fell race, side shows, sheep shearing and show, trade stands, etc.
Contact: K Denton, Publicity Officer, Broad View, Holme, Huddersfield, West Yorkshire. Tel: 01484 682061.
Admission: £2.50 adults; 50p children. **Times**: 9am - 6pm.

20 Jun
THE ANCIENT CEREMONY OF THE ELECTION OF THE MAYOR OF OCK STREET
Outside the Brewery Tap Public House, Ock Street, Abingdon, Oxfordshire.
Ancient election ceremony.
Things to see: A very colourful event which keeps alive an old tradition. The election takes place in Ock Street; after the election the Mayor is chaired along the street. Morris dancing takes place

throughout the day in Abingdon Square and Ock Street.
Contact: Ivan R Henson, 23 Exbourne Rd, Abingdon, Oxfordshire OX14 1DH. Tel: 01235 528024.
Admission: N/A. **Times**: Morris dancers assemble at 10am and the voting station is opened. Voting station closes at 4pm followed by more dancing at 6pm - 8pm.

20 Jun
MARLOW AMATEUR REGATTA
Riverside, Marlow, Buckinghamshire.
Traditional rowing regatta.
Things to see: A high standard of rowing by crews in final preparations for Henley Royal Regatta, plus a traditional funfair.
Contact: A Evans, 12 Sedgmoor Gardens, Flackwell Heath, Buckinghamshire HP10 9AR. Tel: 01628 525977.
Admission: £8. But a mile of towpath is free. **Times**: From 9am.

20 Jun
THE ROUND THE ISLAND RACE
Start at Cowes, round the Isle of Wight, finish at Cowes.
Major yacht race.
Things to see: Approximately 1,500 yachts in a race round the island. Good vantage areas at The Needles, St Catherines Point and Bonchurch, as well as the start and finish at Cowes.
Contact: The Island Sailing Club, High Street, Cowes, Isle of Wight PO31 7RE. Tel: 01983 296621.
Admission: N/A. **Times**: Starts: 7am approx. Finishes from 12 noon - 6.30pm.

20 Jun
PORT OF BRIXHAM INTERNATIONAL TRAWLER RACE & QUAY FESTIVAL
New Fish Quay, Brixham, Devon.
Trawler race.
Things to see: Trawlers racing around Tor Bay. Good vantage points: on board HMS ship in attendance; race control area (Battery Point). Plus exhibitors relating to the fishing industry, stalls, live music, water events, etc.
Contact: Mrs C Beasley, "Whaddon", Crownhill Crescent, Galmpton, Brixham, Devon TQ5 0PS. Tel: 01803 846182/882325. Fax: 01803 882725.
Admission: £1 for programme (proceeds to local charities). **Times**: 9am - 5pm.

20 Jun
SHREWSBURY CARNIVAL & SHOW
The Quarry, Shrewsbury, Shropshire.
Carnival and allied events.
Things to see: Carnival street parade with floats, costumes, etc, plus all-day events in the Quarry.
Contact: Mrs C M Swain, Villa Farm, Bicton, Shrewsbury SY3 8EG. Tel: 01743 850503.
Admission: Free. **Times**: 10am - 6pm.

20 Jun
DEVON COUNTY ANTIQUES FAIR
Salisbury Leisure Centre, The Butts, Hulse Road, Salisbury, Wiltshire.
Antiques fair.
Things to see: Beautiful antiques and collectables among the many items on offer. 140 stands in one hall.
Contact: Val Dennis, Devon Counties Antiques Fairs, The Glebe House, Nymet Tracey, Crediton, Devon EX17 6DB. Tel: 01363 82571.
Admission: £1.50 adults; children free.
Times: 10am - 5pm.

20-21 Jun
FESTIVAL OF GARDENING AT MIDSUMMER
Hatfield House, Hatfield, Hertfordshire.
16th annual show - one of England's best.
Things to see: National flower & plant exhibitors, specialist garden trade stands, gardener's question time, demonstrations, lectures, floral art, arena events, all of the 42 acres of Hatfield's organically managed gardens & the house dressed in flowers.
Contact: The Curator, Hatfield House, Hatfield, Hertfordshire AL9 5NQ. Tel:

01707 262823.
Admission: £5.40 adults; £4.80 OAPs; £1.90 children. **Times**: 10am - 6pm.

20-21 Jun
THOMSON MEMORIAL VINTAGE RALLY WEEKEND
Sat: Baird Park; Sun: Market Square, Stonehaven, Kincardineshire.
Event marking anniversary of birth of Robert William Thomson of Stonehaven, the inventor of the pneumatic tyre in December 1845.
Things to see: Vintage and classic vehicles and stationary engines (latter on Saturday only). Rally in the Market Square on Sunday and vehicle tests in the beautiful setting of Glenbervie House in the afternoon.
Contact: Fred Stephen, 50 Victoria Street, Stonehaven AB3 2LH. Tel: 01569 766363.
Admission: Free. **Times**: Sat: 11am. Sun: 10am for judging of vehicles. 1pm leave for tests at Glenbervie House seven miles to south.

20-21 Jun
WANDSWORTH BOROUGH SHOW
King George's Park, London SW18.
Colourful outdoor show.
Things to see: A range of visual entertainment – arena events, street theatre, music stage, animals, children's art party, stalls, arts and crafts, strolling players, fun fair.
Contact: The Events Team, Room 114, Leisure and Amenities Services, Wandsworth Town Hall, London SW18 2PU. Tel: 0181-871 6363.
Admission: Free. **Times**: 11am - 6pm.

20-26 Jun
BARMOUTH TO FORT WILLIAM THREE PEAKS YACHT RACE
Barmouth - Caernarfon - Ravenglass - Fort William.
Yacht and running race.
Things to see: Mono and multihull racing yachts with crews of five race from Barmouth to Fort William via Caernarfon and Ravenglass, where two from each crew run Snowdon, Scafell and Ben Nevis.
Contact: C P Walker, Tregarn, Barmouth, Gwynedd LL42 1DJ. Tel: 01341 280298.
Admission: N/A. **Times**: Sun: Caernarfon/Snowdon. Mon: Ravenglass/Scafell. Wed/Thurs/Fri: Fort William/Ben Nevis.

20-27 Jun
BROADSTAIRS DICKENS FESTIVAL
Around the town and seafront of Broadstairs, Kent.
Dickens festival.
Things to see: Garden party, country fair, Victorian cricket match and festival dance supper. Characters from the novels of Charles Dickens and many people in Victorian costume. Also music hall, walks, talks, tableaux and the festival play "Pickwick Papers".
Contact: Lee Ault, Rooftops, 58 High Street, Broadstairs, Kent CT10 1JT. Tel: 01843 863453.
Admission: Variable. Some events free.

20-28 Jun
SALTASH CORNWALL 98
Saltash, Cornwall.
Event from the calendar of 'Cornwall '98, The World Watersports Festival'.
Things to see: An extravaganza of maritime celebrations including sailing, gig racing, canoeing and river events as well as a host of entertainments, stalls and fun on the Waterfront.
Contact: Cornwall '98, Trevint House, Strangways Villas, Truro, Cornwall TR1 2PA. Tel: 01872 223527.
Admission: TBA. **Times**: TBA.

21 Jun
HEAVY HORSE DAY
The Historic Dockyard, Chatham, Kent.
Heavy Horses at work.
Things to see: Meet the working Heavy Horses, see hauling the shot and a variety of other working horse trials with arena displays and demonstrations. Other atrractions include, children's games, Punch & Judy and face painting.
Contact: The Historic Dockyard, Chatham, Kent. Tel: 01634 812551.
Admission: £2.50 adults; children free if dressed as a scarecrow! **Times**: 10am - 4pm.

21 Jun
ABERDEEN HIGHLAND GAMES
Hazlehead Park, Aberdeen, Scotland.
Traditional Highland games.
Things to see: Tossing the caber, pipe band competition, tug of war, highland dancing, trade stands, fun fair, etc.
Contact: Dorothy Anderson, Arts & Recreation Department, St Nicholas House, Broad Street, Aberdeen, AB10 1XJ. Tel: 01224 522190.
Admission: £4. **Times**: 10am - 5pm approx.

21 Jun*
BANBURY RUN
Start & finish at Towcester Race Course. Towcester to Oxon and including Sunrising Hill.
Run for pre-1931 motorcycles.
Things to see: Old motorcycles and three-wheeler and sidecar outfits in timed regularity run in picturesque countryside. Frequently ridden by colourful costumed characters. Also, a motorbike autojumble.
Contact: Mrs Ann Davy, Vintage Motor Cycle Club, Allen House, Wetmore Road, Burton on Trent, Staffordshire DE14 1TR.
Admission: N/A. Small parking charge to include programme. **Times**: 10am - 3pm.

21 Jun
BEARS ONLY FAIR
Civic Hall, Stratford-upon-Avon.
Teddy Bear fair.
Things to see: Collectors' teddy bears including limited editions and show specials, and rare antique bears. Free bear making advice centre. Teddy bear making suppliers, Mohair etc. High quality fair for serious bear-collectors, and great family day out. Free valuations from Bonhams of Chelsea.
Contact: Maddy Aldis, 11 Wesley Street, Eccles, Manchester M30 0UQ. Tel: 0161 7077625.
Admission: £3 adults; £2.50 children; £8 family. **Times**: 10.30am - 4.30pm.

21 Jun
MORGAN CAR CLUB MEET AT BEAMISH
The North Of England Open Air Museum, Beamish, Co Durham.
Morgan car rally.

Things to see: Morgan sports cars from throughout the country competing in *concours d'elegance* and autotests. Static displays and exciting action.
Contact: John Macdonald, Howden Works, Lanchester, Co Durham DH7 0QR. Tel: 01207 520916.
Admission: Admission to the event is included within the admission charge to Beamish. **Times**: 10am - 6pm.

21 Jun
THE BRITISH HEART FOUNDATION LONDON TO BRIGHTON BIKE RIDE
London to Brighton.
Europe's largest cycle event for charity.
Things to see: Thousands of cyclists.
Contact: For entry details, Tel: 0891 616077. For other information Tel: 0171-935 0185.
Admission: N/A. **Times**: TBA.

21 Jun
WELSH NSPCC IT'S A KNOCKOUT CHAMPIONSHIPS & SHOW 1998
Bailey Park, Abergavenny, Gwent.
Touring production of "It's A Knockout" for adults and children.
Things to see: Competitors engaging in "Knock Out" games, celebrities, children's characters. Full supporting show with funfair, amusements, etc.
Contact: Mrs E Field, The White House, Llanfoist, Abergavenny, Gwent NP7 9LR. Tel/Fax: 01873 855552.
Admission: £4 adults; £2 children/OAPs. **Times**: 10am - 6pm.

21 Jun
MIDSUMMER POETRY FESTIVAL
Victoria Embankment Gardens, Villiers Street, London WC2.
Open-air poetry festival.
Things to see: Programme of contemporary performance poetry in this attractive garden setting.
Contact: Alternative Arts, 47A Brushfield Street, Spitalfields, London E1 6AA. Tel: 0171-375 0441.
Admission: Free. **Times**: 2pm - 5pm.

21 Jun
BRIDGNORTH LIONS CLUB RAFT REGATTA
Ironbridge to Bridgnorth Severn Park, Shropshire.
Charity raft regatta.
Things to see: Around 1,200 rafters on up to 150 decorated rafts travelling 10 miles through the beautiful Severn Valley. Possibly the largest charity event of its kind.
Contact: D G Whitehead, Bridgnorth Lions Club, PO Box 17, Bridgnorth, Shropshire WV16 4HH.
Admission: N/A for spectators. **Times**: 11am - 5pm approx.

21-26 Jun
MANX INTERNATIONAL CYCLING WEEK
TT Grandstand; TT course; town centres, Isle of Man.
Britian's premier cycling festival.
Things to see: International cycling road races on closed roads, time trials, town centre races, tourist rides. Check race HQ at TT Grandstand for full details.
Contact: Ken Matthews Promotions, 153 Taunton Drive, Aintree, Liverpool L10 8JN. Tel/Fax: 0151-526 8588.
Admission: Mostly free. **Times**: Various.

22 Jun-5 Jul
WIMBLEDON LAWN TENNIS CHAMPIONSHIPS
All England Lawn Tennis Club, Church Road, Wimbledon, London SW19 5AE.
The world's premier tennis tournament.
Things to see: The world's top tennis stars in action and all the excitement of this world-famous event. Flash photography not permitted.
Contact: All England Lawn Tennis Club, Church Road, Wimbledon, London SW19 5AE. Tel: 0181-944 1066.
Admission: To attend the Centre or Number 1 Court apply to enter the public ballot for tickets. Applications can be made from 1 September - 31 December. Only one application per address is

allowed and must be received by midnight on 31 December. Send a sae to: PO Box 98, Church Road, Wimbledon SW19 5AE. Lucky applicants will be informed in mid February. Otherwise queue patiently on the day. **Times**: No play on Sunday 28 June. Check daily press for times of play.

23-24 Jun
CHESHIRE COUNTY SHOW
The Showground, Tabley, Nr Knutsford, Cheshire.
Agricultural show.
Things to see: Many breeds of cattle, sheep, goats, dogs, poultry, rabbits, and large numbers of horses including shires. Plus main ring events, showjumping, ponies, floral competitions, crafts, country sports, 500 trade stands.
Contact: Mr D J Broster, Clay Lane Farm, Marton, Winsford, Cheshire CW7 2QH. Tel: 01829 760020.
Admission: TBA. 1997 guide: £7.50 adults; £6 OAPs; £3 children. Advance tickets available at reduced rates. **Times**: 8.30am - 6pm.

24-25 Jun
LINCOLNSHIRE SHOW
Lincolnshire Showground, Grange-de-Lings, Lincoln.
Agricultural show.
Things to see: Main ring displays, horses, cattle, sheep, pigs, "conservation area" including varied wildlife, exhibitions, a multitude of colourful trade stands, flower show and floral art marquees, farriery demonstrations, etc.
Contact: Mr J P Skehel, Secretary, Lincolnshire Agricultural Society, Lincolnshire Showground, Grange-de-Lings, Lincoln LN2 2NA. Tel: 01522 524240 or 522900.
Admission: 1997 guide: £7-£8 adults; £4.50-£5 children/OAPs. Car parking £3. **Times**: 8.30am - 7.30pm.

Dates can change, events can be cancelled – Please check with the organisers before setting out!

25-28 Jun
ROYAL HIGHLAND SHOW
Royal Highland Centre, Ingliston, Edinburgh.
Scotland's premier agricultural show.
Things to see: Military bands and displays, horses, sheepdog trials, livestock, showjumping, sheep shearing, Food from Scotland exhibition, crafts, forestry events arena and much more.
Contact: The Royal Highland and Agricultural Society of Scotland, The Royal Highland Centre, Ingliston, Edinburgh EH28 8NF. Tel: 0131-333 2444. Fax: 0131-333 5236.
Admission: 1997 guide: £8.50 - £12 adults. **Times**: 8am - 8pm.

26-28 Jun
GARDENERS' WEEKEND
Hever Castle, Edenbridge, Kent.
Floral displays.
Things to see: Displays by horticultural societies and nurseries. Seminars and question time with BBC Radio Kent. Many other things to see such as the Castle itself (Anne Boleyn's childhood home) and award winning gardens – suitable for picnics. New water maze.
Contact: Jan Roberts or Pauline Scott, Hever Castle, Edenbridge, Kent TN8 7NG. Tel: 01732 865224.

Admission: £7 adults; £3.80 children; £6 OAPs; £17.80 family (2 adults, 2 children). **Times**: Gardens open 11am. Castle opens 12 noon. Last admission 5pm. Final exit 6pm.

26-28 Jun
MIDSUMMER FOLK FESTIVAL
Old Leigh and Southend High Street, Essex.
Folk festival.
Things to see: Music, song and dance including folk, Cajun, country & western, and Appalachian dance companies.
Contact: Lisa Tidder, Special Events, Southend Borough Council, PO Box 6, Southend-on-Sea SS2 6ER. Tel: 01702 215166.
Admission: Free and Ticket venues. **Times**: Fri: 8pm - late. Sat/Sun: 11am - late.

27 Jun
OPEN AIR CONCERT
Leeds Castle, Maidstone, Kent.
Summer concert at Leeds Castle.
Things to see: Carl Davis conducts the Royal Liverpool Philharmonic Orchestra in the original summer night classical music concerts, with the "1812", cannons and fireworks as the triumphant finale.
Contact: Leeds Castle, Maidstone, Kent ME17 1PL. Tel: 01622 765400.
Admission: Advance ticket sales only from the box office, Tel: 01622 880008. Open 1 February. Group rates available. **Times**: Gates open 4pm. Entertainment from 5.30pm.

27-28 Jun
MIDDLESEX COUNTY SHOW
Middlesex Showground, Park Road, Uxbridge, Middlesex.
County show.
Things to see: County show with horses, horticulture, dog/goat shows, bands, skurry driving, veteran cars and family attractions.
Contact: M J Grimer, Byron House, Wallingford Road, Uxbridge, Middlesex. Tel: 01895 252131. Or Tel/fax: 01494 862259.
Admission: Saturday £5; £2.50 concessions. Sunday £6; £3 concessions. (in advance from the organisers: £4; £2 concessions). **Times**: 9.30am - 6pm.

27-28 Jun
MIDLAND HILLCLIMB CHAMPIONSHIP
Prescott Hill, Cheltenham, Glos.
Hillclimb competition.
Things to see: Roadgoing sports cars and racing cars ascending a narrow twisting hill road at speeds of up to 110mph. Plus cars in paddock etc.
Contact: Mrs S Ward, Bugatti Owners Club, Prescott Hill, Gotherington, Glos GL52 4RD. Tel: 01242 673136.
Admission: £7 adults. **Times**: 10am - 5pm approx.

27-28 Jun
EVENING GAZETTE MOTOR SHOW
Preston Hall Park, Yarm Rd, Stockton-on-Tees, Cleveland (follow brown signs for Preston Hall Manor).
Motor show and rally.
Things to see: In addition to displays of the latest vehicles from the region's main motor dealers, there will be preserved vehicles including fire eingines from the last century to present day front-line appliances, other motor vehicles from the earliest days of motoring up to the 70's and beyond, stands dedicated to classic cars and single marques stationary engines & agricultural shows, military vehicles and autojumble stands, trade stands, craft marquee, kiddies rides & arena displays.
Contact: Graham Reeves, Events Development Officer, Stockton-on-Tees Borough Council, PO Box 116, Gloucester House, 72 Church Road, Stockton-on-Tees TS18 1YB. Tel: 01642 393939 ext 3911.
Admission: Free. Car Parking £3. **Times**: 10am - 5pm.

27-28 Jun
RAF WADDINGTON INTERNATIONAL AIR SHOW
RAF Waddington, Nr Lincoln (three miles south).
Largest RAF show in UK.
Things to see: A six-hour non-stop international flying display, several static aircraft display parks, Blackpool fun fair, craft fairs, trade stands, bands, major company exhibitions (British Aerospace, Boeing, etc).
Contact: Paul Byram, The Air Show Office, RAF Waddington, Lincoln LN5 9NB. Tel: 01522 726100. Fax: 01522 727170.
Admission: £10 adults; £6 children; under-5s free. In advance £7.50 adults; children £5. Free parking for all vehicles. **Times**: 8.30am - 6pm.

27-28 Jun
DEPOT OPEN DAYS
Midland Railway Centre, Butterley Station, Ripley, Derbyshire.
Steam and diesel rail display.
Things to see: Unique opportunity to view a wide variety of steam and diesel locomotives in action and on display.
Contact: Alan Calladine, Midland Railway Centre, Butterley Station, Ripley, Derbyshire DE5 3QZ. Tel: 01773 747674.
Admission: £7.95 adults; £6.50 OAPs; 2 children free with each adult. **Times**: 11.15am - 4.15pm.

27-28 Jun
NEWBURY GARDEN & LEISURE SHOW
Newbury Showground, Berkshire.
Flower show with other attractions.
Things to see: Large display tents featuring flowers, orchids, crafts, hobbies and small animals.
Contact: J A Bines, Newbury Showground, Hermitage, Thatcham, Berks RG18 9EZ. Tel: 01635 247111.
Admission: TBA. **Times**: 10am - 5pm.

28 Jun
ANNUAL CROQUET TOURNAMENT
Beningbrough Hall, Shipton, Beningbrough, York.
Croquet event.
Things to see: National Trust and local teams competing for the trophy.
Contact: The National Trust, Beningbrough Hall, Shipton, Beningbrough, York YO6 1DD. Tel: 01904 470666.
Admission: Normal admission prices apply. **Times**: 1pm - 4pm.

28 Jun*
ANNUAL PHILIPPINE FESTIVAL
Old RAF Camp, Brookland, Romney Marsh, Kent (A259 South Coast Road).
Celebration of Philippine traditions and culture.
Things to see: National costumes, national dances and Hawaiian dances, Little Miss Philippine beauty contest, games for children, the Philippine jeepney and ethnic food.
Contact: Mr F Trotter, Philippine Village, The RAF Camp, Brookland, Kent TN29 9TF. Tel: 01797 344616 or 01233 732417.
Admission: £1 adults; children free. **Times**: 10am - 7pm.

28 Jun*
BELVOIR CASTLE MEDIEVAL JOUSTING TOURNAMENTS
Belvoir Castle, Lincolnshire.
Medieval jousting tournament.
Things to see: An authentic display of medieval combat, a colourful and excit-

ing event.
Contact: Diane Marshall, The Estate Office, Belvoir Castle, Belvoir, Nr Grantham, Lincolnshire NG32 1PD. Tel: 01476 870262
Admission: £5.50; £4.50 OAPs; £3.50 children. **Times**: 11am - 5pm.

28 Jun
BROMLEY PAGEANT OF MOTORING
Norman Park, Hayes Lane, Bromley, Kent.
The biggest one-day classic car show in the world.
Things to see: Cars of all kinds, arena events, Pick of the Show parade, special displays, club team displays, etc.
Contact: Mr Tony Beadle, Kelsey Publishing Ltd, Kelsey House, 77 High Street, Beckenham, Kent BR3 1AN. Tel: 0181-658 3531.
Admission: In advance: £4.50 adults; £2 children/OAPs. On the day: £6 adults; £3 children/OAPs. **Times**: 9.30am - 6pm.

28 Jun-4 Jul
ALNWICK FAIR
The Market Place, Alnwick, Northumberland.
Medieval fair.
Things to see: On the opening Sunday over 1,000 people parading in costume follow the Herald as he proclaims the Fair open. Plus a week of free entertainment, craft stalls, music.
Contact: Mrs M Frater, 23 St Georges Crescent, Alnwick, Northumberland NE66 1AY. Tel: 01665 605004.
Admission: N/A. **Times**: 10am - 5pm.

29 Jun
WARCOP RUSHBEARING
Warcop village, Cumbria.
Ancient ceremony.
Things to see: Procession through village to parish church with crowns of flowers and crosses of rushes. Military band, girls carrying crowns of flowers and boys carrying rushes.
Contact: Mr R Thompson, Heronwood, Warcop, Appleby-in-Westmoreland, Cumbria CA16 6PU. Tel: 017683 41774.
Admission: N/A. **Times**: 2pm. Church service 3pm.

30 Jun-4 Jul
CLAN DONALD ARCHERY TOURNAMENT
Front Lawn of Armadale Castle, The Clan Donald Visitor Centre, Isle of Skye.
International archery tournament.
Things to see: Event takes place on the lawn in front of Armadale Castle, with 100 top archers competing in this most picturesque setting. There is an open view across the water to the mountains of Knoydart.
Contact: Karen Macaskill, Clan Donald Visitor Centre, Armadale, Sleat, Isle of Skye. Tel: 01471 844305.
Admission: £3.40 **Times**: Tues - Fri: 9am - 5pm. Sat: 10am - 12.30pm.

July

1-2 Jul
ROYAL NORFOLK SHOW
The Showground, Dereham Road, New Costessey, Norwich, Norfolk.
Major agricultural show.
Things to see: Agricultural machinery, livestock, dog show, flower show, conservation and forestry exhibitions, trade stands, art and craft exhibitions, main arena demonstrations.
Contact: Mr John Purling, Chief Executive, The Showground, Dereham Road, New Costessey, Norwich, Norfolk NR5 0TT. Tel: 01603 748931. Fax: 01603 748729.
Admission: TBA. **Times**: 8am - 7pm.

1-5 Jul
HENLEY ROYAL REGATTA
Henley-on-Thames, Oxfordshire.
Rowing regatta and major occasion in the social calendar.
Things to see: International rowing regatta set on one of the most attractive stretches of the Thames. Spectators as well as rowers provide plenty of spectacle.
Contact: The Secretary, Henley Royal Regatta, Regatta Headquarters, Henley-on-Thames, Oxon RG9 2LY. Tel: 01491 572153.
Admission: N/A on the riverbank; enclosure prices unconfirmed. **Times**: Often an 8.30am start, but predominantly 9am, except for Finals Day when racing always starts at 12 noon.

2-6 Jul
ENGLAND V SOUTH AFRICA
Old Trafford, Manchester.
Major five-day international test match between England and South Africa.
Things to see: Top class international cricket for over six hours a day for five days. Membership and corporate hospitality facilities contained within a first class cricketing arena.
Contact: Old Trafford Cricket Ground, Manchester. Tel: 0161 848 7021.
Admission: TBA. **Times**: TBA. No play Sunday.

3-5 Jul
THE NORTH OF ENGLAND MOTORSHOW
The Links, Whitley Bay, Tyne & Wear.
Biggest outdoor regional motorshow of its type in the country.
Things to see: New cars, classic cars, in-car entertainment. Motorsport marquee, sound-off competition, Lamborghini Diablo, plus many more attractions.
Contact: Alan Fairbairn Promotions, Units 1-5 Herbert Terrace, Newcastle Rd, Fulwell, Sunderland SR5 1RL. Tel: 0191 516 0085.
Admission: £3 adults; £1 children. **Times**: 10am - 6pm.

4 Jul
ANNAN RIDING OF THE MARCHES
The Royal Burgh of Annan and its boundaries.
Traditional ceremony and carnival.
Things to see: Various events including traditional inspection on horseback of the 16 miles Royal Burgh boundaries, horse chases, carnival procession and afternoon entertainment, with the spectacular finale of 25 Massed Pipe Bands and handing back of the Burgh Standard. Marchridings were recorded in Annan as early as

1680. Modern-day entertainment combined with an age-old custom combine to make a fine day out for the whole family.
Contact: Don Barty, 10 Seaforth Avenue, Annan, Dumfriesshire DG12 6DX. Tel: 01461 202708.
Admission: N/A. **Times**: 7.45am - 7.30pm.

4 Jul
THORNTON HIGHLAND GATHERING
Memorial Park, Thornton, Fife.
Highland games.
Things to see: Various competitions featuring athletics, cycling, heavyweight events and Highland dancing. Also small funfair, numerous trade stalls, etc. Small display of vintage farm machinery, pipe band contest, etc.
Contact: W Crawford, Secretary, Thornton Highland Gathering, 43 Donald Crescent, Thornton, Kirkcaldy, Fife KY1 4AH.
Admission: £2 adults; £1 children/OAPs. Car park 50p. **Times**: Noon - 6pm approx

4 Jul
OPEN AIR CONCERT
Leeds Castle, Maidstone, Kent.
Summer concert at Leeds Castle.
Things to see: Carl Davis conducts the Royal Liverpool Philharmonic Orchestra in the original summer night classical music concerts, with the "1812", cannons and fireworks as the triumphant finale.
Contact: Leeds Castle, Maidstone, Kent ME17 1PL. Tel: 01622 765400.
Admission: Advance ticket sales only from the box office, Tel: 01622 880008. Open 1 February. Group rates available. **Times**: Gates open 4pm. Entertainment from 5.30pm.

4-5 Jul
DEVON COUNTY ANTIQUES FAIR
Westpoint Exhibition Centre, Clyst St Mary, Exeter, Devon.
Antiques fair.
Things to see: Beautiful antiques and collectables among the estimated one million items on offer. 500 stands in one hall. Plus free lectures, seminars and exhibitions.
Contact: Val Dennis, Devon Counties Antiques Fairs, The Glebe House, Nymet Tracey, Crediton, Devon EX17 6DB. Tel: 01363 82571.
Admission: £3.50 adults; children free. **Times**: Sat: 10am - 5pm. Sun: 10am - 5pm.

4-5 Jul
FOUR SEASONS CRAFTS SHOW
Monument Meadows, Ashridge Estate, Berkhamsted, Herts.
Craft fair.
Things to see: Quality crafts created by experts from all over the country. Robin Hood theme.
Contact: Four Seasons (Events Ltd), 23A Brockenhurst Rd, South Ascot, Berkshire SL5 9DJ. Tel: 01344 874787.
Admission: £2.50-£3.50 adults; £2-£2.50 OAPs; £1 children. **Times**: TBA.

4-5 Jul
SCOTTISH KIT CAR SHOW
Royal Highland Exhibition Centre, Edinburgh.
Kit car show.
Things to see: Thousands of kit cars and replicas, from on the road to *concours* standard.
Contact: Mrs E Cooling, Grosvenor Exhibitions Ltd, Grosvenor House, 81 London Road, Spalding, Lincolnshire. Tel: 01775 712100.
Admission: Approx £6 adult; children £2. **Times**: 9.30am - 6pm.

4-5 Jul
THE GUARDIAN EUROPEAN INTER-CLUB SURF CHAMPIONSHIPS
Sennen, Cornwall.
Event from the calendar of 'Cornwall '98, The World Watersports Festival'.
Things to see: Clubs from all over the UK and Europe in serious surf action at one of the cleanest and most beautiful beaches in Cornwall. There will be a wild

attempt to beat the world record for the most surfers on a single wave.
Contact: Cornwall '98, Trevint House, Strangways Villas, Truro, Cornwall TR1 2PA. Tel: 01872 223527.
Admission: TBA. **Times**: TBA.

4-5 Jul
AMERICAN INDEPENDENCE DAY DISPLAYS
The American Museum, Claverton Manor, Bath, Avon.
Historical military display.
Things to see: Crown forces of 1776 give colourful displays of the drill and way of life of infantry and artillery men.
Contact: Miss Susan Carter, The American Museum, Claverton Manor, Bath, Avon. Tel: 01225 460503.
Admission: To grounds only, which will cover the event. 1997 guide: £2.50 adults; £1.25 children. **Times**: 1pm - 6pm.

4-5 Jul
ELVASTON CASTLE STEAM & TRANSPORT FESTIVAL
Elvaston Castle Country Park, Borrowash, Derby.
Largest steam rally in the Midlands.
Things to see: Vintage vehicles, vintage organs, vintage fairground with gallopers, can-can girls, plus other attractions.
Contact: Mrs E Renshaw, 21 Windsor Drive, Spondon, Derby DE21 7DR. Tel: 01332 673303.
Admission: TBA. **Times**: 10am - 6pm approx.

4-5 Jul
POWDERHAM HORSE TRIALS
Powderham Castle, Kenton, Nr Exeter.
Equestrian competition.
Things to see: Showjumping, dressage, cross country. Walk the cross-country course for a good variety of vantage points.
Contact: Tim Faulkner, The Horse Trials Office, Powderham Castle, Kenton, Exeter EX6 8JQ. Tel: 01626 890243.
Admission: £5 per car. **Times**: 8am - 7pm.

4-5 Jul
SOUTHAMPTON BALLOON AND FLOWER FESTIVAL
Southampton Common, Southampton.
Things to see: A unique family event combining the excitement of approximately 100 hot air balloons with the beauty of the largest horticultural exhibits on the south coast. Also arena entertainment, large trade village, traditional funfair and picnic facilities. Access to main balloon launch area restricted.
Contact: Special Events Unit, Civic Centre, Southampton SO14 7LP. Tel: 01703 832755.
Admission: Free. **Times**: Contact the above for details.

4-5 Jul
STARS & STRIPES WEEKEND
Tatton Park, Knutsford, Cheshire (M56 junction 7; M6 junction 19).
Car show featuring American cars.
Things to see: 1000+ American classic cars on display. Cavalcades of historic cars and static displays including 1950s "Fins 'n' Chrome" era. Ex-US army vehicles in battle-like camps. Plus custom cars, kit cars, American motorcycles and American motorhomes display. Many other American activities throughout the weekend such as music, dancing. Plus monster action stunt team "Big Foot Car Crush".
Contact: Stuart Holmes, Cheshire Auto Promotions, Bridge House, 200 Park Road, Stretford M32 8RB. Tel: 0161-864 2906.
Admission: Sat £4 adults; child free; Sun £5 adults; child free. **Times**: 10am - 5pm.

4-5 Jul*
BEXLEY SHOW
Danson Park, Bexleyheath, Kent.
Family show and events.
Things to see: Spectacular arena events, trade and voluntary stands, vintage and veteran vehicles in motor cavalcade, lake events, clowns, fairground organs, colourful stalls, flower displays, fair-

ground rides, etc.
Contact: Events Manager, Leisure Link, Howbury Centre, Slade Green Road, Slade Green, Kent, DA8 2HX. Tel: 0181-303 7777 ext 3956.
Admission: TBA. **Times**: 10.30am - 6pm.

5 Jul
ATLANTIC ALONE
Falmouth, Cornwall.
Event from the calendar of 'Cornwall '98, The World Watersports Festival'.
Things to see: Be there as some of the world's toughest and most experienced sailors prepare for the greatest challenge of all - circumnavigation of the globe - alone. See the start of this feeder race to the USA and relive the occasion as race news unfolds in the media.
Contact: Cornwall '98, Trevint House, Strangways Villas, Truro, Cornwall TR1 2PA. Tel: 01872 223527.
Admission: TBA. **Times**: TBA.

5 Jul*
OPEN AIR CONCERTS
Leeds Castle, Maidstone, Kent.
Summer concert at Leeds Castle.
Things to see: Carl Davis conducts the Royal Liverpool Philharmonic Orchestra in the original summer night classical music concerts, with the "1812", cannons and fireworks as the triumphant finale.
Contact: Leeds Castle, Maidstone, Kent ME17 1PL. Tel: 01622 765400.
Admission: Advance ticket sales only from the box office. Tel: 01622 880008. Open 1 February. Group rates available. **Times**: Gates open 4pm. Entertainment from 5.30pm.

5 Jul
PADDINGTON PERFORMANCE FESTIVAL
Paddington Recreation Ground, London W9.
Celebration of popular performing arts.
Things to see: Clowns, jugglers, unicyclists, stiltwalkers, musicians, trapeze artists, acrobats, street entertainers and new circus acts.
Contact: Alternative Arts, 47A Brushfield Street, Spitalfields, London E1 6AA. Tel: 0171-375 0441.
Admission: Free. **Times**: 12 noon - 6pm.

5-10 Jul
NEWQUAY 1900 WEEK
Newquay, Cornwall.
A week of Victorian theme events.
Things to see: Civic parade, flora dance, carnival night, torchlight procession, Victorian dress, Queen Victoria, Newquay 1900 Can-Can dancers, fireworks display, etc.
Contact: Ron Hatfield, President, Carnmarth Hotel, Headland Road, Newquay, Cornwall TR7 1HN. Tel: 01637 872519. Fax: 01637 878770.
Admission: N/A. **Times**: TBA.

6-9 Jul
THE ROYAL SHOW
National Agricultural Centre, Stoneleigh Park, Warwickshire.
This is said to be the premier agricultural trade fair in Britain, with visitors from all parts of the world.
Things to see: The biggest celebration of all that's best about the countryside including food, flowers, gardening, country pursuits, equine events, grand ring displays + over 6,000 animals.
Contact: Marketing Department, Royal Agricultural Society of England, National Agricultural Centre, Stoneleigh Park, Warwickshire CV8 2LZ. Tel: 01203 696969.
Admission: TBA. **Times**: TBA.

7-12 Jul
LLANGOLLEN INTERNATIONAL MUSICAL EISTEDDFOD
Royal International Pavilion, Abbey Road, Llangollen.
Traditional music festival.
Things to see: Over 12,000 competitors in national costume, from 47 nations, performing folk dance, folk song and in choral competitions. Floral displays 10ft

high x 120ft long, replenished daily.
Contact: Maureen A Jones, Eisteddfod Office, Llangollen, Clwyd LL20 8NG. Tel: 01978 860236. Fax: 01978 861300.
Admission: £4 adults; £2 OAPs. **Times**: 9am - 10.30pm.

7-12 Jul
THE ROYAL HORTICULTURAL SOCIETY'S HAMPTON COURT PALACE FLOWER SHOW
Home Park of Hampton Court Palace, Surrey.
The world's largest flower show.
Things to see: Extensive floral, horticultural and landscape garden displays. Floral marquees and landscape show gardens plus arts and crafts exhibits, set in over 25 acres of parkland between the Thames and the Long Water and against the backdrop of Sir Christopher Wren's east facade of the Palace.
Contact: Royal Horticultural Society, Vincent Square, London SW1P 2PE. Tel: 0171-649 1885.
Admission: 7/8 Jul: RHS Members only. £17 adults (£10 after 3pm); £5 children. **Times**: 10am - 7.30pm. Closes at 5.30pm on Sunday.

8-12 Jul
THE BRITISH NATIONS CUP & GRAND PRIX
All England Jumping Course, Hickstead, West Sussex.
International showjumping event.
Things to see: The world's top horses and riders in action. Also driving horses and native breed ponies. Over 100 trade stands including country craft fair, children's fair, licensed bars and restaurant.
Contact: British Show Jumping Association, Kenilworth, Warwickshire CV8 2LR. Tel: 01203 698800. Or Mrs Vicky Grinnall, All England Jumping Course, Hickstead, West Sussex RH17 5NU. Tel: 01273 834315.
Admission: £8 - £16 approx. **Times**: 8.30am - 5.30pm.

9-12 Jul*
BRITISH GRAND PRIX
Silverstone Circuit, Silverstone, Northants.
World Championship motor race and supporting events.
Things to see: The highlight of the British motor racing calendar – FIA Formula One Grand Prix with full support programme of races and displays.
Contact: Silverstone Circuits Ltd, Silverstone, Nr Towcester, Northants NN12 8TN. Tel: 01327 857271.
Admission: £10 - £75 adults; £5 - £11 children. Grandstands available. **Times**: 7am - 10pm; Grand Prix race starts 2pm, 12 July*.

10-12 Jul
LORD MAYOR'S STREET PROCESSION '98
Norwich city centre.
City carnival.
Things to see: Procession with bands, entertainers, old time funfair, street

party, outdoor theatre.
Contact: Helen Selleck, Community Arts & Events Officer, Norwich City Council, Gladstone House, 28 St Giles Street, Norwich NR2 1TQ
Admission: N/A. **Times**: TBA.

10-12 Jul
WENLOCK OLYMPIAN GAMES
Much Wenlock Sports Centre, Shropshire.
Three days of sports.
Things to see: Three days of sports beginning on Fri: cricket and karate. Sat: bowls and volleyball. Sun: athletics, track & field, road race, pentathlons, triathlons, bowls, archery, clay pigeon shooting, fencing, and five-a-side. Sunday is the big day.
Contact: Mr N Wood, 5 Slade Lane, Homer, Much Wenlock, Shropshire TF13 6ND. Tel: 01952 727615.
Admission: Free. **Times**: Fri: from 11.30am. Sat/Sun: from 9.30am.

10-14 Jul
WEST CORNWALL MARITIME FESTIVAL
Penzance, Cornwall.
Event from the calendar of 'Cornwall '98, The World Watersports Festival'.
Things to see: A real celebration of maritime heritage and classic sailing. Music stalls and street entertainment make this a must for all the family. Extra excitement as some stunning Tall Ships make a stop in Penzance before the last leg of the journey round the coast to Falmouth for the start of the Cutty Sark Tall Ships' Race 1998.
Contact: Cornwall '98, Trevint House, Strangways Villas, Truro, Cornwall TR1 2PA. Tel: 01872 223527.
Admission: TBA. **Times**: TBA.

11 Jul*
BENSON AND HEDGES CUP FINAL
Lord's Cricket Ground, St John's Wood, London.
Major domestic cricket final.
Things to see: Top level cricket final; 55 overs per side.
Contact: M.C.C., Lord's Ground, London NW8 8QZ. Tel: 0171- 289 1611.
Admission: £20 - £35. **Times**: 10.30am - 7.30pm approx.

11 Jul
DINGWALL HIGHLAND GATHERING
Jubilee Park, Dingwall, Ross-shire.
Highland games.
Things to see: Traditional Highland games with light and heavy track and field events, solo piping, Highland dancing, pipe bands, cycling and side shows.
Contact: A W Miller, 15 Old Evanton Road, Dingwall, Ross-shire IV15 9RA. Tel: 01349 862024.
Admission: £3 adults. £1 children/OAPs **Times**: From 12 noon.

11 Jul
DURHAM MINERS' GALA
City of Durham and racecourse (also cathedral).
Traditional miners' event.
Things to see: Miners' bands and banners march though the streets of the town, plus leading Labour politicians, miners' cathedral service (with bands and banners), political speeches, sideshows, etc. Possibly the most colourful event in the North. Best vantage point probably being outside the Royal County Hotel where all bands and banners converge prior to marching down to the racecourse.
Contact: NUM (Durham Area), PO Box 6, Red Hill, Durham, Co Durham. Tel: 0191 384 3515.
Admission: N/A. **Times**: 9am - 4pm.

11 Jul
INVERNESS HIGHLAND GAMES
Bught Park, Inverness.
Amateur Highland games.
Things to see: Tossing the caber and other heavyweight Scottish events, athletics, cycling, Highland dancing, piping,

craft & trade stalls, etc. Plus children's 'Have-a-go' Highland mini games.
Contact: Jon Hogan, Area Cultural & Leisure Services Manager, Town House, Inverness IV1 1SS. Tel: 01463 724217.
Admission: £2.50. **Times**: 12 noon - 5pm.

11 Jul
THE WORLD CHAMPIONSHIP PEA SHOOTING
The Village Green, Witcham, Nr Ely, Cambridgeshire.
Championship to find the "world's best peashooter".
Things to see: The world's top peashooters in action! Plus a fete, stalls, etc.
Contact: Mrs J A Phillips, 21 The Slade, Witcham, Nr Ely, Cambridgeshire CB6 2LA. Tel: 01353 778363.
Admission: Free. **Times**: 2.30pm - 6pm.

11-12 Jul
DAGENHAM TOWN SHOW
Central Park, Dagenham, Essex.
Largest show of its kind in the South East.
Things to see: Rock concert musical extravaganza, wrestling, horticultural displays, clowns, children's entertainment, floral displays, dog show, showground attractions.
Contact: Lisa Bentley, Events Officer, Frizlands Admin. Offices, Frizlands Lane, Dagenham, Essex RM10 7HX. Tel: 0181-252 8137.
Admission: Free. **Times**: 11am - 7pm.

11-12 Jul
HISTORIC VEHICLE GATHERING
Powderham Castle, Kenton, Nr Exeter, Devon.
Display of historic vehicles of all kinds.
Things to see: A large display of vehicles dating back to the early 1900s, including car club displays and military vehicles. Vintage cars, steam engines, children's events, arena events, craft stalls, autojumble, auction and trade stands.
Contact: Tim Faulkner, Powderham Castle, Kenton, Exeter. Tel: 01626 890243.
Admission: TBA. **Times**: 10am - 5pm approx.

11-12 Jul
MID WALES FESTIVAL OF TRANSPORT
Powis Castle Showground, Welshpool.
Major vehicle rally.
Things to see: 750 – 1000 exhibits, classic, veteran and vintage vehicles of all types plus 100-year-old steam engines, 100+ stationary engines, 100+ motorcycles, arena activities, demonstrations and parades.
Contact: Mike Exton, Seven Stars Road, Welshpool, Powys SY21 7JP. Tel: 01938 553680/553947. Fax: 01938 553680.
Admission: £3.50 adults; children under 16 free. **Times**: Sat: town parade 2.30pm, evening hog roast and disco till 12 midnight. Sun: main rally day with arena activities 10am - 5pm.

11-12 Jul
WOODCOTE RALLY
Woodcote, Nr Reading.
Festival of veteran transport and country pursuits.
Things to see: Steam traction engines, vintage and classic cars and bikes, air display, crafts, street market, country pursuits, entertainment for adults and kids.
Contact: Geoff Capes, Pendeen, Behoes Lane, Woodcote, Reading RG8 0PP. Tel: 01491 680240.
Admission: £5 adults; £2 children/OAPs. **Times**: Sat: 10am - 11pm. Sun: 10am - 6pm.

11-14 Jul
FALMOUTH DRAGON BOAT CHALLENGE
Falmouth, Cornwall.
Event from the calendar of 'Cornwall '98, The World Watersports Festival'.
Things to see: Outstanding entertainment for all the family with teams of up to twenty-one people rowing 40 foot Chinese Dragon Boats over a 200 metre course.

Contact: Cornwall '98, Trevint House, Strangways Villas, Truro, Cornwall TR1 2PA. Tel: 01872 223527.
Admission: TBA. **Times**: TBA.

12 Jul
FUNTASIA!
National Tramway Museum, Crich, Matlock, Derbyshire.
Special children's event.
Things to see: Bouncy castles, clowns, competitions and a whole host of other entertainment!
Contact: Lesley Wyld, Marketing Manager, National Tramway Museum, Crich, Matlock, Derbyshire DE4 5DP. Tel: 01773 852565. Fax: 01773 852326.
Admission: £5.90 adults; children free if you bring a full-paying adult; £5.10 OAPs; £16.20 family ticket. **Times**: 10am - 5.30pm.

12 Jul
MANCHESTER TO BLACKPOOL BIKE RIDE
Start: Albert Square, Manchester. Finish: Sea Front, Blackpool.
Cycle race for cyclists of moderate to expert abilities in aid of charity.
Things to see: Mass start in Manchester, then along a 58 mile route with support vehicles. Marshalls, cyclists, mechanics en route. Finishing cyclists throughout afternoon in Stanley Park, Blackpool. 4,500 cyclists take part.
Contact: Bike Events, PO Box 75, Bath BA1 1BX. Tel: 01225 480130.
Admission: Free to spectators. **Times**: Start from 7am - 10am. Finish throughout afternoon.

12 Jul
MARKET BOSWORTH SHOW
The Park, Market Bosworth, Leicestershire.
Horse show.
Things to see: Horses of all breeds from Shires to Shetlands. Plus dog agility classes, flower show, trade stands, entertainments, vintage and agricultural machinery, crafts.
Contact: Miss M Liddington, Melrose, 32 Atherstone Road, Measham, Swadlincole, Derby DE12 7EG. Tel: 01530 271169.
Admission: £4 adults; £1.50 children/OAPs. **Times**: From 8.30am.

13-18 Jul
ABERDEEN INTERNATIONAL FOOTBALL FESTIVAL
Seaton Park, Aberdeen.
International youth football festival.
Things to see: Up to four competitive football games played simultaneously on grass pitches all located within Seaton Park. Teams attend from all corners of the world. Sections for boys of 16 and under 14. Also girls of 16, plus under-12s seven-a-side.
Contact: Gordon Naismith, Sports, Festivals & Trusts Officer, City Arts and Recreation Department, St Nicholas House, Broad Street, Aberdeen AB9 1XJ. Tel: 01224 522456.
Admission: Free. **Times**: From 1.30pm.

13-16 Jul
SOUTHERN 100 MOTORCYCLE RACES
Billown Circuit, Castletown, Isle of Man.
Motorcycle road racing.
Things to see: Motorcyclists in action on a 4.25 mile course; solos, sidecars and classics.
Contact: George Peach, Secretary, Southern 100, Ellersile, Malew Street, Castletown, Isle of Man. Tel: 01624 822546.
Admission: Free, except main grandstand £1.50. **Times**: Mon - Wed 6pm - 9pm. Thurs 1pm - 6pm.

13-18 Jul
JERSEY FLORAL FESTIVAL
Various venues around Jersey.
A celebration of gardening and flowers.
Things to see: Guided walks, talks and opportunities to visit private gardens, personal appearances by UK gardening personalities.

Contact: Jersey Tourism, Liberation Square, St Helier, Jersey JE1 1BB. Tel: 0171-493 5278.
Admission: Many events are free, but check with programme. **Times**: TBA.

13-19 Jul
CITY OF BELFAST ROSE WEEK
Sir Thomas & Lady Dixon Park, Malone Road, Belfast.
Week of events/activities for adults and children around rose gardens.
Things to see: International rose garden and display, summer rose and flower show, trade stands.
Contact: Alice Blennerhessett, The Cecil Ward Building, 4-10 Linenhall Street, Belfast BT2 8BP. Tel: 01232 320202.
Admission: Free. **Times**: 9am until dusk.

14 Jul
ULSTER HARP DERBY
Maze Racecourse, Lisburn, Co Antrim.
The major flat race meeting in Northern Ireland.
Things to see: Top horses and jockeys in action.
Contact: Maze Racecourse, Lisburn, Co Antrim, Northern Ireland BT27 5BW. Tel: 01846 621256.
Admission: £10 adults; £5 OAPs/students. Car park free. **Times**: From 2.30pm.

14-16 Jul
GREAT YORKSHIRE SHOW
Great Yorkshire Showground, Harrogate, North Yorkshire.
Major agricultural show.
Things to see: More than 8,000 animals, first class flower show, exciting ring events, showjumping and 600 or so trade stands.
Contact: Judy Thompson, Press Officer, Yorkshire Agricultural Society, Great Yorkshire Showground, Harrogate HG2 8PW. Tel: 01423 541000.
Admission: TBA. **Times**: Opens 8am.

16 Jul
NATIONAL BRITISH HILL CLIMB CHAMPIONSHIP
Bouley Bay, Jersey.
Hill climb for cars and motorcycles.
Things to see: Cars, motorcycles and karts in action against the beautiful Bouley Bay scenery.
Contact: Mrs Ellaine Le Cornu, Midway, Croix de Bois, Five Oaks, Jersey JE2 7TU. Tel: 01534 35853.
Admission: £3.50. **Times**: 10am - 6pm approx.

16-18 Jul
KENT COUNTY SHOW
County Showground, Detling, Maidstone, Kent.
Major agricultural show.
Things to see: Livestock, horses and showjumping, British food tent, English wine marquee, sheep shearing, horse shoeing, bee garden and forestry area, veteran and vintage vehicles, steam engines, rural crafts, ring attractions and over 500 trade stands.
Contact: The Secretary, County Showground, Detling, Maidstone, Kent ME14 3JF. Tel: 01622 630975. Fax: 01622 630978.
Admission: TBA. **Times**: 8am - 6pm.

16-18 Jul
1648 CHEPSTOW CASTLE
Chepstow Castle.
Historical spectacular, son et lumiere which tells the story of the siege of Chepstow Castle.
Things to see: Begins with historical fair outside castle. As darkness falls audience go into castle. The production is on a grand scale with 100+ actors, huge image projections, battle scenes, astonishing lighting and effects, pyrotechnics.
Contact: Chepstow Museum. Tel: 01291 625981.
Admission: £7.50 adults; £5 children/OAPs. **Times**: Fair starts 7.30pm. Spectacular: 10.30pm - 12 midnight.

16-19 Jul
CUTTY SARK TALL SHIPS RACE
Falmouth, Cornwall.
Event from the calendar of 'Cornwall '98, The World Watersports Festival'.
Things to see: Few sights are as magnificent as the Start of the Cutty Sark Tall Ships' Race. A unique opportunity to view one hundred of the world's most impressive Square Rigged Ships, Barques and Brigantines with the stunning backdrop of Falmouth Bay. It is also confirmed that the world's most famous cruise liner QE2 will stop over in Falmouth for the Start of the Race on 19 Jul. Also: concerts, south stage, crafts, maritime exhibition, dragon-boat racing, fireworks and all the fun of the fair.
Contact: Cornwall '98, Trevint House, Strangways Villas, Truro, Cornwall TR1 2PA. Tel: 01872 223527.
Admission: TBA. **Times**: TBA.

16-19 Jul
THE OPEN GOLF CHAMPIONSHIP
Royal Birkdale Golf Club, Waterloo Rd, Birkdale, Southport, Merseyside.
Major event in the golfing world calendar.
Things to see: The top golfers in the world competing against one another on this famous and difficult championship course.
Contact: Royal Birkdale Golf Club, Waterloo Rd, Birkdale, Southport, Merseyside. Tel: 01704 567920. Also: Royal & Ancient Golf Club, St Andrews, Fife KY16 9JD. Tel: 01334 472112.
Admission: TBA. **Times**: 7.15am - 8pm approx.

17-19 Jul
NORTHAMPTON TOWN SHOW
Abington Park, Northampton.
Annual town show.
Things to see: Traditional mix of horticultural displays, crafts, exhibitions, trade stands and arena entertainments. Plus evening concerts and grand firework displays.
Contact: Events Team, Cliftonville House, Bedford Road, Northampton NN4 7NR. Tel: 01604 238791.
Admission: Free. Car parking charge.
Times: TBA.

17-19 Jul
FOUR SEASONS CRAFTS SHOW
Ealing Common, London W5.
Craft fair.
Things to see: Quality crafts created by experts from all over the country. Medieval theme.
Contact: Four Seasons (Events Ltd), 23A Brockenhurst Rd, South Ascot, Berkshire SL5 9DJ. Tel: 01344 874787.
Admission: £2.50-£3.50 adults; £2-£2.50 OAPs; £1 children. **Times**: TBA.

17-19 Jul
WAR AND PEACE SHOW
The Hop Farm Country Park, Paddock Wood, Kent.
World's largest gathering of military vehicles, plus large model show.
Things to see: Military vehicles from First World War to the present day, large military model displays, over 250 stalls, three days of arena events, 50+ displays.
Contact: Rex Cadman (on befalf of the Invicta Military Preservation Society), The Old Rectory, Sandwich Rd, Ash, Nr Canterbury, Kent CT3 2AF. Tel: 01304 813128.
Admission: £6 adults; £4.50 OAPs/disabled; £4 children; £18 family ticket.
Times: Gates open 8am Show starts: Fri: 10am - 6pm. Sat: 10am - 6pm. Sun: 10am - 6pm.

17-19 Jul
WEETING STEAM ENGINE RALLY
Fengate Farm, Weeting, Brandon, Suffolk.
Steam engine rally.
Things to see: Large-scale rally on 150 acres with full steam working demonstrations and country crafts.
Contact: R N Parrott, Fengate Farm, Weeting, Brandon, Suffolk. Tel: 01842

810317.
Admission: £5 adults; £4 OAPs; children under 14 free. **Times**: From 9.30am.

17-19 Jul
NATIONAL ROWING CHAMPIONSHIPS OF GREAT BRITAIN
Strathclyde Country Park, N Glasgow.
The National Championship regatta for all UK rowing clubs over 2,000m 6 lane course. The largest 'open regatta' in the UK.
Things to see: 700 crews approximately in competition, half of which are juniors. 9 hours of rowing at 7 minute intervals. Trade exhibition of all major boat builders, oar makers and kit suppliers to the sport.
Contact: Rodney Beer (Chairman) or Jane Beckett (Secretary), c/o Amateur Rowing Association, 6 Lower Mall, Hammersmith, London W6 9DJ. Tel: 0181-748 3632.
Admission: Variable. **Times**: Fri/Sat: 9am - 6pm. Sun: 10am - 5pm.

18 Jul
CLEATOR MOOR SPORTS
Wath Brow Sports Field, Cleator, Cumbria.
Traditional Lakeland sports event.
Things to see: Athletics, Cumberland wrestling, cycling, terrier and lurcher show, ferret show, hound trails, fell races, fun run and a continental cycle race at 7.30pm on Market Square.
Contact: Mr A Kelly, Braith House, Cleator, Cumbria CA23 3DT. Tel: 01946 811656.
Admission: £2 adults; 50p children/OAPs. **Times**: 1pm - 5.30pm.

Dates can change, events can be cancelled – Please check with the organisers before setting out!

18 Jul
RNAS YEOVILTON INTERNATIONAL AIR DAY
Royal Naval Air Station Yeovilton, Yeovil, Somerset.
Major international air show.
Things to see: Military and civilian aircraft, static and flying displays, service displays, traders, caterers, vintage vehicles, military bands, children's rides/fun fair, sideshows etc.
Contact: The Air Day Organiser, Royal Naval Air Station Yeovilton, Yeovil, Somerset BA22 8HT. Tel: 01935 456751.
Admission: TBA. **Times**: 9.30am - 6pm.

19 Jul
HISTORIC VEHICLE RALLY
Newby Hall & Gardens, Ripon, North Yorkshire.
North East Club for pre-war Austins annual rally.
Things to see: Over 800 entries covering vintage, veteran and classic cars, commercial and military vehicles as well as vintage motor cycles.
Contact: Mr R G Alexander, Opening Administrator, Newby Hall, Ripon, North Yorkshire HG4 5AE. Tel: 01423 322583.
Admission: TBA. **Times**: From 10.30am - 5.30pm.

19 Jul
THE SPITALFIELDS COMMUNITY FESTIVAL
The Old Spitalfields Market, Brushfield

St, London E1.
Multicultural celebration in the community of Spitalfields.
Things to see: Music, dance, poetry, plays performed by a wide range of local groups.
Contact: Alternative Arts, 47A Brushfield Street, Spitalfields, London E1 6AA. Tel: 0171-375 0441.
Admission: Free. **Times**: From 11am - 5pm.

19 Jul
WELSH NSPCC IT'S A KNOCKOUT CHAMPIONSHIPS & SHOW 1998
Swansea.
Touring production of "It's A Knockout" for adults and children.
Things to see: Competitors engaging in "Knock Out" games, celebrities, children's characters. Full supporting show with funfair, amusements, etc.
Contact: Mrs E Field, The White House, Llanfoist, Abergavenny, Gwent NP7 9LR. Tel/Fax: 01873 855552.
Admission: £3 adults; £1 children/OAPs. **Times**: 10am - 6pm.

19 Jul
ALFORD CAVALCADE
Grampian Transport Museum, Alford, Aberdeenshire.
Vintage vehicle show.
Things to see: One of Scotland's largest vintage vehicle shows, plus stunt demonstrations and many other attractions.
Contact: Mike Ward, Grampian Transport Museum, Alford, Aberdeenshire AB33 8AD. Tel: 019755 62292. Fax: 019755 62180.
Admission: £3.50 adults; £2 OAPs; £1.50 children. **Times**: 11am - 5pm.

19 Jul
NOSTELL PRIORY COUNTRY FAIR
Nostell Priory, Doncaster Road, Nostell, Wakefield, West Yorkshire.
Country fair.
Things to see: Country pursuits, live bands ranging from jazz to ukulele, sideshows, puppets, rare breeds, showjumping, stalls, craft fair, fishing, etc.
Contact: Living Heritage, PO Box 36, Uttoxeter, Staffs. Tel: 01889 500449.
Admission: TBA. **Times**: 10am - 5pm.

19 Jul
TEDDY BEARS PICNIC
Beningbrough Hall, Shipton, Beningbrough, York.
Teddy Bears' Picnic for children aged 3-12.
Things to see: Teddy bears with picnic. Fun and games for all teddies and keepers. Prizes for Count the Teddy Competition and Best Dressed Teddy.
Contact: The National Trust, Beningbrough Hall, Shipton, Beningbrough, York YO6 1DD. Tel: 01904 470666.
Admission: Normal admission prices apply. **Times**: 12 noon - 4pm.

19 Jul
TOLPUDDLE RALLY
Village of Tolpuddle, Nr Dorchester, Dorset.
Rally in memory of the Tolpuddle Martyrs.
Things to see: The premier rally in the south of England for the workers' movement. Parade of banners, wreath-laying in St John's Church, stalls, music, drama, speeches (high-ranking politicians speak alongside trade unionists), chapel service. TV and press usually present.
Contact: J Northcliffe, T&GWU, 238 Holdenhurst Road, Bournemouth, Dorset BH8 8EG. Tel: 01202 294333.
Admission: N/A. **Times**: 12.30 - 4pm.

19 Jul
VINTAGE VEHICLE & CLASSIC CAR SHOW
Springfields, Spalding, Lincs.
Vintage and classic car rally.
Things to see: Probably the biggest rally in the East of England, with over 450 exhibitors plus music and entertainment.
Contact: Brian Willoughby, Springfield,

Spalding, Lincs PE12 6ET. Tel: 01775 724843/713253.
Admission: £3.50 adults; £3 OAPs; accompanied children free. **Times**: 10am - 5pm.

19-25 Jul
STEAM PACKET INTERNATIONAL FOOTBALL FESTIVAL
Various venues on the Isle of Man.
Football competition.
Things to see: Top football clubs from the Nationwide League in out of season competition.
Contact: Special Events Unit, Grandstand, Douglas, Isle of Man IM2 4TB. Tel: 01624 686766.
Admission: £1 - £4. **Times**: TBA.

19-25 Jul
CITY OF ABERDEEN BOWLING TOURNAMENT
Westburn Park, and other centres in Aberdeen.
Bowls tournament.
Things to see: Bowling tournament with Ladies, Gents, Juniors and Pairs competitions. High standard of play throughout
Contact: Dorothy Anderson, Arts & Recreation Department, St Nicholas House, Broad Street, Aberdeen, AB10 5GU. Tel: 01224 522190.
Admission: Free. **Times**: TBA.

19-25 Jul
THE IAN RUSH INTERNATIONAL SOCCER TOURNAMENT
Aberystwyth, Mid Wales.
Youth soccer tournament with teams from around the world.
Things to see: Over 100 international teams of under 18 years competing in football action morning to night. With opening and closing events etc.
Contact: Colin Mitchell, Murmur Y Coed, Guilsfield, Welshpool, Powys, Mid Wales. Tel: 01938 55 3631.
Admission: £1. **Times**: Sun: opening events and personality visit. Mon - Fri: football days. Sat: finals day and awards ceremony.

20-23 Jul
ROYAL WELSH SHOW
Royal Welsh Showground, Llanelwedd, Builth Wells, Powys.
One of Europe's largest agricultural shows.
Things to see: Wide spectrum of agricultural displays and exhibitions together with a comprehensive range of non-agricultural events to interest the whole family. Livestock: cattle, horses, sheep, goats, pigs, dogs, poultry, pigeons, rabbits, ostriches. Trade stands, forestry, horticulture, produce and handicrafts, horse shoeing and farriery, children's competitions and displays, tug of war, Welsh food hall, sheep dog trials, sheep shearing, sports arena, etc.
Contact: Mr P D Guthrie, Secretary, The Royal Welsh Agricultural Society, Llanelwedd, Builth Wells, Powys LD2 3SY. Tel: 01982 553683.
Admission: TBA. **Times**: 8am - 9pm.

21 Jul
INVERARAY HIGHLAND GAMES
Winterton Park, Castle Grounds, Inveraray, Argyll.
Highland games.
Things to see: Traditional Highland games with heavy events, track events, cycling, piping, dancing, trade and fun stalls, pipe band.
Contact: Mrs M Mather, 16 Upper Riochan, Inveraray, Argyll PA32 8UR. Tel: 01499 302458.
Admission: £3 adults, 50p children; £1.50 OAPs. **Times**: 10.30am - 5.30pm.

21-23 Jul
EAST OF ENGLAND SHOW
East of England Showground, Peterborough.
Major agricultural event.
Things to see: Wide variety of ring displays, cattle, sheep, dogs, horses, art exhibition, craft stalls with working craftspeople, interactive schools area, horse shoeing, etc.
Contact: T Gibson OBE, East of England

Showground, Peterborough PE2 6XE. Tel: 01733 234451. Fax: 01733 370038.
Admission: TBA. **Times**: 9am - 6pm.

21 Jul-2 Aug
THE ROYAL TOURNAMENT
Earls Court Exhibition Centre, London.
The biggest Military Tattoo in the world.
Things to see: The Army, Navy and RAF pit themselves physically and mentally against the clock and each other in grand displays of strength and agility. 1998 is an RAF year and acts will include the Naval Field Gun Competition, the King's Troop and the massed bands of the RAF.
Contact: Laura Heard. Tel: 0171-370 8206.
Admission: TBA. **Times**: Performances begin at 2pm and 7.30pm. Doors open 11am and 5pm respectively.

23-25 Jul
1648 CHEPSTOW CASTLE
Chepstow Castle.
Historical spectacular, son et lumiere which tells the story of the siege of Chepstow Castle.
Things to see: Begins with historical fair outside castle. As darkness falls audience go into castle. The production is on a grand scale with 100+ actors, huge image projections, battle scenes, astonishing lighting and effects, pyrotechnics.
Contact: Chepstow Museum. Tel: 01291 625981.
Admission: £7.50 adults; £5 children/OAPs. **Times**: Fair starts 7.30pm. Spectacular: 10.30pm - 12 midnight.

23-27 Jul
ENGLAND v SOUTH AFRICA
Trent Bridge, Nottingham.
Major five-day international test match between England and South Africa.
Things to see: Top class international cricket for over six hours a day for five days. Membership and corporate hospitality facilities contained within a first class cricketing arena.
Contact: Brian Robson, Secretary, Nottinghamshire C.C.C., Trent Bridge, Nottingham. Tel: 0115 9821525.
Admission: TBA. **Times**: 11am - 6pm daily.

23 Jul-3 Aug
HEADWORX CHERRY COKE SURF FESTIVAL
Fistral Beach, Newquay, Cornwall.
Event from the calendar of 'Cornwall '98, The World Watersports Festival'.
Things to see: Top-name surfing stars in action in the UK's biggest surfing tournament. Also beach entertainment, surf village and live concerts.
Contact: Cornwall '98, Trevint House, Strangways Villas, Truro, Cornwall TR1 2PA. Tel: 01872 223527.
Admission: TBA. **Times**: TBA.

24-26 Jul
FOUR SEASONS CRAFTS SHOW
The Vyne, Sherbourne St John, Basingstoke, Hants.
Craft fair.
Things to see: Quality crafts created by experts from all over the country. Merrie Olde England theme.
Contact: Four Seasons (Events Ltd), 23A Brockenhurst Rd, South Ascot, Berkshire SL5 9DJ. Tel: 01344 874787.
Admission: £2.50-£3.50 adults; £2-£2.50 OAPs; £1 children. **Times**: TBA.

24-26 Jul
CUMBRIA STEAM GATHERING
Cark Airfield, Flookburgh, Grange Over Sands, Cumbria.
Steam engine and vintage vehicle rally.
Things to see: The premier traction engine and vintage vehicle rally in the North of England, with 1200+ exhibits, fairgrounds, circus, brass bands, crafts, exhibitions and displays. Plus collectors' auction sale.
Contact: Tim Holt, South View, Hutton Roof, Via Carnforth, Cumbria LA6 2PF. Tel: 015242 71584.
Admission: £5 adults; £3 OAPs; children free. **Times**: 9.30am - 6pm.

24-26 Jul
NETLEY MARSH STEAM ENGINE RALLY
Netley Marsh, Southampton, Hants (M27 Junction 2, then A326).
Steam engines and vintage vehicles.
Things to see: Steam traction engines, vehicles from 1920s to 1950s, rural craft displays, farm machinery, etc. On-site camping and caravanning area. Evening entertainment.
Contact: Tony Greenham, 38 Water Lane, Totton, Southampton, Hampshire SO40 3DN. Tel: 01703 867882.
Admission: £5 adults. **Times**: Fri: 12 noon - 11.30pm. Sat: 10am - 11.30pm. Sun: 10am - 6pm.

24-26 Jul
ROYAL LANCASHIRE SHOW
Astley Park, Chorley, Lancs.
County show.
Things to see: A major county show featuring livestock classes, including cattle, sheep, goats, pigs, horses and showjumping, sheepdog trials, rural crafts, rare breeds, bandstand and marching bands, trade stands, horticulture and flower arranging, etc.
Contact: The Secretary, Royal Lancashire Agricultural Society, 5 Windmill Cottages, Preston New Road, Mellor Brook, Blackburn BB2 7NT. Tel: 01254 813769.
Admission: £7 adults; £3.50 children/OAPs. Discounts available on advance tickets. **Times**: 9am - 7pm.

25 Jul
LOCHABER HIGHLAND GAMES
An Aird, Fort William.
Highland games.
Things to see: Traditional Highland games with track and field athletics, hill race, heavy events – tug of war, cycling, dancing, pipe band, piping competitions and "Clan" battle displays. Traditional march down High Street at 1pm.
Contact: I Skinner, Secretary, 4 Pobs Drive, Corpach, Fort William PH33 7JP. Tel: 01397 772885.
Admission: £4 adults; £2 children. **Times**: Gates open 10.30am.

25 Jul
AIRTH HIGHLAND GAMES
Airth Park (near Stirling A905 road), Falkirk, Stirlingshire.
Highland games.
Things to see: Traditional Highland games with the usual heavy events, professional athletics, whippet racing, piping and dancing – including the British Open Professional Highland Dancing Championships. Pipe band.
Contact: Alex Dettlaff, Secretary, 36 Paul Drive, Airth, Falkirk, Stirlingshire FK2 8LA. Tel: 01324 831712 or 0850 134129.
Admission: £2.50 adults; £1 children/OAPs. **Times**: From 11am.

25 Jul
BARBON SPRINT HILL CLIMB
Barbon Manor, Nr Kirkby Lonsdale, Cumbria.
Hill climb for motorcycles.
Things to see: A round in the National Hill Climb Association Championships for racing and vintage motorcycles and three wheelers. An exciting hairpin bend offers best vantage point. Also veteran and vintage display and cavalcade.
Contact: P Duff, 218 Burneside Road, Kendal, Cumbria LA9 6EB. Tel: 01539 727828.
Admission: £5 adults; £2 children. **Times**: Practice at 10am; start 2pm.

25 Jul
JOUSTING AT HEVER CASTLE
Hever Castle, Edenbridge, Kent.
Knights of Royal England jousting tournaments in front of King Henry VIII & Anne Boleyn.
Things to see: Knights compete for the hand of a fair maiden. The event includes full gallop jousts, and entertainment from foot soldiers using medieval style weapons. Many other things to see such as the castle – Anne Boleyn's childhood home – and award winning gar-

dens, suitable for picnics.
Contact: Jan Roberts or Pauline Scott, Hever Castle, Edenbridge, Kent TN8 7NG. Tel: 01732 865224.
Admission: TBA. 1997 guide: £6 adults; £3 children; £5.30 OAPs; £15 family (two adults, two children). **Times**: 2pm - 3.30pm approx.

25 Jul
LOCHEARNHEAD, BALQUHIDDER AND STRATHYRE HIGHLAND GAMES
Games Field, Lochearnhead.
Highland games.
Things to see: Highland gathering with full programme of traditional and other events, all in a beautiful lochside setting.
Contact: Mr Angus Cameron, Lochearnhead Hotel, Lochearnhead FK19 8PU. Tel: 01567 830 229.
Admission: TBA. **Times**: From 11.30am.

25 Jul
SOMERTON HORSE SHOW
Home Farm, Kingweston, Somerton, Somerset.
Large one-day horse show.
Things to see: Showjumping at all levels, show horses, dressage, driving turnouts.
Contact: Mrs M Peverley, Locombe Cottage, Yeovilton, Somerset BA22 8EZ. Tel: 01935 840735.
Admission: £2 per car or 25p per pedestrian. **Times**: 9am - 7pm.

25-26 Jul
LITTLEHAMPTON REGATTA
The Seafront Green & River, Littlehampton, West Sussex.
A nautical water festival second only to Cowes.
Things to see: The River Arun comes to life with flotillas of pirate boats, dinghy and bath tub racing, helicopter rides and visiting ships offering you the chance to sail.
Contact: Carolyn Cudmore, Littlehampton Town Council, Church Street, Littlehampton, West Sussex. Tel: 01903 732063.
Admission: N/A. **Times**: Various.

25-26 Jul
THE ROYAL INTERNATIONAL AIR TATTOO 1998
RAF Fairford, Glos.
The world's largest military airshow this year celebrates the 80th anniversary of the Royal Air Force, and will have as its main operational theme "SkyWatch 98" - a meet of reconaissance and surveillance aircraft.
Things to see: Over 400 aircraft from some 35 nations, which gather together to produce a unique and exciting 8-hour flying display, and a static display covering over 2 miles. Entertainment down on the ground also includes a craft fair, arena displays, virtual reality rides and a variety of exhibitors and stalls. An impressive mass release of up to 40 Hot Air Balloons at sunrise and sunset rounds off a truly spectacular event.
Contact: RIAT Information, PO Box 1940, Fairford, Gloucestershire GL7 4NA. Tel: 01285 713456
Admission: TBA. 1997 guide: £20 adults; children under 15 get free admission. Adult tickets £16 if bought in advance. **Times**: Gates open 6.30am. Flying display 10.15am - 6.30pm.

25-26 Jul
INTERNATIONAL MINIATURE TRACTION ENGINE RALLY & STEAM UP
The Tropical Bird Gardens, Rode, Nr Bath, Somerset.
Miniature traction engines, steam trains and birds.
Things to see: Visiting miniature traction engines, steam, diesel and electric locomotives on a very scenic railway route. Plus 280 varieties of birds.
Contact: Mr M D Marshall, Millbrook Cottage, The Hollow, Child Okeford, Blandford Forum, Dorset DT11 8EX. Tel: 01258 861689.
Admission: TBA. **Times**: 11am - 5pm.

25 Jul-2 Aug
LYME REGIS LIFEBOAT WEEK
Marine Parade, Lyme Regis, Dorset.
Fun activities for children and adults.
Things to see: RAF Red Arrows display, RAF Falcons parachute displays, grand firework display, helicopter/lifeboat exercises, open air disco.
Contact: Ken Faragher (Chairman), 9 Springhill Gardens, Lyme Regis, Dorset DT7 3HL. Tel: 01297 443724.
Admission: Free. **Times**: TBA.

25 Jul-8 Aug
GLOUCESTER FESTIVAL
Various venues througout city.
Community arts festival.
Things to see: Procession, fireworks, music, bands, exhibitions, etc.
Contact: Lesley Pritchard, Leisure Services Dept, Herbert Warehouse, Gloucester Docks, Gloucester GL1 2EQ. Tel: 01452 396620.
Admission: Varied, many free. **Times**: Various.

26 Jul
ARCHERY AT HEVER CASTLE
Hever Castle, Edenbridge, Kent.
Archery demonstration.
Things to see: The company of 1415 will demonstrate the use of the longbow as a military weapon. Many other things to see such as the castle and award winning gardens, suitable for picnics.
Contact: Jan Roberts or Pauline Scott, Hever Castle, Edenbridge, Kent TN8 7NG. Tel: 01732 865224.
Admission: TBA. 1996 guide: £6 adults; £3 children; £5.30 OAPs; £15 family (2 adults, 2 children). **Times**: TBA.

Dates can change, events can be cancelled – Please check with the organisers before setting out!

26 Jul
CARTIER INTERNATIONAL POLO
Smith's Lawn, Guards Polo Club, Windsor Great Park, Surrey.
Top class polo action.
Things to see: Top polo action, celebrities/personalities, military band, trade displays, etc.
Contact: Guards Polo Club, Smiths Lawn, Windsor Great Park, Englefield Green, Egham, Surrey TW20 0HP. Tel: 01784 434212.
Admission: Ticket prices approximately £15. **Times**: Play at 2.45pm.

26 Jul
ENGINE MUSEUM OPEN DAY
Prickwillow Engine Museum, Main Street, Prickwillow, Nr Ely, Cambridgeshire.
Museum Open Day.
Things to see: Old drainage engines running, plus many other attractions. **Contact**: Joan Stacey, Prickwillow Engine Trust, Main Street, Prickwillow, Nr Ely, Cambridgeshire CB7 4UN. Tel: 01353 688360.
Admission: £3 adults; £1.50 children; £2 OAPs; £7 family. **Times:** Engines run: 12 noon - 5pm. Museum open 11am - 5pm.

26 Jul*
BELVOIR CASTLE MEDIEVAL JOUSTING TOURNAMENTS
Belvoir Castle, Lincolnshire.
Medieval jousting tournament.
Things to see: An authentic display of medieval combat, a colourful and exciting event.
Contact: Diane Marshall, The Estate Office, Belvoir Castle, Belvoir, Nr Grantham, Lincolnshire NG32 1PD. Tel: 01476 870262.
Admission: £5.50; £4.50 OAPs; £3.50 children. **Times**: 11am - 5pm.

26 Jul
BUCKLER'S HARD VILLAGE FESTIVAL
Bucklers Hard, Hampshire.
Period village festival.
Things to see: An 18th century village

brought to life, with people in traditional costumes and many attractions including theatrical sideshows etc.
Contact: Eric Walters, The Maritime Museum, Buckler's Hard, Beaulieu, Hampshire SO42 7XB. Tel: 01590 616203.
Admission: £4 adults; £3 children. **Times**: 10am - 6pm.

26 Jul*
LONDON TO SOUTHEND CLASSIC CAR RUN
Commences from Cutty Sark, Greenwich, London, and follows route to Southend-on-Sea.
Classic car run.
Things to see: Approximately 150 pre-1970 vehicles recreating a run first held in 1964.
Contact: Lisa Tidder, Special Events, PO Box 6, Southend-on-Sea, Essex SS2 6ER. Tel: 01702 215166/5169.
Admission: N/A. **Times**: Commences from Greenwich 9.30am. Arrives in Southend-on-Sea at 12 noon approx.

26 Jul*
THE TANK MUSEUM BATTLE DAY
The Tank Museum, Bovington, Dorset.
Warfare displays.
Things to see: Tanks and other military vehicles in spectacular battle re-enactments, plus "Living History" encampments and displays of all eras. Tanks of all periods and other military vehicles on display. Now the best show of its kind in the country.
Contact: The Tank Museum, Bovington, Dorset BH20 6JG. Tel: 01929 405 096.
Admission: TBA. **Times**: TBA.

27 Jul-1 Aug
INVERNESS TATTOO
Northern Meeting Park, Inverness.
Military tattoo over 6 nights.
Things to see: A spectacular tattoo involving pipes and drums, military bands, country and Highland dancing, military displays, etc.
Contact: Bob Shanks, 26 Midmills Road, Inverness, IV2 3NY. Tel: 01463 242915 (evening).
Admission: 1997 guide: £3 outside, £4 stand ticket. **Times**: 8pm - 10pm approx.

28-30 Jul
NEW FOREST & HAMPSHIRE COUNTY SHOW
The Showground, New Park, Brockenhurst, Hampshire.
County show.
Things to see: The biggest agricultural and equestrian event in Hampshire. Livestock, showjumping and extensive horse classes, exhibitions, arena displays, etc, taking place on a 42 acre site.
Contact: The New Forest Agricultural Show Society, The Showground, New Park, Brockenhurst, Hampshire SO42 7QH. Tel: 01590 622400. Fax: 01590 622637.
Admission: TBA. **Times**: 8.30am - 6pm.

28 Jul-1 Aug
GLORIOUS GOODWOOD
Goodwood Racecourse, Chichester, West Sussex.
Horse racing and entertainment.
Things to see: Top class horse racing, plus steel and jazz bands. Children's playground and creche.
Contact: Racecourse Office, Goodwood Racecourse, Chichester, West Sussex PO18 0PS. Tel: 01243 755022.
Admission: From £5.50 (TBA). **Times**: 11am - 6pm.

30 Jul-1 Aug
SCOTTISH NATIONAL SHEEP DOG TRIALS
Braco, Stirling.
Sheep dog trials.
Things to see: Sheep dogs in action.
Contact: A Philip Hendry, Secretary: ISDS, Chesham House, 47 Bromham Road, Bedford MK40 2AA. Tel: 01234 352672.
Admission: £4 adults; £2 concessions. **Times**: 8am - 5pm approx.

30 Jul-2 Aug
STOCKTON RIVERSIDE INTERNATIONAL FESTIVAL
Various venues in and around Stockton High Street/Riverside Park.
Probably the largest street theatre/world music event in the country.
Things to see: The best street theatre and music from around the world. International (ethnic) craft fair.
Contact: Graham Reeves, Events Development Officer, Stockton Council Leisure Services, 72 Church Road, Stockton-on-Tees TS18 1YB. Tel: 01642 393911.
Admission: Most events are free. **Times**: TBA.

31 Jul*
AMBLESIDE SPORTS
Rydal Park, Ambleside, Cumbria.
Traditional sports event.
Things to see: Various traditional Lakeland sports including Cumberland and Westmorland wrestling, hound trials, guide races, fell races, cycle races, and track events. Rydal Park provides a beautiful setting in the centre of the Lake District.
Contact: Christine Laidler, Secretary Ambleside Sports Association, 8 Oldfield Court, Windermere, Cumbria LA23 2HH. Tel: 015394 45531.
Admission: TBA. 1997 guide: £2.50 adults; £1 children. **Times**: Gates open 10.30am. First event 12 noon.

31 Jul
LANGHOLM COMMON RIDING
Langholm, Dumfriesshire.
Traditional ceremonies and games.
Things to see: Ceremonial procession led by the "Cornet" and his mounted supporters, accompanied by brass, pipe and flute bands and emblem bearers. Spectacular mounted chase up hill slope and fair-crying in the Market Place. Followed by a programme of horse racing, athletic games, Highland dancing and Cumberland wrestling. Evening open air dance and parade.
Contact: R Hill, Secretary, Langholm Common Riding, Bank of Scotland Buildings, Langholm, Dumfriesshire DG13 0AD. Tel: 013873 80428.
Admission: N/A. **Times**: From 8.30am.

Dates can change, events can be cancelled – Please check with the organisers before setting out!

31 Jul-1 Aug
THE ULSTER RALLY
Northern Ireland – all six counties.
Special stage rally.
Things to see: Rally cars at speed on closed public roads.
Contact: Robert Harkness, 134 Coagh Road, Stewartstown, Co Tyrone, Northern Ireland.
Admission: N/A. **Times**: Start and finish Belfast. Start: 2pm, 31 Jul. Finish: 4pm, 1 Aug.

31 Jul-2 Aug
FOUR SEASONS CRAFTS SHOW
Charlecote Park, Nr Stratford-upon-Avon, Warks.
Craft fair.
Things to see: Quality crafts created by experts from all over the country. Robin Hood theme.
Contact: Four Seasons (Events Ltd), 23A Brockenhurst Rd, South Ascot, Berkshire SL5 9DJ. Tel: 01344 874787.
Admission: £2.50-£3.50 adults; £2-£2.50 OAPs; £1 children. **Times**: TBA.

31 Jul-2 Aug*
THE SOUTH EAST GARDEN FESTIVAL
The Historic Dockyard, Chatham, Kent.
Gardens and gardening event.
Things to see: Covered floral displays, craft marquees and feature gardens with many specialist displays including

alpines, conifers, miniature roses, heathers, fuchsia, herbs, bonsai and cactus. Also over 100 commercial displays exhibiting everything from plants to greenhouses, fences to mowers and garden furniture to handtools.
Contact: The Historic Dockyard, Chatham, Kent ME4 4TE. Tel: 01634 812551.
Admission: £2.50 adults; children free.
Times: 10am - 4pm.

31 Jul-2 Aug
8th WESTON SUPER HELIDAYS
Sea Front, Weston-super-Mare, Avon.
Helicopter and military vehicle show
Things to see: Large helicopter fly-in, military and classic vehicle line-up, stalls and sideshows, etc.
Contact: Elfan ap Rees, Avia Press Associates, 75 Elm Tree Road, Locking, Weston-super-Mare, Avon BS24 8EL.
Admission: £1. **Times**: 10am - 6pm.

August

1 Aug
DEVON COUNTY ANTIQUES FAIR
Matford Centre in the Exeter Livestock Centre, Matford Park Rd, Marsh Barton, Exeter, Devon.
Antiques fair.
Things to see: Beautiful antiques and collectables among the many items on offer. 430 stands in all.
Contact: Val Dennis, Devon Counties Antiques Fairs, The Glebe House, Nymet Tracey, Crediton, Devon EX17 6DB. Tel: 01363 82571.
Admission: £2 adults; children free. **Times**: 10am - 5pm.

1 Aug
NAIRN FARMERS' SHOW
Farmers' Showfield, Nairn.
Agricultural show.
Things to see: Traditional agricultural and horticultural competitions, exhibitions and events; stock judging, grand parade of prize winners, pipe band, Highland dancers, SWRI craft exhibitions, horticulture classes, poultry.
Contact: Mrs M Forbes (Secretary), Broadley Farm Nairn IV12 5QU. Tel/fax: 01667 453368.
Admission: TBA. **Times**: 9am - 5pm.

1 Aug
BRITISH CLASSIC MOTORBOAT RALLY
Windermere Steamboat Museum, Rayrigg Road, Windermere, Cumbria.
Classic boat rally.
Things to see: The largest gathering of traditional river and lake craft, touring motorboats, ski boats, racing and record-breaking boats in the country. Classic motorboats of every description, dating from 1900 onwards, on display and in action. Many participating crews in period costume.
Contact: Bob Henson, Windermere Steamboat Museum, Rayrigg Road, Windermere, Cumbria LA23 1BN. Tel: 015394 45565.
Admission: Normal museum entry fees apply. **Times**: 10am - 5pm.

1 Aug
CAPEL BANGOR & DISTRICT AGRICULTURAL & HORTICULTURAL SHOW
Maesbangor Field, Capel Bangor, Aberystwyth.
Large agricultural show.
Things to see: Shire horses, Welsh cobs, mountain ponies, mountain and moorland, Arab class, Shetlands, palominos. Dressage competitions, harness classes, fancy dress on horseback, children's riding classes, dog show, Welsh black cattle, 10 classes for breeds of sheep, pet lamb classes, shearing by hand and machine.
Contact: Mrs Bethan Bebb, Blaendyffry, Goginan, Aberystwyth. Tel: 01970 880228.
Admission: £3 adults; £1 children. **Times**: 10am - 4pm.

1 Aug
JOUSTING AT HEVER CASTLE
Hever Castle, Edenbridge, Kent.
Knights of Royal England traditional jousting tournaments in front of King Henry VIII & Anne Boleyn.
Things to see: Knights competing for the hand of a fair maiden. The event includes full gallop jousts, and entertainment

from foot soldiers using medieval style weapons. Many other things to see such as the castle and award winning gardens, suitable for picnics.
Contact: Jan Roberts or Pauline Scott, Hever Castle, Edenbridge, Kent TN8 7NG. Tel: 01732 865224.
Admission: TBA. 1997 guide: £6 adults; £3 children; £5.30 OAPs; £15 family (2 adults, 2 children). **Times**: 2pm - 3.30pm approx.

1 Aug
LEICESTER CARIBBEAN CARNIVAL
Victoria Park, Leicester.
Carnival procession.
Things to see: A large procession of floats, dance troupes, costumes, limbo dancers, etc. Caribbean food stalls plus many other ethnic dishes.
Contact: Herdle White, Co-ordinator, 138 Charles Street, Leicester LE1 1LB. Tel: 0116 2530491.
Admission: Free. **Times**: Open to general public 10am - 8pm. Procession leaves the park at 1pm. Other events do take place throughout the week. Contact the organiser for further details.

1 Aug
MALDON & DISTRICT CARNIVAL
The Promenade Park, Maldon, Essex.
Grand carnival day and firework display.
Things to see: Various events culminating in a major firework display, said to be the premier display in East Anglia. A highly acclaimed Craft Fayre containing over 30 pitches. Continuous entertainment throughout the afternoon, lasting approximately four hours.
Contact: Lyn Smith, 21 Park Drive, Maldon, Essex CM9 5JQ. Tel: 01621 852147.

Dates can change, events can be cancelled – Please check with the organisers before setting out!

Admission: £2 adults; 50p children/OAPs; £5 per vehicle including occupants. **Times**: Day commences 12 noon; firework display 9.30 - 10pm.

1-2 Aug*
ANNUAL FIRE ENGINE RALLY
Bressingham Steam Museum, Bressingham, Diss, Norfolk.
Demonstration of firefighting of all eras.
Things to see: Display of fire engines and fire fighting equipment through the ages with fire drills taking place on Saturday afternoon and all day Sunday.
Contact: Jonathan Wheeler, Bressingham Steam Museum, Bressingham, Diss, Norfolk. Tel: 01379 687386.
Admission: Normal entry prices. **Times**: 10.30am - 5.30pm.

1-2 Aug
CLASSIC CAR AND COUNTRY SHOW
Loseley House, Nr Guildford, Surrey.
Large display of old vehicles plus country activities and antiques fair.
Things to see: Over 1000 veteran, vintage and classic cars, commercial vehicles, motorcycles, fire appliances and army vehicles. Variety of country pursuits and trade exhibitions. All in the grounds of this attractive Elizabethan stately home. There is a recognised camping/caravan site in the grounds.
Contact: Tim Williams, Queen Elizabeth's Foundation for the Disabled, Leatherhead Court, Leatherhead, Surrey KT22 0BN. Tel: 01372 842204.
Admission: All proceeds to the charity. **Times**: 10am - 6pm.

1-2 Aug*
FESTIVAL OF FREE FLIGHT
Middle Wallop, Stockbridge, Hants.
Paragliding, kiting, buggying, land yachting, parascending.
Things to see: Watch or try your hand at any or all of the above activities.
Contact: Janet Houlton, Press & PR Officer, Museum of Army Flying, Middle

Wallop, Stockbridge, Hants SO20 8DY. Tel: 01980 674421. Fax: 01264 781694.
Admission: £3 adults per day or £5 for the weekend. **Times**: Gates open 12 noon. Flying display starts 2pm.

1-2 Aug
VINTAGE SPORTS CAR CLUB HILLCLIMB
Prescott Hill, Cheltenham, Glos.
Vintage sports car contest.
Things to see: Vintage sports cars ascending a narrow twisting hill road at high speed to gain the quickest times, cars on display in paddock, etc.
Contact: Mrs S Ward, Bugatti Owners Club, Prescott Hill, Gotherington, Glos GL52 4RD. Tel: 01242 673136.
Admission: TBA. 1996 guide £8 adults. **Times**: 10am - 5pm approx.

1-2 Aug*
A VINTAGE WEEKEND IN HEBDEN BRIDGE
Hebden Bridge, West Yorkshire.
Transport rally.
Things to see: Vehicles dating from 1890 to 1970: cars, commercials, motorcycles, bicycles, stationary engines. Cavalcade of vehicles leaves Old Town each day at 12 noon. Opportunities to see vehicles on the move in stunning scenery.
Contact: Brian Collins, Automobilia Transport Museum, The Heritage Centre, Leeds Road, Huddersfield HD1 6QA.
Admission: TBA. 1996 guide: £1 adults; 50p children. **Times**: 12 noon - 5pm.

1-2 Aug
ENFIELD STEAM & COUNTRY SHOW
Trent Country Park.
North London's largest steam extravaganza.
Things to see: Steam engines, craft fayre, teddy bears' picnic, falconry, arena events, folk music, country crafts, etc.
Contact: Helen Winchester, Tourism Development Officer, PO Box 58, Civic Centre, Enfield. Tel: 0181-982 7788.
Admission: £4 adults; £2.50 children/OAPs. **Times**: 10am - 5pm.

1-2 Aug
HISTORY IN ACTION III
Kirkby Hall, Northamptonshire (4 miles NE of Corby, off the A43).
English Heritage's largest historical festival of the year and the largest event of its kind in Europe.
Things to see: Re-enactments, living history and other displays from the Romans to D-Day. Over 1,500 performers from 50 top groups, a full day of displays each day including Grand Parade of all participants.
Contact: Head Custodian, Kirby Hall, Nr Deene, Northants NN1 5EN. Tel: 01536 402840.
Admission: £8 adults; £6 OAPs; £4 children. English Heritage members are free. **Times**: 10am - 5pm.

1-2 Aug*
SOUTHEND ANNUAL JAZZ FESTIVAL
Various venues around Southend, Essex.
Jazz festival.
Things to see: Variety of famous jazz musicians performing around the town.
Contact: Lisa Tidder, Special Events, Southend Borough Council, PO Box 6, Southend-on-Sea SS2 6ER. Tel: 01702 215166/5169.
Admission: N/A. **Times**: 11am - late.

1-8 Aug
SKANDIA LIFE COWES WEEK
Cowes, Isle of Wight.
Yacht racing.
Things to see: A colourful week for the yachting enthusiast. 900 yachts in 29 classes take part in races.
Contact: Captain D J Bradby, RN, Cowes Combined Clubs, 18 Bath Road, Cowes, Isle of Wight PO31 7QN. Tel: 01983 295744/293303.
Admission: N/A. **Times**: Races start 10.30am daily.

1-9 Aug
FRIENDS OF THOMAS THE TANK ENGINE
Midland Railway Centre, Butterley Station, Ripley, Derbyshire.
Family fun day with Thomas the Tank Engine theme.
Things to see: A theme event based on the Thomas the Tank Engine character with locomotives decorated as Thomas's friends, with "Oswald" the talking engine plus the Fat Controller.
Contact: Alan Calladine, Midland Railway Centre, Butterley Station, Ripley, Derbyshire DE5 3QZ. Tel: 01773 747674.
Admission: £7.50 adults; £6.50 OAPs; 2 children free withh each adult. **Times**: 10.30am - 4.15pm.

1-31 Aug*
ANGLO-SAXON FESTIVAL
West Stow Country Park and Anglo-Saxon Village, Bury St Edmunds, Suffolk.
Festival bringing to life the reconstructed Anglo-Saxon village.
Things to see: Saxons in costume in and around the reconstructed buildings; watch and have a go at their everyday crafts; listen to storytellers; join guided tours of the village; and more. No two days will be the same.
Contact: Liz Proctor, The Visitor Centre, West Stow Country Park, Icklingham Road, West Stow, Bury St Edmunds, Suffolk IP28 6HG. Tel: 01284 728718.
Admission: (provisional) £4.50 adults; £3 children/OAPs; £12.50 families (up to 5, max 2 adults).

2 Aug
DRUMMOND CASTLE GARDENS OPEN DAY
Drummond Estate, By Crieff, Perthshire.
Annual open day.
Things to see: The beauty of the largest Italianate Gardens in Scotland. Bands and other attractions, prize draw and teas.
Contact: Crieff Tourist Information Centre, Town Hall, High Street, Crieff, Perthshire PH7 3HU. Tel: 01764 652578.
Admission: £3 adults; £2 OAPs; £1 children. **Times**: 2pm - 6pm.

2 Aug
LEIGHTON BUZZARD RAILWAY MODEL MANIA
Page's Park Station, Billington Road, Leighton Buzzard, Beds.
Model cars, trains and boats.
Things to see: Remote control model car grand prix on specially contructed circuit; a large selection of model boats and sailing displays on pond; several model railway layouts operated by local clubs.
Contact: Mr Graham Stroud, Leighton Buzzard Railway, Page's Park Station, Billington Road, Leighton Buzzard, Beds LU7 8TN. Tel: 01525 373888.
Admission: Train fare £4.50 adults; £1 children. Displays free. **Times**: 11am - 5pm.

2 Aug
LIONS BLACKPOOL CARNIVAL SPECTACULAR
The Promenade and Stanley Park Showground, Lawsons Road, Blackpool.
Carnival procession and allied events.
Things to see: Floats, bands, dance troupes, etc. On site: competitions for dance troupes, jazz bands, majorettes, army displays, funfair, dog show, baby show.
Contact: Ken Ogden, 18 Lulworth Ave, Blackpool FY3 9SN. Tel: 01253 693661 or 312708.
Admission: Free. **Times**: 10.30am - 6pm (approx).

2-7 Aug
FIREBALL NATIONAL CHAMPIONSHIPS
Looe, Cornwall.
Event from the calendar of 'Cornwall '98, The World Watersports Festival'.
Things to see: Top-notch dinghy sailing in this highly acclaimed monohull class.
Contact: Cornwall '98, Trevint House, Strangways Villas, Truro, Cornwall TR1

2PA. Tel: 01872 223527.
Admission: TBA. **Times**: TBA.

2,9, 16, 23, 30,31 Aug
ARCHERY AT HEVER CASTLE
Hever Castle, Edenbridge, Kent.
Archery demonstration.
Things to see: The company of 1415 demonstrate the use of the longbow as a military weapon. Many other things to see such as the castle and award winning gardens, suitable for picnics.
Contact: Jan Roberts or Pauline Scott, Hever Castle, Edenbridge, Kent TN8 7NG. Tel: 01732 865224.
Admission: TBA. 1996 guide: £6 adults; £3 children; £5.30 OAPs; £15 family (two adults, two children). **Times**: TBA.

4 Aug
ROYAL GUN SALUTE FOR THE BIRTHDAY OF HM QUEEN ELIZABETH THE QUEEN MOTHER
The Tower of London and in Hyde Park.
Gun salutes to mark the anniversary of the birthday of the Queen Mother.
Things to see: Gun salutes are fired in London by the King's Troop Royal Artillery in Hyde Park at 1200 hours (41 Gun Royal Salute) and by the Honourable Artillery Company at the Tower of London at 1300 hours (62 Gun Royal Salute).
Contact: The Information Officer, Public Information Office, Headquarters London District, Chelsea Barracks, London SW1H 8RF.
Admission: Free. **Times**: See above.

4-8 Aug
GREAT BRITISH BEER FESTIVAL
Grand Hall, Olympia, London.
Beer festival.
Things to see: "The biggest pub in the world" – the largest choice of real ales to be found anywhere. Also some Continental beers. Pub games, live entertainment, etc.
Contact: Mike Bener, CAMRA, 230 Hatfield Road, St Albans, Herts AL1 4LW. Tel: 01727 867201.
Admission: TBA. **Times**: TBA.

5 Aug
INTERNATIONAL AIR DAY
RAF St Mawgan, Newquay, Cornwall.
Air show.
Things to see: Military and civil flying displays and many static displays.
Contact: Air Day Coordinator, RAF St Mawgan. Tel: 01637 872201 ext 7385.
Admission: £7 in advance. £9 on the day. A ticket admits 1 adult and 1 child under 15. Ticket line: 01637 850931. **Times**: Gates open 8am. Flying display starts 11am.

5 Aug
ISLE OF SKYE HIGHLAND GAMES
Games Field, Portree, Isle of Skye.
Traditional Highland games.
Things to see: Traditional Highland games against spectacular scenery.
Contact: A Stewart, 8 Wentworth Street, Portree, Isle of Skye. Tel: 01478 612540.
Admission: TBA. **Times**: 10am - 5pm.

6 Aug
BRISTOL BALLOON FIESTA NIGHTGLOW
Ashton Court Estate, Long Ashton, Bristol.
Hot air balloon event and concert.
Things to see: Tethered hot air balloons glowing as night falls. Choreographed to music, the burners are lit or extinguished to create a stunning visual spectacle. Followed by fireworks. Also trade stands, entertainers and concert.
Contact: Susan Armstrong-Brown, Bristol Balloon Fiesta Ltd, St Johns Street, Bedminster, Bristol BS3 4NH. Tel: 0117 953 5884.
Admission: £4. **Times:** 2pm - 10.30pm.

6-8 Aug
WELSH NATIONAL SHEEP DOG TRIALS
Newport, Gwent.
Sheep dog trials.

Things to see: Sheep dogs in action.
Contact: A Philip Hendry, Secretary: ISDS, Chesham House, 47 Bromham Road, Bedford MK40 2AA. Tel: 01234 352672.
Admission: £4 adults; £2 concessions. **Times**: 8am - 5pm approx.

6-10 Aug
ENGLAND v SOUTH AFRICA
Headingley, Leeds.
Major five-day international test match between England and South Africa.
Things to see: Top class international cricket for over six hours a day for five days. Membership and corporate hospitality facilities contained within a first class cricketing arena.
Contact: Headingley Cricket Ground, St Michaels Lane, Leeds, West Yorkshire LS6 3BU.
Admission: TBA. **Times**: TBA.

7 Aug
KIRKISTOWN SPRINT
Kirkistown, Co Down, Northern Ireland.
Part of the Knockdene Ford Speed Weekend.
Things to see: A range of motor vehicles from vintage to specialist single seater racing cars sprinting around a race track.
Contact: The Ulster Automobile Club, 29 Shore Road, Holywood, Northern Ireland BT18 9HX. Tel: 01232 426262. Fax: 01232 421818.
Admission: N/A. **Times**: 10.30am - 6pm.

7-8 Aug
WARGRAVE & SHIPLAKE REGATTA
Regatta Field, Shiplake, Oxfordshire.
Traditional regatta.
Things to see: Traditional river sports and fireworks display.
Contact: Mr Peter Symons, Wargrave & Shiplake Regatta, River Home, Willow Lane, Wargrave, Reading RG10 8LH. Tel: 0118 9403413.
Admission: £2.50 for weekend. **Times**: Fri: 9am - 8pm. Sat: 8.30am - 7.30pm. Fireworks 10.30pm.

7-9 Aug
FOUR SEASONS CRAFTS SHOW
Runnymede Riverside Meadows, Egham, Surrey.
Craft fair.
Things to see: Quality crafts created by experts from all over the country. Runnymede Pageant.
Contact: Four Seasons (Events Ltd), 23A Brockenhurst Rd, South Ascot, Berkshire SL5 9DJ. Tel: 01344 874787.
Admission: £2.50-£3.50 adults; £2-£2.50 OAPs; £1 children. **Times**: TBA.

7-9 Aug
INTERNATIONAL BRISTOL BALLOON FIESTA
Ashton Court Estate, Long Ashton, Bristol.
Highlight of the European ballooning calendar.
Things to see: Mass ascent of 150 hot air balloons, including many special shape balloons. Plus various arena and village green events, trade stands and entertainments.
Contact: Susan Armstrong-Brown, Bristol Balloon Fiesta Ltd, St Johns Street, Bedminster, Bristol BS3 4NH. Tel: 0117

Dates can change, events can be cancelled – Please check with the organisers before setting out!

953 5884.
Admission: £4 car parking charge only. **Times:** Ascents approximately 6.30am and 6pm.

7-9 Aug
LOWTHER HORSE DRIVING TRIALS & COUNTRY FAIR
Lowther, Penrith, Cumbria.
Horse trials and country fair.
Things to see: The largest event of its kind in the UK featuring the traditional driving trials and country fair will be host to a number of new attractions. Attracts many of the top performers in their class and sport.
Contact: Francesca Aked, Tony Brunskill Associates, PR House, 13 Friargate, Penrith CA11 7XR. Tel: 01768 864190.
Admission: TBA. **Times**: 9am - 6pm.

7-9 Aug
PORTSMOUTH & SOUTHSEA SHOW
Southsea Common, Southsea, Hants.
Big family show.
Things to see: Floral marquee, ideal home exhibition, trade stands, dog shows, arena displays, farm trail, bandstand, motor show.
Contact: Guildhall Entertainments Manager, Guildhall, Guildhall Square, Portsmouth PO1 2AB. Tel: 01705 834146.
Admission: £3.75. Advance tickets from Box Office, Tel: 01705 824355 from July. **Times**: 10am - 7pm.

7-29 Aug
EDINBURGH TATTOO
Edinburgh Castle.
Military Tattoo.
Things to see: A unique blend of music, ceremony, entertainment and theatre, set against the spectacular backdrop of Edinburgh Castle. Flash photography forbidden during show.
Contact: The Tattoo Office, 32 Market Street, Edinburgh EH1 1QB. Tel: 0131-225 1188. Fax: 0131-225 8627.
Admission: £8.50 - £20. **Times**: Mon-Fri 9pm; Saturdays 7.30pm and 10.30pm.

8 Aug
JOUSTING AT HEVER CASTLE
Hever Castle, Edenbridge, Kent.
Knights of Royal England traditional jousting tournaments in front of King Henry VIII & Anne Boleyn.
Things to see: Knights competing for the hand of a fair maiden. The event includes full gallop jousts, and entertainment from foot soldiers using medieval style weapons. Many other things to see such as the castle and award winning gardens, suitable for picnics.
Contact: Jan Roberts or Pauline Scott, Hever Castle, Edenbridge, Kent TN8 7NG. Tel: 01732 865224.
Admission: TBA. 1997 guide: £6 adults; £3 children; £5.30 OAPs; £15 family (two adults, two children). **Times**: 2pm - 3.30pm approx.

8 Aug
RIPLEY SHOW
Ripley Castle Park, Nr Harrogate.
Agricultural and horticultural show.
Things to see: Showing classes (cattle, horses, donkeys, sheep, etc), gymkhana, sheepdog trials, carriage driving, gun dog tests, marquees with produce, flowers and handicrafts. Trade stands, children's entertainment etc. All in the setting of Ripley Castle gardens and lake with its tropical plants. Ripley is also one of Britain's most beautiful and historic villages.
Contact: Hon. Sec. Mrs F M Skelton, 15 Leadhall Drive, Harrogate HG2 9NL. Tel: 01423 871975.
Admission: TBA. 1996 guide: £4 adults; £1 children. **Times**: 9.00am - 6pm.

8 Aug
SLALEY SHOW & RUN
Townhead Field, Slaley, Northumberland.
Agricultural show and fun run.
Things to see: Various events including sheep judging, craft demonstrations, pony events, jumping rings, main ring attractions, floral and industrial tents.

Fun run/fell race through the countryside and forests around Slaley.
Contact: Secretary, Slaley Show Society, Slaley, Hexham, Northumberland.
Admission: £2.50 adults; £1 OAPs. Children and car parking free. **Times**: 9.30am - 5pm; run start at 12.30pm. Senior run 1pm.

8 Aug
STRATHPEFFER HIGHLAND GATHERING
Castle Leod, Strathpeffer.
Highland games.
Things to see: Full range of Highland games against a spectacular backdrop.
Contact: G R Spark, Glenesk, Strathpeffer IV14 9AT. Tel: 01997 421348.
Admission: £3 adults; £1 children. **Times**: Starts 10.30am.

8 Aug
CRAIGANTLET HILL CLIMB
Craigantlet, Belfast, Northern Ireland.
Second oldest hill climb in Britain.
Things to see: A range of motor vehicles from vintage to specialist single seater racing cars in hill-climbing action. Limited access to good vantage points.
Contact: The Ulster Automobile Club, 29 Shore Road, Holywood, Northern Ireland BT18 9HX. Tel: 01232 426262. Fax: 01232 421818.
Admission: N/A. **Times**: 10.30am - 6.30pm.

8-9 Aug
THE RIVER THAMES FLOWER SHOW
Beale Park, Lower Basildon, Reading, Berkshire.
Flower Show.
Things to see: Nationally selected nurserymen displaying their blooms, floral art displays, Q and A forum by the Gardening Roadshow, a panel of well known radio and TV gardening experts, display gardens, craft village, trade stands and much more.
Contact: Beale Park, The Child-Beale Trust, Lower Basildon, Reading, Berkshire RG8 9NH. Tel: 0118 984 5172.
Admission: £4 adults; £3 OAPs; £2.50 children. **Times**: 10am - 6pm.

8-9 Aug
THE YEOVIL FESTIVAL OF TRANSPORT
Yeovil Showground, Yeovil, Somerset.
Display of all types of transport through the ages.
Things to see: 1300+ vintage & veteran vehicles, steam engines, hot air balloons. Main ring attractions, one-make club stands (about 75), American car section, custom cars. Hundreds of trade stands, autojumble, crafts, helicopter rides, fairground, etc.
Contact: The Administrator, PO Box 40, Yeovil, Somerset. Tel: 01935 422319.
Admission: £5 adults; £3 children/OAPs. **Times**: 10am - 6pm.

8-17 Aug
SANQUHAR RIDING OF THE MARCHES
Sanquhar (various venues around town).
Ancient custom of inspection of Burgh Boundaries.
Things to see: Various activities and dances with the actual March Riding on Saturday 15 August. 6am: Townsfolk walk through the town from Pipers Thorn to Gallows Knowe. 8am: Swearing in of Cornet and Principals at Tolbooth. 8.20am - 11.30am: Ride out round Burgh Boundaries, including Chases. 11.45am: Ride out round town including procession of bands and floats. 2pm: Various events at primary school field. 5.15pm: Parade of massed bands.
Contact: James Pirrie, 14 West Lothian, Sanquhar DG4 6DQ. Tel: 01659 58287.
Admission: Free. **Times**: As above.

9 Aug
NUTTS CORNER SPRINT
Nutts Corner, Co Antrim, N Ireland.
Part of the Knockdene Ford Speed Weekend.

Things to see: A range of motor vehicles from vintage to specialist single seater racing cars sprinting around a race track.
Contact: The Ulster Automobile Club, 29 Shore Road, Holywood, Northern Ireland BT18 9HX. Tel: 01232 426262. Fax: 01232 421818.
Admission: N/A. **Times**: 10.30am - 6pm.

9 Aug
KIRKLEES HISTORIC VEHICLE PARADE
From Leeds to Greenhead Park, Huddersfield, West Yorkshire.
Vehicle parade and display.
Things to see: Around 100 vintage vehicles assemble at the Wallace Arnold coach depot in Leeds from 10.30am. Parade travels 17 miles to Huddersfield, arriving 12.30pm onwards. Good vantage point at the Badger Inn, Bradley Road, two miles from Huddersfield.
Contact: A D Hanson, 23 George Street, Lindley, Huddersfield HD3 3LY. Tel: 01484 655452.
Admission: Free. **Times**: Starts 11.30am.

9 Aug
TREGONY HEAVY HORSE SHOW
Tregony Sports Field, Tregony, Truro, Cornwall.
Horse show.
Things to see: Horse show with heavy horses, donkeys, Shetland ponies, etc, plus trade stands.
Contact: D Mennear, 20 Tregony Hill, Tregony, Truro, Cornwall. Tel: 01872 530357.
Admission: TBA. **Times**: Starts 10am.

9 Aug-5 Sep
EDINBURGH INTERNATIONAL FESTIVAL & EDINBURGH FESTIVAL FRINGE
Edinburgh.
The world's largest festival of the arts.
Things to see: A wealth of arts and entertainment with many international stars – theatre, music, dance, opera and visual arts. Plus the Festival Fringe events including 600 indoor theatre productions, dance, music, musicals & workshops, comedy, children's events, exhibitions.
Contact: Edinburgh Festival Society, 21 Market Street, Edinburgh EH1 1BW. Tel: 0131-226 4001. Fax: 0131-225 1173. Fringe Office, 180 High Street, Edinburgh EH1 1QS. Tel: 0131-226 5257.
Admission: Various. **Times**: Various.

10-11 Aug
ROYAL OCEAN RACING CLUB COWES-FALMOUTH-LISBON RACE
Falmouth, Cornwall.
Event from the calendar of 'Cornwall '98, The World Watersports Festival'.
Things to see: One of the most prestigious of all yacht races. Enjoy the wonderful views as these leading international sailors complete the race from Cowes and set sail for Lisbon.
Contact: Cornwall '98, Trevint House, Strangways Villas, Truro, Cornwall TR1 2PA. Tel: 01872 223527.
Admission: TBA. **Times**: TBA.

11-12 Aug
ANGLESEY COUNTY SHOW
The Showground, Gwalchmai, Holyhead, Anglesey.
North Wales' premier agricultural show.
Things to see: Livestock, shire horses, heavy horse teams, showjumping, main ring attractions, fashion show.
Contact: Mr A W Hughes, Show Administrator, "Ty Glyn Williams", The Showground, Gwalchmai, Nr Holyhead, Anglesey LL65 4RW. Tel: 01407 720072.
Admission: TBA. **Times**: 8.30am-6.30pm.

12-15 Aug
BINHAM PAGEANT & SON ET LUMIERE
Binham, Nr Fakenham, Norfolk.
Historical pageant with sound & light and actors.
Things to see: The history of Binham Priory unfolds with battle scenes and historic drama.

Contact: Andrew Cuthbert, The Ford House, Binham, Fakenham, Norfolk NR21 0DJ. Tel: 01263 711736.
Admission: £5 - £20. **Times**: 9pm - 11pm approx.

13 Aug
BALLATER HIGHLAND GAMES
Monaltrie Park, Ballater, Aberdeenshire.
Highland games.
Things to see: Full range of traditional Highland games in a picturesque setting.
Contact: Edward Anderson, PO Box 2, Ballater, Aberdeenshire AB35 5RZ. Tel: 013397 55771.
Admission: £3.50. **Times**: Starts 12.30pm.

13-15 Aug
ENGLISH NATIONAL SHEEP DOG TRIAL
Muncaster Castle, Ravenglass, West Cumbria.
Sheep dog trial.
Things to see: Sheep dogs in action.
Contact: A Philip Hendry, Secretary, ISDS, Chesham House, 47 Bromham Road, Bedford MK40 2AA. Tel: 01234 352672.
Admission: £4 adults; £2 concessions. **Times**: Starts 8am.

13-14 Aug
JERSEY BATTLE OF FLOWERS
Jersey.
Famous floral parade.
Things to see: A grand parade with colourful floats decorated with masses of flowers, carnival queens and many other events, including a Moonlight Parade and a firework display.
Contact: T M Avery. Tel: 01534 639000. Fax: 01534 68985.
Admission: TBA. **Times**: TBA. Thurs: Floral Parade. Fri: Moonlight Parade.

13-14 Aug
UNITED COUNTIES SHOW
Carmarthen, Carmarthenshire.
Agricultural show.
Things to see: Main ring events, dairy and beef cattle, sheep, goats, pigs, horses, trade stands, etc.
Contact: Byrnan Davies, Secretary, U.C.A.S, The Showground, Carmarthen, Carmarthenshire. Tel: 01267 232141.
Admission: £6 adults; £3 OAPs; £2.50 children. **Times**: 9am - 7.30pm daily.

14 Aug
SOUTH AFRICA V SRI LANKA
Trent Bridge, Nottingham.
The Triangular Tournament. The first game in a Tri-Nation tournament of 1 day cricket internationals between England, South Africa and Sri Lanka.
Things to see: Top class international cricket.
Contact: Brian Robson, Secretary, Nottinghamshire C.C.C., Trent Bridge, Nottingham. Tel: 0115 9821525.
Admission: TBA. **Times**: 11am - 6pm daily.

14-15 Aug
SHREWSBURY FLOWER SHOW
Quarry Park, Shrewsbury, Shropshire.
Horticultural show and large programme of events.
Things to see: Floral displays, floral art, bands, arena events, showjumping, fireworks, etc.
Contact: Mr P C Road-Night, SHS, Quarry Lodge, Shrewsbury, SY1 1RN. Tel: 01743 364051. Fax: 01743 233555.
Admission: TBA. 1997 guide: advance day ticket £7.50. **Times**: Fri: 10.30am - 10.15pm. Sat: 10am - 10.15pm.

14-16 Aug
NORTHAMPTON BALLOON FESTIVAL
The Racecourse Park, Northampton.
Hot air balloon event.
Things to see: Large display of hot air balloons with full ground entertainment programme and trade area.
Contact: Events Team, Cliftonville House, Bedford Road, Northampton NN4 7NR. Tel: 01604 238791.

Admission: Free. Car parking charge. **Times**: Balloon flights 6.30am and 6.30pm.

14-16 Aug
CARDIGAN BAY REGATTA
New Quay Pier, Cardigan.
Sailing regatta.
Things to see: Sailing for dinghies and cruisers, ocean races, passage races, swimming events. Particularly colourful at the start of races when waiting for the gun. Also crabbing and model boat building (material provided), sand building and modelling, treasure quiz, barrel filling (teams of four). The bay is very picturesque and a school of dolphins may often be seen early morning and evening.
Contact: Mrs M Aline Horton, Rhiwig, Penwig Lane, New Quay, Dyfed, SA45 9NQ. Tel: 01545 561019.
Admission: N/A. **Times**: 9.30am - 6pm.

14-16 Aug
FOUR SEASONS CRAFTS SHOW
Aldenham Country Park, Nr Elstree, Herts.
Craft fair.
Things to see: Quality crafts created by experts from all over the country. Medieval theme.
Contact: Four Seasons (Events Ltd), 23A Brockenhurst Rd, South Ascot, Berkshire SL5 9DJ. Tel: 01344 874787.
Admission: £2.50-£3.50 adults; £2-£2.50 OAPs; £1 children. **Times**: TBA.

14-22 Aug
SOUTHEND CARNIVAL WEEK
Various venues around Southend-on-Sea, Essex.
Carnival processions plus other events.
Things to see: Evening procession, fancy dress competition, dog show, beautiful toddlers competition, etc.
Contact: Tourist Information Centre, High Street, Southend-on-Sea, Essex. Tel: 01702 215120.
Admission: Various. **Times**: TBA.

15 Aug
JOUSTING AT HEVER CASTLE
Hever Castle, Edenbridge, Kent.
Knights of Royal England traditional jousting tournaments in front of King Henry VIII & Anne Boleyn.
Things to see: Knights competing for hand of a fair maiden. The event includes full gallop jousts, and entertainment from foot soldiers using medieval style weapons. Many other things to see such as the castle and award winning gardens, suitable for picnics.
Contact: Jan Roberts or Pauline Scott, Hever Castle, Edenbridge, Kent TN8 7NG. Tel: 01732 865224.
Admission: TBA. 1997 guide: £6 adults; £3 children; £5.30 OAPs; £15 family (two adults, two children). **Times**: 2pm - 3.30pm approx.

15 Aug
HURLEY REGATTA
Mill Lane Meadows, Hurley, Berkshire.
Fun Regatta for all the family with land-based entertainment and competitions. All proceeds to charity.
Things to see: Canoe, raft, punt, skiff, dragon boat, children's races, team events and individual events, novelty events, funfair, charity stalls, team competitions. Visitors can picnic on river bank while watching Regatta.
Contact: Mrs J Burfitt, Kumara, Mill Lane, Hurley, Berkshire. Tel: 01628 825615.
Admission: TBA. **Times**: 9am - 6pm.

15 Aug
THE WORLD PIPE BAND CHAMPIONSHIPS
Venue TBA. Possibly Glasgow Green, Glasgow.
The major event of its kind in the world.
Things to see: Over 190 pipe bands competing in seven competition arenas. Pipe bands and dancers in full Highland dress (competing in various events). Host of other attractions including strongman events, Highland dancing, drum majors.

Contact: J Mitchell Hutcheson, Royal Scottish Pipe Band Association, 45 Washington Street, Glasgow G3 8AZ. Tel: 0141-221 5414. Fax: 0141-221 1561.
Admission: £3 adults; £1.50 children/OAPs. **Times**: 9am - 6.30pm.

15-16 Aug
DE HAVILLAND MOTH CLUB ANNUAL FLY-IN
Grounds of Woburn Abbey, Bedfordshire.
Air show.
Things to see: A grand meeting of over 90 Tiger Moth aeroplanes, with displays, aerobatics and parachuting.
Contact: P A Gregory, Woburn Abbey, Woburn, Beds MK43 OTP. Tel: 01525 290666.
Admission: £5 per car. **Times**: 9am - 6pm both days.

15-16 Aug
DIESEL & STEAM WEEKEND
Midland Railway Centre, Butterley Station, Ripley, Derbyshire.
Railway event.
Things to see: Train services featuring both steam and diesel power, narrow-gauge and model railways, museum, country park, farm park, etc.
Contact: Alan Calladine, Midland Railway Centre, Butterley Station, Ripley, Derbyshire DE5 3QZ. Tel: 01773 747674.
Admission: £7.95 adults; £6.50 OAPs; 2 children free with each adult. **Times**: 10.30am - 4.15pm.

15-16 Aug
MEDIEVAL CRAFT SHOW
Beale Park, Lower Basildon, Reading, Berkshire.
Over 100 nationally selected craftsmen.
Things to see: Craftsmen demonstrating and selling their crafts and skills; twice daily jousting and falconry displays, wandering minstrels and period singers.
Contact: Beale Park, The Child-Beale Trust, Lower Basildon, Reading, Berkshire RG8 9NH. Tel: 0118 984 5172.
Admission: £4 adults; £3 OAPs; £2.50 children. **Times**: 10am - 6pm.

15-16 Aug
BRITISH TOURING CAR CHAMPIONSHIP RACING
Knockhill Racing Circuit, By Dunfermline.
Britain's biggest and most spectacular motor racing series.
Things to see: Spectacular top motor-sport action – British Touring Car Championship double-header races, plus full support race programme of premier national racing series. No public transport to the venue – nearest town is Dunfermline with its bus and railway stations.
Contact: Stewart Gray, Knockhill Racing Circuit, By Dunfermline, Fife KY12 9TF. Tel: 01383 723337.
Admission: £20 adults (£17 if paid in advance). **Times**: Qualifying on 2nd with racing action on 3rd starting around 9am.

15-22 Aug
BILLINGHAM INTERNATIONAL FOLKLORE FESTIVAL
Various venues in Billingham Town Centre, Cleveland.
World-renowned folklore festival.
Things to see: The best performers of traditional folk dance and music from across the globe. International craft fair runs in conjunction with the festival. The event culminates in a display of fireworks.
Contact: Mr Graham Reeves, Events Development Officer, Stockton-on-Tees Borough Council, PO Box 116, Gloucester House, 72 Church Road, Stockton-on-Tees TS18 1YB. Tel: 01642 393939 ext 3911.
Admission: TBA. **Times**: TBA.

15-31 Aug
EDINBURGH BOOK FESTIVAL
Charlotte Square Gardens, Edinburgh.
Housed in a tented village of summer marquees, this is the biggest book event

for the public in Europe.
Things to see: Packed programme of around 400 events in 17-day festival with extensive programme for children. All sorts of writers meet their public in demonstrations, workshops and talks. Thousands of books on display in the book tents.
Contact: The Director, EBF, 137 Dundee Street, Edinburgh EH11 1BG. Tel: 0131 228 5444.
Admission: From £1 (-£5 for events). Advance programme information available in April. Full diary of events available June. **Times**: 10am - 9pm daily.

16 Aug
BASILDON HORSE SHOW
Beale Park, Lower Basildon, Reading, Berkshire.
A popular local show with a multitude of classes.
Things to see: Mostly show jumping.
Contact: Beale Park, The Child-Beale Trust, Lower Basildon, Reading, Berkshire RG8 9NH. Tel: 0118 984 5172.
Admission: Free. **Times**: 8am - 6pm.

16 Aug
COMBE MILL IN STEAM
Combe Mill (just off the A4095 at Long Handborough, Oxfordshire).
Special steam day.
Things to see: An 18thC beam engine and three other steam engines in steam. Plus working museum featuring blacksmiths and wood turners. Delightful riverside picnic area.
Contact: F A Huddleston, Braemar, The Ridings, Stonesfield, Witney, Oxfordshire OX8 8EA. Tel: 0993 891785.
Admission: £2.50 adults; £1 children/OAPs. **Times**: 10am - 5pm.

Dates can change, events can be cancelled – Please check with the organisers before setting out!

16 Aug
ENGLAND V SRI LANKA
Lord's Cricket Ground, St John's Wood, London.
The Triangular Tournament. The second game in a Tri-Nation tournament of 1 day cricket internationals between England, South Africa and Sri Lanka.
Things to see: Top class international cricket.
Contact: M.C.C., Lord's Ground, London NW8 8QZ. Tel: 0171-289 8979.
Admission: TBA. **Times**: 10.30am - 7.30pm approx.

16 Aug
CRIEFF HIGHLAND GATHERING
Market Park, King Street, Crieff, Perthshire.
Highland games.
Things to see: Traditional Highland games with the usual piping, dancing, sports and heavy events.
Contact: Crieff Tourist Information Centre, Town Hall, High Street, Crieff, Perthshire PH7 3HU. Tel: 01764 652578.
Admission: TBA. **Times**: From 11.30am.

16 Aug
DUMFRIES & GALLOWAY HORSE SHOW
Wheatcroft, Castle Douglas.
Horse show.
Things to see: Horse and pony showing classes, showjumping, driving, Clydesdale showing classes, etc.
Contact: Mrs J Milligan, Culvennan, Castle Douglas, Scotland. Tel: 01556 670254.
Admission: TBA. **Times**: 9.30am - 5pm.

16-22 Aug
FOWEY ROYAL REGATTA WEEK
Fowey, Cornwall.
Carnival week and regatta.
Things to see: Many events including carnival, floral dancing, raft races, sailing, children's sport and Red Arrows flying display (unconfirmed).
Contact: Miss S Baker, Flat 1, 5 Trafalgar Square, Fowey, Cornwall PL23 1AZ. Tel:

01726 832047.
Admission: N/A. **Times**: Various.

17 Aug
ALDEBURGH OLDE MARINE REGATTA & CARNIVAL
Seafront and town centre, Aldeburgh, Suffolk.
Traditional carnival.
Things to see: Lifeboat launch, air sea rescue display, carnival and lantern processions, firework display.
Contact: Mrs J Gowen, 3 Grundisburgh Road, Woodbridge, Suffolk IP12 4HJ. Tel: 01394 444333.
Admission: Generous donations requested. **Times**: 9am - 10pm.

18 Aug
ENGLAND V SOUTH AFRICA
Edgbaston County Ground, Birmingham.
The Triangular Tournament. The last game in a Tri-Nation tournament of 1 day cricket internationals between England, South Africa and Sri Lanka.
Things to see: Top class international cricket.
Contact: Warwickshire County Cricket Club, Edgbaston, Birmingham B5 7QU. Tel: 0121-446 4422.
Admission: From £17 per person. **Times**: 10.45am - 7pm.

19 Aug
VENTNOR CARNIVAL PROCESSION
Ventnor, Isle of Wight.
Carnival procession and displays.
Things to see: Procession with floats and costumed characters.
Contact: Mrs J Busbridge, 2 Shaftesbury Cottage, Beaconsfield Rd, Ventnor, Isle of Wight.
Admission: Free. **Times**: Children's Procession 2pm start. Main Procession 7pm.

19 Aug
WEYMOUTH CARNIVAL DAY
Weymouth Seafront, Dorset.
Carnival procession and displays.
Things to see: Procession with floats and costumed characters, Red Arrows flying display, firework display, etc.
Contact: Mr H G Bailey, Leisure & Entertainments General Manager, Pavilion Complex, The Esplanade, Weymouth, Dorset DT4 8ED. Tel: 01305 772444.
Admission: Free. **Times**: Contact Weymouth Tourist Information Centre for event update and programme on 01305 785747.

20 Aug
THE TRIANGULAR TOURNAMENT FINAL
Lord's Cricket Ground, St John's Wood, London.
Final between either England, South Africa or Sri Lanka.
Things to see: Top class international cricket.
Contact: M.C.C., Lord's Ground, London NW8 8QZ. Tel: 0171-289 8979.
Admission: TBA. **Times**: 10.30am - 7.30pm approx.

20-22 Aug
IRISH NATIONAL SHEEPDOG TRIALS
Limavady, Londonderry, Northern Ireland.
Sheepdog trials.
Things to see: Sheepdogs in action.
Contact: A Philip Hendry, Secretary: ISDS, Chesham House, 47 Bromham Road, Bedford MK40 2AA. Tel: 01234 352672.
Admission: £4 adults; £2 concessions. **Times**: 8am - 5pm approx.

21-22 Aug
BILLINGHAM SHOW
John Whitehead Park, Billingham, Cleveland.
Long established show.
Things to see: Arena events, stalls and trade stands, horticultural and homecraft competitive classes.
Contact: Graham Reeves, Events Development Officer, Stockton-on-Tees Borough Council, PO Box 116, Gloucester

House, 72 Church Road, Stockton-on-Tees TS18 1YB. Tel: 01642 393939 ext 3911.
Admission: Free. **Times**: TBA.

21-23 Aug
FOUR SEASONS CRAFTS SHOW
Kingston Lacey House, Wimborne, Dorset.
Craft fair.
Things to see: Quality crafts created by experts from all over the country. Robin Hood theme.
Contact: Four Seasons (Events Ltd), 23A Brockenhurst Rd, South Ascot, Berkshire SL5 9DJ. Tel: 01344 874787.
Admission: £2.50-£3.50 adults; £2-£2.50 OAPs; £1 children. **Times**: TBA.

21-23 Aug*
BRITISH HORSE TRIALS CHAMPIONSHIP
Gatcombe Park, Minchinhampton, Stroud, Gloucestershire.
Equestrian competition.
Things to see: Horse trials consisting of dressage, cross-country and showjumping. Also main arena attractions. Check with organisers which days are set for dressage, showjumping or cross-country. Access into main arena and close proximity to cross country fences prohibited.
Contact: Mrs G Dale, The Estate Office, Bramham Park, Wetherby, West Yorkshire LS23 6ND. Tel: 01937 541811.
Admission: Details and ticket application forms available from June at the above address. **Times**: TBA.

21-31 Aug
ARUNDEL FESTIVAL
Arundel, West Sussex.
An internationally acclaimed arts Festival.
Things to see: Variety of events in the open air theatre of Arundel Castle including Shakespeare, Jazz, drama, classical concerts, and a spectacular firework display.
Contact: Box Office, The Marygate, Arundel, West Sussex BN18 9AT. Tel: 01903 883690.
Admission: N/A. **Times**: Various.

21-31 Aug
ARUNDEL FESTIVAL FRINGE
Arundel, West Sussex.
A range of outdoor entertainment for all the family to compliment the Arundel Festival.
Things to see: Bath tub racing, art exhibitions, illuminated procession and free fireworks display, plus many other activities.
Contact: Mr Don Ayling, 3 Causeway Villas, Arundel, West Sussex. Tel: 01903 882904.
Admission: N/A. **Times**: Various.

22 Aug
JOUSTING AT HEVER CASTLE
Hever Castle, Edenbridge, Kent.
Knights of Royal England traditional jousting tournaments in front of King Henry VIII & Anne Boleyn.
Things to see: Knights competing for the hand of a fair maiden. The event includes full gallop jousts, and entertainment from foot soldiers using medieval style weapons. Many other things to see such as the castle and award winning gardens, suitable for picnics.
Contact: Jan Roberts or Pauline Scott, Hever Castle, Edenbridge, Kent TN8 7NG. Tel: 01732 865224.
Admission: TBA. 1997 guide: £6 adults; £3 children; £5.30 OAPs; £15 family (2 adults, 2 children). **Times**: 2pm - 3.30pm approx.

22 Aug
ILLUMINATIONS SWITCH ON & FIREWORKS SPECTACULAR
Marine Parade, Southend-on-Sea, Essex.
Illuminations and fireworks.
Things to see: A celebrity switches on the famous seafront illuminations, followed by a large fireworks display.
Contact: Lisa Tidder, Special Events, PO Box 6, Southend-on-Sea, Essex SS2 6ER.

Tel: 01702 215166/5169.
Admission: N/A. **Times**: Commences 8.30pm approx.

22-23 Aug
LINCOLNSHIRE STEAM & VINTAGE RALLY
County Showground (A15 north of Lincoln).
Steam and vintage rally.
Things to see: Steam engines, organs, vintage tractors, models, miniatures, commercials, cars, classic cars, oil engines, trade stands. 100+ engines, 1,400 exhibits in all.
Contact: D G Macdonald, 21 Linden Walk, Louth, Lincs LN11 9HT. Tel: 01507 605937.
Admission: £4 adults; £2 children/OAPs; under 5's free. **Times**: 9am - 6pm.

22-23 Aug
VINTAGE CLASSIC & SPORTSCAR SHOW
Tatton Park, Knutsford, Cheshire (Junction 19 of the M6, Junction 7 of the M56).
Huge vintage, classic and sportscar rally.
Things to see: Vintage pre-1950 motorcars and motorcycles, sportscars and supercars, club displays, over 1000 classic and vintage cars, etc.
Contact: Stuart Holmes, Bridge House, Park Road, Stretford M32 8RB. Tel: 0161-864 2906.
Admission: £5 adults; children free. **Times**: 9am - 5pm.

22-23 Aug*
EGHAM ROYAL SHOW
Runnymede, Egham, Surrey.
Agricultural show.
Things to see: Animals, horticultural exhibits, traction engines, showjumping, arena events, etc.
Contact: T Diggens, 33 Spring Avenue, Egham, Surrey TW20 9PJ.
Admission: £6 adults; £3 children/OAPs. **Times**: 9am - 6pm.

Dates can change, events can be cancelled – Please check with the organisers before setting out!

22-24 Aug
CITY OF PORTSMOUTH INTERNATIONAL KITE FESTIVAL
Southsea Common, Southsea, Hants.
Major kite festival for all, from professionals to small children.
Things to see: Sat & Sun: internationally famous kites and fliers, fighting kites, stunt kite displays, parachuting teddy bears. Mon: free-fly day for the public, Woofers and Tailwaggers Dog Show. All weekend: workshops, craft marquee, kite stalls, trade stands, refreshments.
Contact: Guildhall Entertainments Manager, Guildhall, Guildhall Square, Portsmouth PO1 2AB. Tel: 01705 834146.
Admission: Free. **Times**: 10am - 5pm.

22-24 Aug
NORMAN ROCHESTER
Rochester Castle Gardens, Rochester, Kent.
Norman festival.
Things to see: The Castle gardens transformed to Norman times, with displays of falconry, archery, trial by combat, etc.
Contact: Visitor Information Centre, 95 High Street, Rochester, Kent ME1 1EW. Tel: 01634 843666.
Admission: Free. **Times**: 10am - 5pm.

22-24 Aug*
THE DERBYSHIRE COUNTRY SHOW
Hartington Moor Showground (on the A515 Ashbourne to Buxton Road, seven miles north of Ashbourne).
Country show.
Things to see: Horse trials, dressage and showing (Sat & Mon), sheep dog trials (Sun), vintage vehicles and steam engines. 300 exhibits, two arenas.
Contact: Frank Marchington, Barren Clough Farm, Buxworth, High Peak,

Derbyshire SK23 7NS. Tel: 01663 732750.
Admission: £4 adults; £2 children/OAPs.
Times: 10am - 6pm.

22-28 Aug
WHITBY FOLK WEEK
Whitby, North Yorkshire.
Folk festival.
Things to see: Lots of traditional music, dance and street events.
Contact: Malcolm Storey, PO Box 44, Selby, North Yorkshire YO8 9YP. Tel: 01757 708424.
Admission: Various. **Times**: 10am - 1am.

22-28 Aug
CELTIC WATERSPORTS FESTIVAL
Bude, Cornwall.
Event from the calendar of "Cornwall '98, The World Watersports Festival".
Things to see: A dozen different watersports - including canoeing, rowing, sailing and surfing, plus a wealth of singing, music and all-out merriment.
Contact: Cornwall '98, Trevint House, Strangways Villas, Truro, Cornwall TR1 2PA. Tel: 01872 223527.
Admission: TBA. **Times**: TBA.

22-30 Aug
LLANDRINDOD WELLS VICTORIAN FESTIVAL
Llandrindod Wells, Powys.
Festival recreating the Victorian life.
Things to see: Costumes, torchlight procession, firework display and varied other events, all in a very picturesque setting. Non-stop street entertainment.
Contact: Mandy Davies, Festival Adminstrator. Tel: 01597 823441.
Admission: Various; street events free. **Times**: Starts 10.30am daily.

Dates can change, events can be cancelled – Please check with the organisers before setting out!

23 Aug
GREAT SCOTTISH RUN
Venue TBA, Glasgow.
Mass run.
Things to see: The UK's third largest mass participation fun run, a 13-mile half marathon with approximately 9,500 participants and almost 10,000 attending.
Contact: Fiona Ross, Marketing Officer, Parks & Recreation, Glasgow City Council, 37 High Street, Glasgow G1 1LX. Tel: 0141-287 3773. Fax: 0141-287 5557.
Admission: N/A. **Times**: TBA.

23 Aug
BOGNOR BIRDMAN - THE ORIGINAL
The Pier & Esplanade, Bognor Regis, West Sussex.
Now in it's 25th year, this event attracts crowds from all over the world.
Things to see: Those magnificent men in their flying machines as they leap from Bognor Regis Pier in an attempt to win a jackpot prize of £15,000. A colourful carnival atmosphere is guaranteed with the Grand Street Parade, air displays and family entertainment.
Contact: Mr Bill Nunton, Arun District Council, Maltravers Rd, Littlehampton, West Sussex BN17 5LF. Tel: 01903 716133.
Admission: N/A. **Times**: 10am - 5pm.

23 Aug
ENGINE MUSEUM OPEN DAY
Prickwillow Engine Museum, Main Street, Prickwillow, Nr Ely, Cambridgeshire. Museum Open Day.
Things to see: Old drainage engines running, plus many other attractions. **Contact**: Joan Stacey, Prickwillow Engine Trust, Main Street, Prickwillow, Nr Ely, Cambridgesire CB7 4UN. Tel: 01353 688360.
Admission: £3 adults; £1.50 children; £2 OAPs; £7 family. **Times:** Engines run: 12 noon - 5pm. Museum open 11am - 5pm.

23 Aug
HORSE DAY
National Coal Mining Museum for England, Caphouse Colliery, New Road, Overton, Wakefield, West Yorkshire.
A celebration of the horse.
Things to see: Horses of every type and size and many horse-related crafts.
Contact: Tina Jamieson, National Coal Mining Museum for England, Caphouse Colliery, New Road, Overton, Wakefield, West Yorkshire WF4 4RH. Tel: 01924 848806.
Admission: Free. **Times**: 10.30am - 4.30pm.

24-25 Aug
OULD LAMMAS FAIR
Ballycastle, Co Antrim, N Ireland.
Two day traditional fair.
Things to see: Market stalls, fun fair, street entertainers, horse trading, stalls selling traditional local delicacies such as dulse (edible seaweed) and yellow man.
Contact: Peter Mawdsley, Chief Executive Health Officer, Moyle District Council, Sheskburn House, 7 Mary St, Ballycastle Northern Ireland. Tel: 012657 62225.
Admission: Free. **Times**: All day.

26 Aug-1 Sep
BEATLES WEEK FESTIVAL
Various venues, Liverpool, Merseyside.
Annual celebration of Beatles music.
Things to see: Music and entertainment connected with the Fab Four.
Contact: Mr Bill Heckle, Cavern City Tours Ltd, The Cavern Club, 10 Mathew Street, Liverpool L2 6RE. Tel: 0151-236 9091.
Admission: TBA. **Times**: TBA.

27-29 Aug
PORT OF DARTMOUTH ROYAL REGATTA
Dartmouth, Devon.
Variety of waterborne and land-based events.
Things to see: Sailing and rowing, water and land-based sporting events, Red Arrows display, firework displays, funfair, craft fair etc.
Contact: Mrs Wendy Rendle, Hon Sec, 7 Ferndale, Dartmouth, Devon TQ6 9QU. Tel: 01803 832435.
Admission: Free. **Times**: 9am - 11pm daily.

27-30 Aug
BOWMORE BLAIR CASTLE HORSE TRIALS
Blair Castle, Pitlochry, Perthshire.
International equestrian three day event.
Things to see: Dressage, show jumping and cross country all around Blair Castle.
Contact: The Horse Trials Office, Estates Office, Blair Atholl, Pitlochry, Perthshire PH18 5TH. Tel: 01796 481 543.
Admission: £3 - £5. **Times**: 9am - 6pm.

27-31 Aug
ENGLAND VS SRI LANKA
The Oval, Kennington, London.
Major five-day international test match.
Things to see: Top class international cricket for over six hours a day for five days. Membership and corporate hospitality facilities contained within a first class cricketing arena.
Contact: Surrey County Cricket Club, The Oval, Kennington, London SE11 5SS.
Admission: TBA. **Times**: 11am - 6pm daily.

28-31 Aug
CHILTERNS CRAFT SHOW
Stonor Park, Henley-on-Thames, Oxon.
Craft show.
Things to see: Over 170 quality modern and traditional craftsmen demonstrating and selling hand-made British crafts. Held under marquee, it offers a family day out to see rural crafts, bands and dancers.
Contact: ICHF Ltd, Dominic House, Seaton Road, Highcliffe, Dorset. Tel: 01425 272711.
Admission: £4.50 adults; £3.50 OAPs; £1 children. **Times**: 10am - 6pm.

28-31 Aug
GLASTONBURY CHILDREN'S FESTIVAL
Abbey Park Playground, Fishers Hill, Glastonbury, Somerset.
Event designed for children.
Things to see: Puppeteers, clowns, jugglers, magicians, storytellers, etc.
Contact: Arabella Churchill, Children's World Charity, 2 St Edmunds Cottages, Glastonbury, Somerset BA6 8JD. Tel: 01458 832925.
Admission: TBA. **Times**: 10.30am - 5pm.

29 Aug
DENBIGH FLOWER SHOW
Lon Felin Field, Ystrad Road, Denbigh, Denbighshire.
Horticultural show and large programme of events.
Things to see: Floral displays, dog show, Silver Band, morris dancing, children's amusements, 5-a-side football competitions (10 & under) and other displays.
Contact: Emrys Williams, Highfield, 2 Llewelyn's Estate, Denbigh, Denbighshire LL16 3NR. Tel: 01745 812724.
Admission: £3 adults; £2 OAPs; £1 children. **Times**: 10am - 7pm (approx).

29 Aug*
SOUTHEND SAILING BARGE RACE
Southend Pier, Southend-on-Sea, Essex.
Classic barge race.
Things to see: The splendour of a bygone era with sailing barges racing for various trophies.
Contact: Lisa Tidder, Special Events, PO Box 6, Southend-on-Sea, Essex SS2 6ER. Tel: 01702 215166.
Admission: Normal Pier admission. **Times**: 9am - 3pm approx.

29 Aug
WENSLEYDALE SHOW
Moor Road, Leyburn, North Yorkshire.
Traditional agricultural show.
Things to see: Cattle, heavy horses, ponies, sheep, sheepdog trials, trade stands, children's games, main ring entertainment. Fine views over Wensleydale and Pen Hill.
Contact: Miss H Percy, Thorngill, Coverham, Leyburn, North Yorks DL8 4TJ. Tel: 01969 640261.
Admission: £4 adults; £2 children/OAPs. Free parking. **Times**: 10am - 5pm.

29 Aug
JOUSTING AT HEVER CASTLE
Hever Castle, Edenbridge, Kent.
Knights of Royal England traditional jousting tournaments in front of King Henry VIII & Anne Boleyn.
Things to see: Knights competing for the hand of a fair maiden. The event includes full gallop jousts, and entertainment from foot soldiers using medieval style weapons. Many other things to see such as the castle and award winning gardens, suitable for picnics.
Contact: Jan Roberts or Pauline Scott, Hever Castle, Edenbridge, Kent TN8 7NG. Tel: 01732 865224.
Admission: TBA. 1997 guide: £6 adults; £3 children; £5.30 OAPs; £15 family (2 adults, 2 children). **Times**: 2pm - 3.30pm approx.

29-30 Aug
THE ROYAL HORTICULTURAL SOCIETY OF SCOTLAND FLOWER SHOW
Duthie Park, Riverside Drive, Aberdeen.
Flower show.
Things to see: Almost 400 classes of entries.
Contact: Mrs H Main, Treorchy, Hillside, Portlethen, Aberdeenshire, AB12 4RB. Tel: 01224 781171.
Admission: 1997 guide: £2 adults; £1.50 OAPs; 75p children. **Times**: Sat: 12 noon - 7pm. Sun: 11am - 5pm.

29-30 Aug
INVERNESS FLOWER & GARDEN FESTIVAL
Inverness Sports Centre, Bught Park, Inverness.
Inverness's largest flower and garden

festival.
Things to see: Competition entries from Floral Art to Bee-keeping. Also trade stands, garden diplays, workshops, demonstrations and Gardeners' Question Times.
Contact: Jon Hogan, Events & Promotions Officer, Highland Council, Town House, Inverness IV1 1JJ. Tel: 01463 724262.
Admission: £2.50 adults; £1 children; £5 family. **Times**: TBA.

29-31 Aug
FESTIVAL OF TRANSPORT
Broad Farm, Hellingly, Sussex.
Large transport show including aerial display.
Things to see: Up to 1500 vintage vehicles on a 25-acre site. All pre-1950s including steam engines and various working vintage exhibits.
Contact: Mrs D M Hymans, 8 North Close, Polegate, East Sussex BN26 6HH. Tel: 01323 484926.
Admission: £4 adults; £1 children. **Times**: 10am - 5.30pm.

29-31 Aug
THE TOWN & COUNTRY FESTIVAL
National Agricultural Centre, Stoneleigh Park, Warwickshire.
Country show.
Things to see: Festival of Motoring: classic cars, motorbikes, military. Festival of the Countryside: farm animals, country crafts, country sports fair. Festival of Entertainment: grand ring attractions, fun fair, dogs in action. Festival of Leisure & Shopping: hobbies, crafts, antiques, food.

Dates can change, events can be cancelled – Please check with the organisers before setting out!

Contact: Jayne Spence, Royal Agricultural Society of England, National Agricultural Centre, Stoneleigh Park, Warwickshire CV8 2LZ. Tel: 01203 696969.
Admission: TBA. **Times**: TBA.

29-31 Aug
WEST INDIAN CARNIVAL
Potternewton Park, Leeds.
The biggest carnival in the UK to rival Notting Hill.
Things to see: Carnival procession, costumes and atmosphere with thousands of people enjoying a party and reggae concert in the park.
Contact: Tourist Information, The Arcade, Leeds City Station, Leeds LS1 1PL. Tel: 0113 242 5242.
Admission: Free. **Times**: TBA.

29-31 Aug
FOUR SEASONS CRAFTS SHOW
Wakehurst Place, Ardingly, Nr Haywards Heath, West Sussex.
Craft fair.
Things to see: Quality crafts created by experts from all over the country. Robin Hood theme.
Contact: Four Seasons (Events Ltd), 23A Brockenhurst Rd, South Ascot, Berkshire SL5 9DJ. Tel: 01344 874787.
Admission: £2.50-£3.50 adults; £2-£2.50 OAPs; £1 children. **Times**: TBA.

29-31 Aug*
SURFERS AGAINST SEWAGE OCEAN FESTIVAL
Fistral Beach, Newquay, Cornwall.
Event from the calendar of 'Cornwall '98, The World Watersports Festival'.
Things to see: Beach Festival and serious surfing action. A festival of family entertainment that also puts a spotlight on the need for clean seas and environmental awareness.
Contact: Cornwall '98, Trevint House, Strangways Villas, Truro, Cornwall TR1 2PA. Tel: 01872 223527.
Admission: TBA. **Times**: TBA.

29-31 Aug
STOCKTON SUMMER CARNIVAL
Preston Hall Park, Stockton, Cleveland.
Local carnival.
Things to see: In addition to the usual array of trade stands, stalls, sideshows and funfair, the event has now added a two-day showjumping event with both affiliated and unaffiliated classes, plus arena displays.
Contact: Mr Graham Reeves, Events Development Officer, Stockton-on-Tees Borough Council, PO Box 116, Gloucester House, 72 Church Road, Stockton-on-Tees TS18 1YB. Tel: 01642 393939 ext 3911.
Admission: Car park charge. **Times**: 10am - 5pm.

30-31 Aug
ADVENTURE SPORTS SPECIAL
Crealy Country Park, Clyst St Mary, Exeter, Devon.
Adventure sports activity day.
Things to see: Canoeing on the Dragonfly Lake, abseiling from the Buzzard's Tower and archery. Plus pony rides.
Contact: Crealy Country Park, Sidmouth Road, Clyst St Mary, Nr Exeter, Devon EX5 1DR. Tel: 01395 233200.
Admission: £4.50 adults; £3.75 children/OAPs. **Times**: TBA.

30-31 Aug
BANK HOLIDAY TREASURE HUNT
Beningbrough Hall, Shipton, Beningbrough, York.
Treasure Hunt for children aged 3-12.
Things to see: Follow the treasure hunt and find all the clues.
Contact: The National Trust, Beningbrough Hall, Shipton, Beningbrough, York YO6 1DD. Tel: 01904 470666.
Admission: Normal admission prices apply. **Times**: 12 noon - 4pm.

30-31 Aug
A NATIONAL FESTIVAL OF TRANSPORT
National Tramway Museum, Crich, Matlock, Derbyshire.
Tramcars in operation.
Things to see: Some static - most moving! All kinds of vintage traffic drives, displays, & jostles for street space with vintage trams.
Contact: Lesley Wyld, Marketing Manager, National Tramway Museum, Crich, Matlock, Derbyshire DE4 5DP. Tel: 01773 852565. Fax: 01773 852326.
Admission: £5.90 adults; £3 children; £5.10 OAPs; £16.20 family ticket. **Times**: 10am - 5.30pm.

30-31 Aug
STEAM UP
Coldharbour Mill, Working Wool Museum, Uffculme, Cullompton, Devon.
Steam event.
Things to see: 1910 300hp mill engine in steam, Lancashire boilers, steam pumps. Also turn-of-the-century spinning and weaving machinery. Beam engine and New world tapestry.
Contact: Miss Jill Taylor, Coldharbour Mill, Uffculme, Cullompton, Devon EX15 3EE. Tel: 01884 840960.
Admission: £5 adults; £2.50 children. **Times**: 10.30am - 5pm.

30-31 Aug*
BELVOIR CASTLE MEDIEVAL JOUSTING TOURNAMENTS
Belvoir Castle, Lincolnshire.
Medieval jousting tournament.
Things to see: An authentic display of medieval combat, colourful and exciting.
Contact: Diane Marshall, The Estate Office, Belvoir Castle, Belvoir, Nr Grantham, Lincolnshire NG32 1PD. Tel: 01476 870262
Admission: £5.50; £4.50 OAPs; £3.50 children. **Times**: 11am - 5pm.

30-31 Aug*
BRAEMORE HOUSE CLASSIC CAR SHOW
Braemore House, Braemore, Fordingbridge, Hants.
Classic car show.

Things to see: 900 gleaming classic cars, plus autojumble, trade stands, live commentary, children's entertainments, concours competition.
Contact: Sally Greenwood, Greenwood's Exhibitions, PO Box 49, Aylesbury, Bucks HP22 5FF. Tel: 01296 631181/632040. Fax: 01296 630394.
Admission: £4 adults; £3 OAPs/children.
Times: 10am - 5pm.

30-31 Aug*
KNEBWORTH 98 CLASSIC CAR SHOW
Knebworth Park, Stevenage, Herts.
Classic car show.
Things to see: 2,000 classic cars, autojumble, trade stands, live commentary, children's entertainments, concours competition.
Contact: Sally Greenwood, Greenwood's Exhibitions, PO Box 49, Aylesbury, Bucks HP22 5FF. Tel: 01296 631181/632040. Fax: 01296 630394.
Admission: £5.50 adults; £4 OAPs/children. **Times**: 10am - 5pm.

30-31 Aug
MILITARY VEHICLE RALLY
DLI Museum, Aykley Heads, Durham City.
Annual vehicle rally.
Things to see: At least 50 military vehicles including trucks, jeeps, motorbikes, etc. Plus militaria stalls.
Contact: Stephen D Shannon, DLI Museum, Aykley Heads, Durham City DH1 5TU. Tel: 0191 3842214.
Admission: Free. **Times**: 10am - 5pm.

30-31 Aug
MILL AND FARM OPEN DAYS
Worsbrough Country Park, Worsbrough Bridge, Barnsley.
Open days at Worsbrough Corn Mill and Wigfield Open Farm.
Things to see: Water-powered corn milling, bread baking demonstrations, shire horse show and ploughing match, goat shearing, cattle foot trimming, brass bands, clowns, puppet shows, craft fair, etc. Set in 200 acre Worsbrough Country Park.
Contact: Debra Bushby, Worsbrough Country Park, Off Park Road, Worsbrough Bridge, Barnsley, South Yorkshire S70 5LJ. Tel: 01226 774527.
Admission: Farm: £1.50 adults; 75p children/OAPs. Mill: 50p adults; 25p children/OAPs.**Times**: 12 noon - 5pm.

30-31 Aug
NOTTING HILL CARNIVAL '98
Streets of Notting Hill & Ladbroke Grove, London.
Europe's largest street festival of arts and culture.
Things to see: Spectacular procession of Mas' (costume) bands. Fantastic and creative costumes. Hugely popular event, attended by over 1.5 million people over two days. Three live stages, hundreds of food and craft stalls, 45 static sound systems on the streets. Plus certain events during pre-carnival run-up – children's costume gala, adult costume gala, Calypso Monarch final, Steelband Panorama competition.
Contact: Notting Hill Carnival Ltd, Unit 35, Grand Union Centre, 332 Ladbroke Grove, London W10 5AH. Tel: 0181-964 0544. Fax: 0181-964 0545.
Admission: N/A for two-day carnival on the road. However, entry fee charged for some pre-carnival events. **Times**: 10am - 7pm.

31 Aug
SAINT MONDAY FESTIVAL
Weavers' Triangle Visitor Centre, 85 Manchester Road, Burnley, Lancs.
Saint Monday Festival.
Things to see: Stalls, games, entertainment, refreshments.
Contact: The Curator, Weavers' Triangle Visitor Centre, 85 Manchester Road, Burnley, Lancs BB11 1JZ. Tel: 01282 452403.
Admission: Free. **Times**: 11am - 4pm.

31 Aug
SEDAN CHAIR RACE
The Pantiles, Royal Tunbridge Wells, Kent.
Fun race around the famous Pantiles.
Things to see: Wacky fun event in which local teams, some in fancy dress, have to run with Sedan chairs around a course of the Pantiles stopping at various points to take the spring waters, eat a piece of cake, bob for apples, drink a jug of ale. Gets very crowded but good viewing area. Also additional entertainment with street entertainers and a folk band.
Contact: Yvonne Sayer, Tourism & Marketing Assistant, Tunbridge Wells Borough Council, The Town Hall, Royal Tunbridge Wells, Kent TN1 1RS. Tel: 01892 526121 ext 3294.
Admission: Free. **Times**: 12 noon - 7pm. Races start at 2pm.

31 Aug
WORLD BOG SNORKELLING CHAMPIONSHIPS
Llanwrtyd Wells, Powys.
Wacky event.
Things to see: The championships take place in a bog on the outskirts of Llanwrtyd Wells, where a trench 60 yards long has been dug out. Competitors must swim two lengths of the bog with flippers and snorkels.
Contact: Gordon Green, The Neuadd Arms Hotel, The Square, Lllanwrtyd Wells, Powys. Tel: 01591 610236.
Admission: TBA. **Times**: TBA.

31 Aug
CIRCUS SKILLS
East Riddlesden Hall, Bradford Rd, Keighley, West Yorkshire.
Juggling, diablo and circus show.
Things to see: Try your hand at circus skills. Join in the fun.
Contact: Events Co-ordinator, East Riddlesden Hall, Bradford Rd, Keighley, West Yorkshire BD20 5EL. Tel: 01535 607075.
Admission: £3.20 adults; £1.70 children; £8 family. **Times**: 12 noon - 4pm. Circus show at 3pm.

31 Aug
MANX GRAND PRIX
TT mountain course, Isle of Man.
Motorcycle road racing.
Things to see: Motorcycle road racing on the 37.73 mile TT mountain course. Races for solos from 250cc to 1000cc and classic bikes from 175cc to 500cc.
Contact: Caroline Etherington, M.M.C.C. Ltd, Race Office, Grandstand, Douglas, Isle of Man. Tel: 01624 627979.
Admission: Free. Except for grandstands £3 - £5. **Times**: 8.30am - 2pm.

September

2 Sep
MUKER SHOW
Muker, North Yorkshire.
Traditional agricultural and horticultural show.
Things to see: Show in a stunning showground surrounded by beautiful Swaledale, a picturesque setting in itself. Special events include a fell race, children's fancy dress/races and sheepdog trials.
Contact: Mrs M Rutter, Jubilee House, Dyke Heads, Gunnerside, Richmond, North Yorkshire DL11 6JG. Tel: 01748 886330.
Admission: £2. **Times:** From 10am.

2, 4 Sep
MANX GRAND PRIX
TT mountain course, Isle of Man.
Motorcycle road racing.
Things to see: Motorcycle road racing on the 37.73 mile TT mountain course. Races for solos from 250cc to 1000cc and classic bikes from 175cc to 500cc.
Contact: Caroline Etherington, M.M.C.C. Ltd, Race Office, Grandstand, Douglas, Isle of Man. Tel: 01624 627979.
Admission: Free. Except for grandstands £3 - £5. **Times**: 8.30am - 2pm.

2-6 Sep
GREAT DORSET STEAM FAIR
South Down, Tarrant Hinton, Blandford, Dorset.
The leading steam/preservation event in the UK and Europe, regularly attended by 175,000 visitors.
Things to see: Over 2,000 working exhibits on a 500 acre site. Working steam engine demonstrations involving heavy haulage, woodsawing, threshing, plouging and road making. An old time steam funfair, heavy horses, rural crafts, working bygones, vintage tractors, vintage cars and motorcycles. Old commercial and army vehicles, trade stands, auto jumble.
Contact: Show Secretary, Mr M F Oliver, Dairy House Farm, Child Okeford, Blandford, Dorset DT11 8HT. Tel: 01258 860361.
Admission: TBA. 1997 guide: £7.50 adults; £6 OAPs; £3 children. **Times**: 9am - until late.

3 Sep
BUCKS COUNTY SHOW
Weedon Park, Aylesbury, Bucks.
Agricultural show.
Things to see: Dairy, cattle, sheep, horses, trade stands, rural crafts, domestic & horticultural.
Contact: Mrs Caroline Griffith, Agriculture House, Ardenham Lane, Aylesbury, Bucks HP19 3DA. Tel: 01296 483734.
Admission: TBA. **Times:** 8.30am - 6pm.

3-5 Sep
LONGSHAW SHEEP DOG TRIALS CENTENARY
Longshaw Pastures, Longshaw Lodge, Grindleford, Nr Sheffield.
Sheep dog trials.
Things to see: Thurs: open class; double dogs; best conditioned and most typical dog/bitch classes; hound trail. Fri: open class; double dogs. Sat: local class and championship with a double gather.
Contact: Mrs S M Humphreys, Secretary, 1 Moorland Road, Hathersage, Nr Sheffield S30 1BH. Tel: 01433 651852.
Admission: £1.50 adults; 50p children. **Times**: 7.30am - 6.30pm.

4-6 Sep
DUNDEE FLOWER SHOW
Camperdown Country Park, Dundee.
Flower show.
Things to see: Scotland's premier flower show incorporates colourful display of flowering exhibits, food, trade and craft fair. Full entertainment programme for children and adults. All exhibits under cover in tented village.
Contact: Colin Ainsworth, Dundee City Council, Leisure and Parks Department, Tayside House, Crichton Street, Dundee DD1 3RB. Tel: 01382 433815.
Admission: 1997 guide: £4 adults, £2.50 children/OAPs. **Times:** Friday 1pm - 8pm, Saturday 10am - 8pm, Sunday 10am - 6pm.

4-6 Sep*
THE NATIONAL AMATEUR GARDENING SHOW
Royal Bath and West Showground, Shepton Mallet, Somerset.
Horticultural event for everyone who takes an interest in gardening.
Things to see: Flower, fruit & vegetable displays and competitions, lectures and demonstrations, advice from gardening experts, craft fair, show gardens, plant stalls and trade stands.
Contact: The Secretary, The Royal Bath and West of England Society, The Showground, Shepton Mallet, Somerset BA4 6QN. Tel: 01749 822200. Fax: 01749 823169.
Admission: TBA. **Times**: 9.30am - 5.30pm.

4 Sep-8 Nov
BLACKPOOL ILLUMINATIONS
Promenade, Blackpool. Starr Gate to Red Bank Road.
Famous night-time illuminations.
Things to see: Six miles of illuminations, festoons and features – 500,000 lamps in all. Spectacular display includes the newest technology, including fibre-optics and low voltage neon to complement the traditional lamps. Plus illuminated tramcars.
Contact: Tourism Services, 1 Clifton Street, Blackpool, Lancashire FY1 1LY. Tel: 01253 25212.
Admission: Free. **Times:** Dusk to 11.30pm (later at weekends).

5 Sep
BEN NEVIS RACE
Start: New Town Park, Fort William, Scotland.
Race to the top of Britain's highest mountain.
Things to see: Around 400 runners (men and women) racing to the top of the mountain and back, a picturesque combination of runners and mountain scenery. Two recommended vantage points are Red Burn, and the aluminium bridge, both on the Ben Nevis Path.
Contact: Mr G MacFarlane, 16 Grange Terrace, Fort William PH33 6JG.
Admission: £1.50. **Times:** Race starts at 2pm. Last runner returns at 5pm approx.

5 Sep
SHERIFF'S RIDE
Market Square/Freeford Park/Guildhall, Lichfield, Staffs.
Historical tradition of Lichfield.
Things to see: The sheriff and his entourage assemble at the Guildhall and, followed by upwards of 120 horseriders and vehicles commence the 20 mile circuit of the City boundary.
Contact: Mr P Young, Town Clerk, Lichfield City Council, City Council Offices, Guildhall, Lichfield, Staffordshire WS13 6LX. Tel: 01543 250011.
Admission: Free. **Times:** Ride leaves Market Square at 10.30am. Arrival at Freeford Park for lunch at 1pm. Ride concludes at Guildhall at 6.30pm.

5 Sep
BRAEMAR ROYAL HIGHLAND GATHERING
Braemar, Aberdeenshire.
Highland gathering.
Things to see: Traditional Highland

gathering and sports events. The best vantage point for viewing this event is at ringside seat sections D or E.
Contact: W Meston, Coilacriech, Ballater, Aberdeenshire AB35 5UH.
Admission: Seats - grandstand £17.50, uncovered stand £10, ringside £8. **Times:** 9.30am - 5pm.

5 Sep
ILSINGTON SHEEPDOG TRIALS
Halshanger Manor, Nr Ashburton, Devon.
Sheepdog trials and other events.
Things to see: Dog trials including the West of England and Devon County Championships. As well as the dogs, there is a vintage and veteran car display, children's sports, ferret racing, archery, and local stalls with home-made cakes, jams, etc.
Contact: Dick Wills, Honorary Secretary, Narracombe Farm, Ilsington, Devon TQ13 9RD. Tel: 01364 661243.
Admission: £3 adults; children free. **Times:** 9.30am - 6pm.

5 Sep*
NAT WEST TROPHY
Lord's Cricket Ground, St John's Wood, London.
Premier domestic cricket final.
Things to see: Top level cricket final; 60 overs per side.
Contact: M.C.C., Lord's Ground, London NW8 8QZ. Tel: 0171- 432 1066.
Admission: £20 - £35. **Times**: 10.30am - 7.30pm approx.

5-6 Sep
RAINBOW CRAFT FAIR
Newby Hall & Gardens, Ripon, North Yorkshire.
200 top quality crafts people from throughout Britain.
Things to see: Crafts people demonstrating skills and goods on sale to public.
Contact: Mr R G Alexander, Opening Administrator, Newby Hall, Ripon, North Yorkshire. Tel: 01423 322583.
Admission: TBA. **Times**: From 10am - 5.30pm.

5-6 Sep
SOWERBY BRIDGE RUSHBEARING FESTIVAL
Town of Sowerby Bridge and environs, Yorkshire.
Traditional procession.
Things to see: Procession of rushcart and pullers, and morris dancers, over a nine-mile route through scenic countryside. Formal presentation of rushes at churches, dancing outside pubs, plus mummers and other street entertainment. Saturday route runs from the village of Warley through Sowerby Bridge to Sowerby; on Sunday from Sowerby through Mill Bank to Ripponden.
Contact: Mr F J Knights, 9 Bright Street, Sowerby Bridge, West Yorkshire, HX6 2ES.
Admission: N/A. **Times**: Start 11am Saturday; finish 5pm Sunday.

5-6 Sep
VICTORIAN FAIR WEEKEND
Kirkby Lonsdale Town, Cumbria.
Outdoor fair in Victorian costume.
Things to see: People dressed in Victorian costume, street entertainers, colourful stalls selling/demonstrating Victorian crafts etc.
Contact: K.L.T.I.C., 24 Main Street, Kirkby Lonsdale, Cumbria LA6 2AE.
Admission: N/A. However, there is a £5 parking fee per vehicle. **Times:** 10am until evening.

5-6 Sep
AUTOJUMBLE AND AUTOMART
Beaulieu Abbey, Beaulieu, Brockenhurst, Hampshire.
Europe's biggest autojumble event.
Things to see: Over 1,500 stalls for everything connected with motoring and motorcycling plus more than 100 cars in the automart.
Contact: Stephen Munn, Marketing Manager, Beaulieu Abbey, Beaulieu,

Brockenhurst, Hampshire SO42 7ZN. Tel: 01590 612345.
Admission: TBA. **Times**: From 10am.

5-6 Sep
BRISTOL INTERNATIONAL KITE FESTIVAL
Ashton Court Estate, Bristol.
Two-day kite flying festival.
Things to see: Continuous programme of kite displays, demonstrations, competitions and battles, with kites of all shapes and sizes. Also stalls, children's kite-making workshops, free flying area for public.
Contact: Festival Office, 5 Lilymead Avenue, Bristol BS4 2BY. Tel: 0117 9745010.
Admission: Free; £4 for cars to enter the Estate. **Times**: 11am - 5.30pm.

5-6 Sep
GLOSSOP VICTORIAN WEEKEND
Glossop, Derbyshire.
Recreation of Victorian times.
Things to see: The whole town become Victorian – people in Victorian costume, shire horses, traction engines, street organs, Victorian fairground, penny farthings, vintage cars, street entertainers, crafts stalls, brass bands, Punch & Judy, etc.
Contact: Tourist Information Centre, The Gatehouse, Victoria Street, Glossop, Derbyshire. Tel: 01457 855920.
Admission: Free. **Times**: 10am - 5.30pm daily.

5-6 Sep
BRITISH & MIDLAND HILLCLIMB CHAMPIONSHIPS
Prescott Hill, Cheltenham, Glos.
Hillclimb competition for cars.
Things to see: Roadgoing sports cars and racing cars ascending a narrow twisting hill road at speeds of up to 110mph.
Contact: Mrs S Ward, Bugatti Owners Club, Prescott Hill, Gotherington, Glos GL52 4RD. Tel: 0242 673136.
Admission: £7 adults. **Times**: 10am - 5pm approx.

5-6 Sep
DEVON COUNTY ANTIQUES FAIR
Westpoint Exhibition Centre, Clyst St Mary, Exeter, Devon.
Major antiques fair.
Things to see: Beautiful antiques and collectables among the estimated one million items on offer. 500 stands in one hall. Plus free lectures, seminars and exhibitions.
Contact: Val Dennis, Devon Counties Antiques Fairs, The Glebe House, Nymet Tracey, Crediton, Devon EX17 6DB. Tel: 01363 82571.
Admission: £3.50 adults; children free. **Times**: Sat: 10am - 5pm. Sun: 10am - 5pm.

5-6 Sep
LEIGHTON BUZZARD RAILWAY AUTUMN STEAM UP
Page's Park Station, Billington Road, Leighton Buzzard, Beds.
Largest gathering of the year at this venue.
Things to see: Up to eight steam locos in operation, plus heritage diesels, visiting locos, cavalcades, regular passenger train service, displays and family entertainment.
Contact: Mr Graham Stroud, Leighton Buzzard Railway, Page's Park Station, Billington Road, Leighton Buzzard, Beds LU7 8TN. Tel: 01525 373888.
Admission: Train fare £4.50 adults; £1 children. **Times**: 11am - 5pm.

5-13 Sep
FILEY FISHING FESTIVAL
Filey Brigg and Filey Bay, Yorkshire.
Fishing festival.
Things to see: Six boat fishing events, eight shore fishing events. Best vantage point from the beach at Coble Landing, and Carr Naze on the Brigg.
Contact: Mrs K Marshall, 87 Scarborough Rd, Filey, North Yorkshire YO14 9NQ. Tel: 01723 515745.
Admission: N/A. **Times**: From 9am.

6 Sep
THE FINAL 'MANE' EVENT
National Tramway Museum, Crich, Matlock, Derbyshire.
Horse-trams in operation.
Things to see: Last chance of the year to rumble along the rails on one of the museum's enchanting horse-trams.
Contact: Lesley Wyld, Marketing Manager, National Tramway Museum, Crich, Matlock, Derbyshire DE4 5DP. Tel: 01773 852565. Fax: 01773 852326.
Admission: £5.90 adults; £3 children; £5.10 OAPs; £16.20 family ticket. **Times**: 10am - 5.30pm.

6 Sep
THE IMECHE COVENTRY RUN
Start and finish: Coombe Country Park, Brinkton Rd, Coventry. Towns en route: Kenilworth, Solihull, Henley, Stratford, Warwick, Royal Leamington Spa.
480 veteran, vintage & classic cars provide Europe's biggest touring event..
Things to see: The largest collection of cars from 1896 to 1997 touring Warwickshire on mobile display in front of crowds in excess of 100,000. Plus on return a giant picnic with celebrity prizegiving, aerobatic displays, hot air balloons, jazz bands, morris dancers.
Contact: International Festival Services (UK) Ltd, Vintage House, Kings Lane, Broom, Alcester, Warwickshire. Tel: 01789 772298.
Admission: Car Park Ticket. **Times**: Depart: 10am. Return: 2pm.

6 Sep
MONMOUTH CONSERVATIVE ASSOCIATION ANNUAL CHARITY RAFT RACE
From Monmouth Boat House to Tump Farm, Whitebrook, Gwent.
Raft race and fun day.
Things to see: Around 150 rafts racing over a six mile course, plus supporting programme.
Contact: Don Beddoes or Mrs Diane Davies, 55 Bridge Street, Usk, Monmouthshire NP5 1BQ. Tel: 01291 672780.
Admission: £2 per car. **Times**: 11am - 5pm; first rafts sail at 12 noon.

6 Sep
RAMSGATE VICTORIAN STREET FAIR
Addington Street, Ramsgate, Kent.
Costume street fair and entertainments.
Things to see: Over 50 stalls with all stallholders and some visitors in period costume, folk music and dancing, juggling and magic, vintage cars, traditional crafts, barbershop singing, Victorian melodrama, street theatre.
Contact: Penny Warn, 7 Liverpool Lawn, Ramsgate, Kent CT11 9HJ. Tel: 01843 596288.
Admission: N/A. **Times**: 10.30am - 5pm.

6 Sep
SHEPWAY AIRSHOW
The Leas, Folkestone, Kent.
Airshow.
Things to see: Displays of static and flying aircraft, plus an extensive ground-based exhibition.
Contact: Lisa Holden, Events Manager, Shepway District Council, Civic Centre, Castle Hill Avenue, Folkestone, Kent CT20 2QY. Tel: 0303 850388.
Admission: Free. **Times**: 9am - 6pm.

10-12 Sep
INTERNATIONAL SHEEP DOG TRIALS
Biggar, Lanarkshire.
International sheepdog competition.
Things to see: The major international sheepdog trials with the best in the world competing.
Contact: Mr A Philip Hendry, Secretary,

Dates can change, events can be cancelled – Please check with the organisers before setting out!

International Sheep Dog Society, Chesham House, 47 Bromham Road, Bedford MK40 2AA. Tel: 0234 352672.
Admission: £5 adults; £2.50 concessions. **Times**: From 8am.

10-13 Sep
THE BLENHEIM INTERNATIONAL HORSE TRIALS
Blenheim Palace, Woodstock, Oxfordshire.
International three-day event horse trials.
Things to see: Dressage on Thursday and Friday; cross country on Saturday; showjumping on Sunday. Plus over 150 trade stands, great shopping, celebrity challenges, children's fair.
Contact: Horse Trials Secretary, Blenheim Palace, Woodstock, Oxford OX20 1PS. Tel: 01993 813335. Fax: 01993 813337. Box Office: 01993 813255
Admission: TBA. **Times**: 9am - 5pm.

10-14 Sep*
MANX INTERNATIONAL CAR RALLY
Stages all over the Isle of Man.
International and historic car rally.
Things to see: One of the top rallies in Europe, with rally cars at high speed on closed roads. 30 stages all over the island.
Contact: Richard Bargery, Memorial Hall, Union Mills, Isle of Man IM4 4AD. Tel: 01624 852440. Fax: 01624 852441.
Admission: N/A. **Times**: TBA.

11-13 Sep
WEALD OF KENT CRAFT SHOW
Penshurst Place, Nr Tonbridge, Kent.
Craft show.
Things to see: Over 170 quality modern and traditional craftsmen demonstrating and selling hand-made British crafts. Held under marquee, it offers a family day out to see rural crafts, bands and dancers.
Contact: ICHF Ltd, Dominic House, Seaton Road, Highcliffe, Dorset. Tel: 01425 272711.
Admission: £4.50 adults; £3.50 OAPs; £1 children. **Times**: 9.30am - 5.30pm.

Dates can change, events can be cancelled – Please check with the organisers before

11-13 Sep
SEA SHANTY FESTIVAL
Deal, Kent.
A celebration of Deal's maritime history incorporating a programme of free entertainment.
Things to see: Nautical encounters with treaure hunting pirates, sea-dog singalongs and spirited ghost walks. Also special events for children including story telling and puppetry performances.
Contact: Lisa Webb, Arts Development Officer, Dover District Council, White Cliffs Business Park, Dover, Kent CT16 3PD. Tel: 01304 872058.
Admission: TBA. **Times**: TBA.

11-13 Sep
PATCHWORK & QUILTING EXHIBITION
Hever Castle, Edenbridge, Kent.
Patchwork and quilting displays.
Things to see: Magnificent display of patchwork quilts and wall hangings. Many other things to see such as the castle and award winning gardens, suitable for picnics.
Contact: Jan Roberts or Pauline Scott, Hever Castle, Edenbridge, Kent TN8 7NG. Tel: 01732 865224.
Admission: TBA. 1996 guide: £6 adults; £3 children; £5.30 OAPs; £15 family (two adults, two children). **Times**: TBA.

12 Sep
CASTLETON SHOW
Castleton Cricket Field, Nr Whitby, North Yorkshire.
Country show.
Things to see: Flowers and vegetables,

craft stalls, pony sports, children's sports, fancy dress and terrier show.
Contact: Mrs Linda Raw, 62 High Street, Castleton, Nr Whitby, North Yorkshire YO21 2DA.
Admission: £1.50 approx. **Times**: From 1pm.

12 Sep
EXETER CARNIVAL GRAND ILLUMINATED PROCESSION
City centre, Exeter, Devon.
Major carnival procession with fringe events.
Things to see: A fully illuminated carnival procession with over 150 entries – the largest procession in Devon, Cornwall and Dorset. The line-up and judging area is on the Marsh Barton Trading Estate; there are likely to be fewer crowds in this area than along the procession route.
Contact: Arthur Dyke, 37 Laburnum Road, Wonford, Exeter, Devon EX2 6EF. Tel: 01392 276619.
Admission: N/A. **Times**: Fringe events start 9am. Judging takes place from 6pm; procession starts 7.30pm.

12 Sep
PLOUGHING MATCH & PRODUCE SHOW
North Somerset (venue TBA).
Ploughing competition.
Things to see: Horses, vintage and modern tractors, in ploughing action. Plus produce and rural crafts.
Contact: Keith Pulman, Show Office, East Dundry, Bristol. Tel: 01179 643498.
Admission: Free. **Times**: 10am - 3pm.

12 Sep
USK SHOW
The Showground, Gwernesney, Usk, Gwent
Agricultural show.
Things to see: Cattle, sheep, horses, dogs, poultry, goats, rabbits, cage birds, homecraft and horticultural exhibits, craft fayre, steam engines, vintage tractors and engines, classic cars, trade stands, Llangibby hounds and grand parade.
Contact: Mrs G J Rogers, Lower Church Farm, Llantrisant, Usk, Gwent NP5 1LG. Tel: 01291 672379.
Admission: £4 adults; £2 OAPs; £1 children. **Times**: 9am - 6pm.

12-13 Sep
FOUR SEASONS CRAFTS SHOW
Apps Court Farm, Walton-on-Thames, Surrey.
Craft fair.
Things to see: Quality crafts created by experts from all over the country. Merrie Olde England theme.
Contact: Four Seasons (Events Ltd), 23A Brockenhurst Rd, South Ascot, Berkshire SL5 9DJ. Tel: 01344 874787.
Admission: £2.50-£3.50 adults; £2-£2.50 OAPs; £1 children. **Times**: TBA.

12-13 Sep
ESSEX STEAM RALLY & CRAFT FAIR
Barleylands Farm, Barleylands Road, Billericay, Essex.
Steam rally and rural fair.
Things to see: 80 steam engines, many rural demonstrations such as blacksmiths and basket-makers, heavy horses, 150 craft stands, old time fair, three arenas, food hall, vintage tractors, cars, commercials and motorbikes, plus much more.
Contact: Mrs J Philpot/Mrs J Cowell, Barleylands Farm, Barleylands Road, Billericay, Essex CM11 2UD. Tel: 01268 532253.
Admission: TBA. **Times**: 10am -5pm.

12-13 Sep
DIESEL SPECTACULAR
Midland Railway Centre, Butterley Station, Ripley, Derbyshire.
Diesel rail event.
Things to see: Unique opportunity to view a wide variety of diesel locomotives in action.
Contact: Alan Calladine, Midland Railway Centre, Butterley Station, Ripley, Derbyshire DE5 3QZ. Tel: 01773 747674.

Admission: £7.95 adults; £6.50 OAPs; 2 children free with each adult. **Times**: 11.15am - 4.15pm.

12-13 Sep
LUTON SHOW
Stockwood Country Park, Luton.
Horticultural and livestock show.
Things to see: Various floral, horticultural and small livestock exhibits. Also arena entertainment, trade stands, pet show, exemption dog show.
Contact: Luton Borough Council, Leisure & Cultural Department, Arts Division (Promotions), 146 Old Bedford Road, Luton LU2 7HH. Tel: 01582 746037.
Admission: £3 adults; £1.20 children approx. Family tickets available. **Times**: Sat: 12 noon - 6pm. Sun: 10am - 6pm approx.

12-20 Sep
SOUTHAMPTON INTERNATIONAL BOAT SHOW
Western Esplanade, Southampton, Hants.
The world's largest on-water boat show.
Things to see: A large selection of boats and other craft covering all aspects of the leisure marine industry. Over 600 exhibitors.
Contact: National Boat Shows Ltd, Meadlake Place, Thorpe Lea Road, Egham, Surrey TW20 8HE. Tel: 01784 473377.
Admission: TBA. **Times**: 10am - 7pm daily. Sun 21st: 10am - 6pm.

13 Sep
WISCOMBE PARK SPEED HILL CLIMB
Wiscombe Park, Southleigh, Colyton, Devon (RAC signposted).
Speed hill climb for cars.
Things to see: Racing, sports and saloon cars being driven at high speed on a narrow and tortuous track. Speeds in excess of 100mph recorded. Cars of great mechanical interest can be viewed static in the pits.
Contact: Dr R A Willoughby, Tudor Cottage, Sulhamstead, Reading RG7 4BP. Tel: 01734 302439.
Admission: £3 - £4. **Times**: 9am - 5.30pm.

13 Sep
IN LIVING MEMORY
National Tramway Museum, Crich, Matlock, Derbyshire.
Special event at the National Tramway Museum.
Things to see: Free admission today if you arrive in full Edwardian or Victorian period costume.
Contact: Lesley Wyld, Marketing Manager, National Tramway Museum, Crich, Matlock, Derbyshire DE4 5DP. Tel: 01773 852565. Fax: 01773 852326.
Admission: £5.90 adults; £3 children; £5.10 OAPs; £16.20 family ticket. **Times**: 10am - 5.30pm.

13 Sep*
HARDRAW SCAR BRASS BAND CONTEST
Grounds of The Green Dragon Inn, Hardraw, Hawes, North Yorkshire.
Traditional brass band contest.
Things to see: Up to 20 brass bands performing in a very attractive Dales setting of a natural amphitheatre, first held in 1881. Finale of massed bands in impromptu concert of marches/hymn tunes, with audience singing hymns. Added attraction is the picturesque Hardraw Force waterfall. The provided seating is limited so please bring your own seat/rug.
Contact: Dennis Hill, 33 Newport Road, North Cave, East Yorkshire HU15 2NU. Tel: 01430 423451.
Admission: TBA. **Times**: 10.30am - 6pm approx.

13 Sep
GREAT AUTUMN PLANT FAIR
Beningbrough Hall, Shipton, Beningbrough, York.
Sale of plants.

Things to see: Rare and unusual plants on sale.
Contact: The National Trust, Beningbrough Hall, Shipton, Beningbrough, York YO6 1DD. Tel: 01904 470666.
Admission: TBA. **Times**: 11am - 4pm.

13 Sep
BATTLE OF BRITAIN OPEN DAY
Biggin Hill Airport, Kent.
One of the world's finest flying displays at famous Battle of Britain fighter base.
Things to see: Five-hour flying display – military, civilian, old and new. Static aircraft park, exhibition, funfair, etc. Patrons enclosure with marquee, grandstand, seating and uninterrupted view.
Contact: Air Displays International, Biggin Hill Airport, Biggin Hill, Kent TN16 3BN. Tel: 01959 540959.
Admission: TBA. **Times:** 9am - 5pm.

15-16 Sep
CITY OF LONDON FLOWER SHOW
Guildhall, Gresham Street, London EC2.
Flower show.
Things to see: Large variety of flowers, fruit and vegetables on display.
Contact: Show Secretary, Corporation of London, Parks & Gardens Dept, West Ham Park, Upton Lane, London E7 9PU. Tel: 0181-472 3584.
Admission: TBA. **Times**: TBA.

17 Sep
THAME SHOW
Thame Showground, Oxfordshire (on the Northern Bypass of Thame).
Agricultural show.
Things to see: Showjumping, cattle, sheep, goats, donkeys, horses, dogs, etc. Demonstrations, trade stands.
Contact: Mr Mike Howes, Starbank House, 23 High Street, Thame, Oxfordshire OX9 2BZ. Tel: 01844 212737.
Admission: TBA. **Times**: From 8am.

18-20 Sep
BRITISH CRAFT SHOW
Luton Hoo, Luton, Beds.
Craft show.
Things to see: Over 170 quality modern and traditional craftsmen demonstrating and selling hand-made British crafts. Held under marquee, it offers a family day out to see rural crafts, bands and dancers.
Contact: ICHF Ltd, Dominic House, Seaton Road, Highcliffe, Dorset. Tel: 01425 272711.
Admission: £4.50 adults; £3.50 OAPs; £1 children. **Times**: 9.30am - 5.30pm.

18-20 Sep
HARROGATE AUTUMN FLOWER SHOW
Great Yorkshire Showground, Harrogate, North Yorkshire.
Major flower show.
Things to see: Meet the country's finest nurserymen, talented craftspeople and purveyors of some of the finest foods. Displays by 12 specialist societies, vegetables, honey and many more delights including the National Onion Championships! Country crafts and fine country foods.
Contact: North of England Horticultural Society, 4A South Park Road, Harrogate, North Yorkshire. Tel: 01423 561049. Fax: 01423 536880.
Admission: TBA. **Times:** Fri: 9.30am - 6pm. Sat: 9.30am - 6pm. Sun: 9.30am - 5.30pm.

19 Sep
DR JOHNSON BIRTHDAY CELEBRATIONS
Market Square, Lichfield, Staffs.
Commemorative of the birth of Dr Johnson, Lichfield's most famous son.
Things to see: The Mayor and civic party

Dates can change, events can be cancelled – Please check with the organisers before setting out!

accompanied by the President and members of the Johnson Society and staff and pupils from King Edward VI school (Dr Johnson's old school) walk in procession from the Guildhall to the Johnson statue on The Market Square. A short service takes place in which the mayor places a laurel wreath on the statue and the choir from St Michaels church sing Johnson's 'Last Prayer'. The Johnson Birthplace Museum is decorated with flowers and bunting and the public can visit the museum free of charge.
Contact: Mr P Young, Town Clerk, Lichfield City Council, City Council Offices, Guildhall, Lichfield, Staffordshire WS13 6LX. Tel: 01543 250011.
Admission: Free. **Times:** Dr Johnson Birthday Celebrations: 11.45am - 12.15pm. Johnson Birthplace Museum: 11.30am - 5pm.

19 Sep
EGREMONT CRAB FAIR AND SPORTS
Main Street, Market Hall and Baybarrow Sports Field, Egremont, Cumbria.
Traditional Lakeland events.
Things to see: Traditional regional events including fell race, hound trails, dog show, Cumberland & Westmorland wrestling, climbing greasy pole, hunting songs, horn blowing, clay pipe smoking, World Gurning Championship.
Contact: Mr Alan Clements, 14 Dent View, Egremont, Cumbria CA22 2ET. Tel/fax: 01946 821554.
Admission: £2.50 sports field; voluntary collections elsewhere. **Times:** 8am - 10pm.

19 Sep
EGGLESTON AGRICULTURAL SOCIETY ANNUAL SHOW
High Shipley Farm, Eggleston, Nr Barnard Castle, Co Durham.
Agricultural show.
Things to see: Cattle, sheep, horses, BSJA leaping, harness racing, poultry, pigeons, rabbits, cavies, cage birds, flowers, vegetables, floral art, cakes, bread, needlework, photography, art, children's classes, stone walling.
Contact: Mr G Lawson, Secretary, 56 Galgate, Barnard Castle, Co Durham DL12 8BH. Tel: 01833 638749.
Admission: £3 adults; £1 children. **Times**: 9am - 6.30pm.

19 Sep
INVERCHARRON TRADITIONAL HIGHLAND GAMES
A836 Balblair Farm, Bonar Bridge/Lairg Road, Sutherland.
Highland games.
Things to see: Piping, Highland dancing, track and field, heavies events, tug of war, whippet racing, clay pigeon shooting. Plus various children's amusements, etc.
Contact: Mrs M Chalmers, "Migdale Mill", Bonar Bridge, Sutherland IV24 3AR. Tel: 01863 766521.
Admission: £3. **Times**: 10am - 5.30pm.

19 Sep
LOSSIEMOUTH AUTUMN FLOWER SHOW
Lossiemouth Community Centre, Coulardbank Road, Lossiemouth, Moray.
Autumn flower show.
Things to see: Plants and flowers of all kinds in season, floral art, baking, handiwork (both adults and children), alpines, etc.
Contact: Mr J Millar, 23 South Covesea Terrace, Lossiemouth IV31 6NA. Tel: 01343 813912.
Admission: TBA. **Times**: 1pm - 4.30pm.

19 Sep
DEVON COUNTY ANTIQUES FAIR
Matford Centre in the Exeter Livestock Centre, Matford Park Rd, Marsh Barton, Exeter, Devon.
Antiques fair.
Things to see: Beautiful antiques and collectables among the many items on offer. 430 stands in all.
Contact: Val Dennis, Devon Counties

Antiques Fairs, The Glebe House, Nymet Tracey, Crediton, Devon EX17 6DB. Tel: 01363 82571.
Admission: £2 adults; children free. **Times**: 10am - 5pm.

19 Sep
SOUTH COAST ROWING CHAMPIONSHIPS
Stithians Lake, Cornwall.
Event from the calendar of 'Cornwall '98, The World Watersports Festival'.
Things to see: Join upwards of 600 competitors and thousands of spectators for the climax of the South Coast Rowing events.
Contact: Cornwall '98, Trevint House, Strangways Villas, Truro, Cornwall TR1 2PA. Tel: 01872 223527.
Admission: TBA. **Times**: TBA.

19-20 Sep
FOUR SEASONS CRAFTS SHOW
Lloyd Park, Coombe Rd, South Croydon, Surrey.
Craft fair.
Things to see: Quality crafts created by experts from all over the country. Robin Hood theme.
Contact: Four Seasons (Events Ltd), 23A Brockenhurst Rd, South Ascot, Berkshire SL5 9DJ. Tel: 01344 874787.
Admission: £2.50-£3.50 adults; £2-£2.50 OAPs; £1 children. **Times**: TBA.

19-20 Sep
NEWBURY & ROYAL COUNTY OF BERKSHIRE SHOW
Newbury Showground, Berkshire.
County agricultural show.
Things to see: Large county show with many attractions. Contact the organisers nearer the time for further details of events.
Contact: Newbury Showground, Priors Court, Hermitage, Thatcham, Berkshire RG18 9QZ.
Admission: £8 adult; £4 children/OAPs. **Times**: Saturday 8.30am - 6pm, Sunday 9am - 6pm.

Dates can change, events can be cancelled – Please check with the organisers before setting out!

19-20 Sep
STEAM & VINTAGE RALLY
The Tropical Bird Gardens, Rode, Nr Bath, Somerset.
Trains and vintage vehicles.
Things to see: Steam, diesel and electric locomotives, traction engines, steam rollers, vintage vehicles, steam engines, stationary engines. Plus 280 varieties of birds.
Contact: Mr M D Marshall, Millbrook Cottage, The Hollow, Child Okeford, Blandford Forum, Dorset DT11 8EX. Tel: 01258 861689.
Admission: TBA. **Times**: 11am - 5pm.

19-20 Sep
STEAM THRESHING
Cogges Manor Farm Museum, Nr Witney, Oxon.
Steam engine event.
Things to see: Steam engine driving the museum's restored threshing drum. Cotswold farm buildings with displays and traditional farm animals. Manor house with room displays & cooking in the Victorian kitchen.
Contact: Carol Nightingale, Site Manager, Cogges Manor Farm Museum, Church Lane, Cogges, Nr Witney, Oxon OX8 6LA. Tel: 01993 772602.
Admission: £3.25 adults; £2 OAPs; £1.75 children; £9 family. **Times**: Sat/Sun: 12 noon - 5.30pm. Mon: 10.30pm - 5.30pm.

19 Sep-1 Nov
WALSALL ILLUMINATIONS
Walsall Arboretum, Walsall, West Midlands.
Illuminations and light show.

Things to see: This spectacular lights and laser show for all the family is held in the beautiful setting of Walsall Arboretum, with around 35 acres of lakes, trees and gardens.
Contact: Adrian King, Marketing Section, Walsall Leisure & Community Services, Walsall MBC, Civic Centre, Darwall Street, Walsall WS1 1TZ. Tel: 01922 653148.
Admission: TBA. **Times**: 19 Sep-1 Oct: 7.30pm - 9.30pm. 5 Oct-18 Oct: 7pm-9.30pm. 19 Oct-1 Nov: 6.30pm - 9pm.

20 Sep
BORROWDALE SHEPHERDS MEET & SHOW
Yew Tree Farm, Rosthwaite, Borrowdale, Cumbria.
Sheepdog trials and country show.
Things to see: Plenty of animals to see. Sheep, sheepdog trials; ponies, dogs, etc.
Contact: Mr M Roulson, Yew Tree Farmhouse, Stonethwaite, Borrowdale, Keswick, Cumbria CA12 5XG. Tel: 017687 77322.
Admission: £2.50 adults; £1 children. **Times**: TBA.

20 Sep
HYDE PARK HORSEMEN'S SUNDAY
St John's Church, Hyde Park Crescent, London W2.
Annual equestrian gathering and church service.
Things to see: Church service with usually about 60 horses, both ridden and driven. Both vicar and congregation take the service on horseback. Following the service there is an orderly procession of all the horses, coming up in groups to receive commemorative rosettes before riding off to the famous Rotten Row in Hyde Park. Morris dancers at beginning of procession.
Contact: Ross Nye, 8 Bathurst Mews, London W2 3SB. Tel: 0171-262 3791 or 01483 535910.
Admission: N/A. **Times**: Service begins 12 noon.

20 Sep
THE SPITALFIELDS SHOW
The Old Spitalfields Market, Brushfield St, London E1.
Annual horticultural show.
Things to see: Displays of fruit, flowers, vegetables, home-made produce and handicrafts.
Contact: Alternative Arts, 47A Brushfield Street, Spitalfields, London E1 6AA. Tel: 0171-375 0441.
Admission: Free. **Times**: From 12 noon - 4pm.

20 Sep
LEUKAEMIA RESEARCH FUND VINTAGE CAR RALLY
Tredegar House & Park, Newport, Gwent.
Display of vintage vehicles.
Things to see: Vintage, classic and sports cars; commercial vehicles; military vehicles; motor cycles; stationary engines. Plus amusements, arena events.
Contact: Mr & Mrs B N Womack, 8 Cwm Cwddy Drive, Bassaleg, Newport, Gwent NP1 9JA. Tel: 01633 895145.
Admission: £4 adults; £2 children; £10 family ticket. **Times**: 11.30am - 6pm.

21 Sep
NIDDERDALE SHOW
Bewerley Park, Pateley Bridge, North Yorkshire.
Agricultural show.
Things to see: Showjumping, cattle, sheep, pigs, goats, pigeons, poultry and rabbits. Plus trade stands, craft marquee, food marquee with cookery demonstrations.
Contact: Mrs Susan Monk, 80 Westville Oval, Harrogate, North Yorkshire HG1 3JW. Tel: 01423 525460.
Admission: £4 adults; £4 car parking. **Times:** Judging commences at 9am.

23 Sep
AUTUMN EQUINOX CEREMONY
At the top of Primrose Hill, London.
Druid celebration of the harvest.

Things to see: Processions, trumpet-call, sheathing of the sword, entry of Ceridwen, "Mother Earth", bearing Cornucopia and fruits of the harvest, libation to the Earth, scattering of fruit and call of peace. Best vantage point is on the western side of the ceremony. Spectators are asked not to cross the processions, enter or crowd the circle. Best to use entrance into Primrose Hill from Primrose Hill Road.
Contact: Honorary Secretary, The Druid Order, 23 Thornsett Road, Anerley, London SE20 7XB. Tel: 0181-659 4879.
Admission: N/A. **Times:** 1250hrs BST.

23-27 Sep
HORSE OF THE YEAR SHOW
Wembley Arena, Empire Way, Wembley, London.
Premier showjumping event.
Things to see: Top showjumping event with leading riders from the UK and around the world. Plus Shetland Pony Grand National and fun events involving lots of horses. Many trade stands.
Contact: Show Secretary, British Showjumping Association, British Equestrian Centre, Stoneleigh, Coventry CV8 2LR. Tel: 01203 693088.
Admission: TBA. **Times**: TBA.

26-27 Sep
MODELLERS WEEKEND
The National Waterways Museum, Llanthony Warehouse, Gloucester Docks.
Models display.
Things to see: Model steam engines/model boats in action, model engines.
Contact: Mary Mills, Media/PR, National Waterways Museum, Llanthony Warehouse, Gloucester Docks, Gloucester GL1 2EH. Tel: 01452 318054.
Admission: £4.50 adults; £3.50 children/OAPs; £10-£12 Family tickets.
Times: 10am - 5pm approx.

27 Sep
ENGINE MUSEUM OPEN DAY
Prickwillow Engine Museum, Main Street, Prickwillow, Nr Ely, Cambridgeshire. Museum Open Day.
Things to see: Old drainage engines running, plus many other attractions. **Contact**: Joan Stacey, Prickwillow Engine Trust, Main Street, Prickwillow, Nr Ely, Cambridgeshire CB7 4UN. Tel: 01353 688360.
Admission: £3 adults; £1.50 children; £2 OAPs; £7 family. **Times:** Engines run: 12 noon - 5pm. Museum open 11am - 5pm.

October

1-3 Oct
NOTTINGHAM GOOSE FAIR
The Forest Recreation Ground, Hyson Green, Nottingham.
Europe's largest travelling fair.
Things to see: One of the oldest traditional funfairs in Britain, offering all the fairground attractions, both traditional and modern.
Contact: Victoria Market Office, Glasshouse St, Nottingham, Notts. Tel: 0115 941 7324.
Admission: Free. **Times**: 12 noon - 12 midnight.

1-4 Oct
CREATIVE STITCHES & CRAFTS ALIVE
Westpoint Exhibition Centre, Devon Showground, Clyst St Mary, Nr Exeter, Devon.
Needlecraft and rural crafts show.
Things to see: Two shows in one venue. Quality hand-made British crafts alongside a wide variety of needlecraft, sewing and knitting supplies including fabrics, kits and machinery.
Contact: ICHF Ltd, Dominic House, Seaton Road, Highcliffe, Dorset. Tel: 01425 272711.
Admission: £5.20 adults; £4.20 OAPs; £1 children. **Times**: 9.30am - 5.30pm (Sunday 5pm).

Dates can change, events can be cancelled – Please check with the organisers before setting out!

2-4 Oct
SPECIAL NEEDLEWORK AND LACE EXHIBITION
Blair Castle, Pitlochry, Perthshire.
Annual exhibition of the castle's work and lace collection.
Things to see: One of the finest needlework exhibitions in the country, most of which is attributed to Lady Evelyn Stewart Murray (1868 -1940). In all over 120 pieces of lace and embroidery.
Contact: Geoff G Crerar, Adminstrator, Blair Castle, Blair Atholl, Pitlochry, Perthshire PH18 5TL. Tel: 01796 481 207.
Admission: TBA.**Times**: TBA.

2-4 Oct
THOMAS THE TANK ENGINE
Didcot Railway Centre, Oxfordshire.
Railway fun day for children with Thomas the Tank Engine theme.
Things to see: Thomas and friends in steam, the Fat Controller, face painting, Punch and Judy. Also story telling, refreshments and souvenir shop.
Contact: Jeanette Howse, Didcot Railway Centre, Didcot, Oxfordshire OX11 7NJ. Tel: 01235 817200.
Admission: £6.50 adults, £5.50 children/OAPs. **Times**: 10am - 5pm.

3 Oct
DEVON COUNTY ANTIQUES FAIR
Salisbury Leisure Centre, The Butts, Hulse Road, Salisbury, Wiltshire.
Antiques fair.
Things to see: Beautiful antiques and collectables among the many items on offer. 140 stands in one hall.
Contact: Val Dennis, Devon Counties Antiques Fairs, The Glebe House, Nymet

Tracey, Crediton, Devon EX17 6DB. Tel: 01363 82571.
Admission: £1.50 adults; children free. **Times**: 10am - 5pm.

3-4 Oct
ERIDGE HORSE TRIALS
Eridge Park, Nr Tunbridge Wells, Kent.
Major equestrian event.
Things to see: Horse trials featuring novice, open intermediate horses including international riders.
Contact: Mrs J Nolan, South Eastern Equestrian Services, Oatridges, Best Beech, Wadhurst, East Sussex TN5 6JL. Tel: 01892 783227.
Admission: £8 per car. **Times**: From 9am.

4 Oct
BICTON HORSE TRIALS
Bicton Arena, East Budleigh, Devon.
Horse trials.
Things to see: Horses jumping fences over a cross country course.
Contact: A C Stevens, St Giles Cottage, Northleigh, Colyton, Devon EX13 6BL. Tel: 01404 871296.
Admission: £5 per car to include occupants. **Times**: 8.30am - 6pm.

4 Oct
DULVERTON CARNIVAL
Dulverton, Somerset.
Town carnival.
Things to see: Illuminated evening carnival procession with numerous floats, costumes, etc. A good vantage point would be at Exmoor House, where the judging will take place.
Contact: Jan Ross, The Cedars, Jury Road, Dulverton, Somerset.
Admission: N/A. **Times**: Starts 6.30pm.

4 Oct
PEARLY HARVEST FESTIVAL
St Martin-in-the-Fields, Trafalgar Square, London.
Traditional church service.
Things to see: The Pearly Kings and Queens attending in their colourful costumes.
Contact: The Rev David Monteith, St Martin-in-the-Fields, St Martin's Place, London WC2. Tel: 0171-930 0089.
Admission: Free. **Times**: 3pm - 4pm.

4 Oct
PUNCH & JUDY OPEN AIR FESTIVAL
Covent Garden Piazza, London WC2.
Puppet festival.
Things to see: Performances of traditional Punch & Judy puppets, plus folklore puppets from other countries.
Contact: Percy Press, 16 Templeton Road, London N15 6RY. Tel: 0181-802 4656.
Admission: N/A. **Times**: 10.30am - 5.30pm.

4 Oct*
BRITISH & INTERNATIONAL CRAFT FAIR
Cocksmoors Woods Leisure Centre, Alcester Road, Kings Heath, Birmingham.
International crafts.
Things to see: Crafts of all kinds from Britain and overseas.
Contact: Joyce Towers, 8 Fiery Hill Road, Barnt Green, Birmingham B45 8LF. Tel: 0121-445 3967.
Admission: N/A. **Times**: 9.30am - 5pm.

8 Oct
INTERNATIONAL BALLROOM DANCE CHAMPIONSHIPS
Royal Albert Hall, London.
Ballroom & Latin American dance.
Things to see: The International Professional Modern and Latin American Championships, the International Amateur Modern and Latin American Championships, plus the world famous "Giants in Cabaret".
Contact: Dance News Special Projects Ltd, Hamble House, Meadrow, Godalming, Surrey GU9 3HJ. Tel: 01483 428679.
Admission: £12 - £28. **Times**: 5.45pm - 1am.

9-11 Oct
CIRCUIT RETROSPECTIVE
Start near Belfast, Northern Ireland; finish in the Republic of Ireland.
Classic car trial.
Things to see: A large variety of old cars on the road and competing in numerous autotests.
Contact: Ulster Automobile Club, 29 Shore Road, Holywood, Northern Ireland BT18 9HX. Tel: 01232 426262. Fax: 01232 421818.
Admission: N/A. **Times**: Contact the U.A.C.

10 Oct
DEVON COUNTY ANTIQUES FAIR
Matford Centre in the Exeter Livestock Centre, Matford Park Rd, Marsh Barton, Exeter, Devon.
Antiques fair.
Things to see: Beautiful antiques and collectables among the many items on offer. 430 stands in all.
Contact: Val Dennis, Devon Counties Antiques Fairs, The Glebe House, Nymet Tracey, Crediton, Devon EX17 6DB. Tel: 01363 82571.
Admission: £2 adults; children free. **Times**: 10am - 5pm.

10 Oct
WASDALE HEAD SHOW AND SHEPHERDS' MEET
Wasdale Head, Cumbria.
Traditional shepherds' meet and show.
Things to see: Show of Herdwick sheep and shepherd's dogs, hound trails, Cumberland and Westmorland style wrestling, dog show, terrier show, fell races, childrens' sports, displays and rural crafts, shepherds' crooks and stick show.
Contact: Mr D Smith, 6 Hardingill, Gosforth, Seascale, Cumbria CA20 1AQ. Tel: 019467 25340.
Admission: £2.50 **Times**: 10am - 6pm.

Dates can change, events can be cancelled – Please check with the organisers before setting out!

10-11 Oct
TWO DAY MOTOCROSS
Sorel Headland, St John, Jersey.
Motorcycle motocross.
Things to see: Motocross action for juniors and seniors (solos), with backdrop of landscape view of headland and sea.
Contact: Mrs Ellaine Le Cornu, Midway, Croix de Bois, Five Oaks, Jersey JE2 7TU. Tel: 01534 35853.
Admission: TBA. **Times**: 10am - 5.30pm approx.

10-11 Oct
BRITISH NATIONAL PLOUGHING CHAMPIONSHIPS
Adstone, Towcester, Northamptonshire.
A two day event which shows competitive ploughing at its best.
Things to see: Approx 250 ploughmen from around the UK compete in World style ploughing, reversible ploughing, horse ploughing and vintage classes. Plus demonstrations of agricultural machinery and crafts.
Contact: Mr Ken Chappell, The Society of Ploughmen, Quarry Farm, Loversall, Doncaster, South Yorkshire DN11 9DH. Tel: 01302 852469.
Admission: TBA. **Times**: 9am - 5pm daily.

10-11 Oct
DIESEL & STEAM WEEKEND
Midland Railway Centre, Butterley Station, Ripley, Derbyshire.
Railway event.
Things to see: Train services featuring both steam and diesel power, narrow gauge and model railways, museum, country park, farm park, etc.
Contact: Alan Calladine, Midland Rail-

way Centre, Butterley Station, Ripley, Derbyshire DE5 3QZ. Tel: 01773 747674.
Admission: £7.95 adults; £6.50 OAPs; two children free with each adult. **Times**: 10.30am - 4.15pm.

11 Oct
BEARS ONLY FAIR
Town Hall, Loughborough.
Teddy Bear fair.
Things to see: Collectors' teddy bears including limited editions and show specials, and rare antique bears. Free bear making advice centre. Free valuations from Bonhams of Chelsea. High quality fair for serious bear-collectors and great family day out.
Contact: Maddy Aldis, 11 Wesley Street, Eccles, Manchester M30 0UQ. Tel: 0161 7077625.
Admission: £3 adults; £2.50 children; £8 family. **Times**: 10.30am - 4.30pm.

11 Oct
AUTUMN VINTAGE GATHERING
Amberley Museum, Amberley, Arundel, West Sussex.
Vintage vehicle gathering.
Things to see: Grand end-of-season gathering of steam engines, vintage cars, motorcycles, lorries, buses, fire engines, cycles, stationary engines and other items. In addition to the event itself, visitors can enjoy all the usual museum attractions, including craftsmen at work, train rides, vintage bus rides, etc.
Contact: Howard Stenning, Amberley Museum, Amberley, Arundel, West Sussex BN18 9LT. Tel: 01798 831370.
Admission: TBA. 1997 guide: £5 adults; £4.50 OAPs; £2.50 children. **Times**: 10am - 5pm.

11 Oct*
PEARL WORLD CONKER CHAMPIONSHIPS
Ashton, Nr Oundle, Peterborough.
Conker championships and "fun day".
Things to see: Men's, women's and children's World Conker Championship contest, plus entertainments, stalls, etc. Takes place on the village green which together with the thatched houses provides a very attractive backdrop.
Contact: John Hadman, 22 New Road, Oundle, Peterborough PE8 4LB. Tel: 01832 272735.
Admission: £1.50 adults; 50p OAPs; children free. Free car parking. **Times**: 9.30am - 3pm.

17 Oct
BUTTERMERE SHEPHERDS' MEETING & SHOW
Croft Farm, Buttermere, Cumbria.
Traditional Lakeland shepherds' meet.
Things to see: Sheep, sheepdogs, terriers, fellracing, hound trails, walking sticks, Cumberland and Westmorland wrestling, singing, hallowing and horn blowing. Also a bowler hat competition. All in a superb scenic setting.
Contact: D Norman, Crag Farm, Buttermere, Cockermouth, Cumbria. Tel: 0176 8770204.
Admission: £2. **Times**: 10am - 6pm (approx).

17-18 Oct
BISHOP BURTON HORSE TRIALS
Bishop Burton College, Bishop Burton, Beverley, East Yorkshire.
BHS horse trials.
Things to see: Top level dressage, showjumping and cross country. Trade stands, refreshments and licensed bar.
Contact: Miss L Johnson, Secretary, Bishop Burton College, Bishop Burton, Beverley, East Yorkshire. Tel: 01964 553085.
Admission: £5 per car approx. **Times**: 9am - 5pm approx.

17-18 Oct
NATIONAL CHAMPIONSHIP SERIES
River Dee, Llangollen, Clwyd, Wales.
Final event for Premier & Division 1.
Things to see: Canoe slalom competitions in superb surroundings on a spectacular stretch of the River Dee.
Contact: Slalom Development Officer,

BCU, Adbolton Lane, West Bridgford, Nottingham NG2 5AS. Tel: 01636 705363. Fax: 01636 701910.
Admission: N/A. **Times**: Racing takes place each day for most of the day.

18 Oct
COMBE MILL IN STEAM
Combe Mill (just off the A4095 at Long Handborough, Oxfordshire).
Special steam day.
Things to see: An 18thC beam engine and three other steam engines in steam. Plus working museum featuring blacksmiths and wood turners. Delightful riverside picnic area.
Contact: F A Huddleston, Braemar, The Ridings, Stonesfield, Witney, Oxfordshire OX8 8EA. Tel: 0993 891785.
Admission: £2.50 adults; £1 children/OAPs. **Times**: 10am - 5pm.

18 Oct
SHAKESPEARE IN SPITALFIELDS
The Old Spitalfields Market, Brushfield St, London E1.
Shakespeare event.
Things to see: Talented thespians perform their favourite bits of the bard.
Contact: Alternative Arts, 47A Brushfield Street, Spitalfields, London E1 6AA. Tel: 0171-375 0441.
Admission: Free. **Times**: From 12 noon - 3pm.

Dates can change, events can be cancelled – Please check with the organisers before setting out!

18 Oct*
SEA CADET CORPS TRAFALGAR DAY PARADE
Trafalgar Square, London.
Sea Cadets' parade and service.
Things to see: Parade of nearly 500 young people (Sea Cadets), service of commemoration, wreath laying and march past, with two bands – guard and colour party. Plus international representatives, a VIP reviewing officer, a young cadet reading Nelson's prayer.
Contact: Mark Mallon, Head of PR, 202 Lambeth Road, London SE1 7JF. Tel: 0171-928 8978.
Admission: N/A. **Times**: 11am - 1pm.

18-19 Oct
BEALE MODEL BOAT TRADE SHOW
Beale Park, Lower Basildon, Reading, Berkshire.
Show concentrating on providing a forum for buyers, traders and makers.
Things to see: This show makes great use of the variety of waters at Beale Park, includes demonstrations and many trade stands.
Contact: Beale Park, The Child-Beale Trust, Lower Basildon, Reading, Berkshire RG8 9NH. Tel: 0118 984 5172.
Admission: £4 adults; £3 OAPs; £2.50 children. **Times**: 10am - 6pm.

19-23 Oct*
WINDERMERE RECORD ATTEMPTS
By Low Wood Hotel, Windermere, Cumbria.
Watersport record attempts.
Things to see: World and National record attempts by all classes of craft and waterskiers.
Contact: Phyllis M Berry, Helm Rock, Annisgarth Park, Windermere, Cumbria

LA23 2HF. Tel: 015394 42595.
Admission: Free. **Times**: 8am - 6pm daily.

19-25 Oct
APPLE WEEK
Beningbrough Hall, Shipton, Beningbrough, York.
One of the largest collection of "top fruit" in a National Trust Walled Garden.
Things to see: Visit the fruit display and taste home cooked apple and fruit recipes in the restaurant all week.
Contact: The National Trust, Beningbrough Hall, Shipton, Beningbrough, York YO6 1DD. Tel: 01904 470666.
Admission: Normal admission prices apply. **Times**: TBA.

19-31 Oct
AUTUMN COLOURS WEEK
Fairhaven Garden Trust, South Walsham, Norfolk (nine miles NE of Norwich on B1140).
Gardens open for autumn colours.
Things to see: Trees and shrubs in their lovely autumn hues. Also plants for sale, boat trips on the Broad and a bird sanctuary for ornithologists.
Contact: Mr G E Debbage, Resident Warden, The Fairhaven Garden Trust, 2 The Woodlands, Wymers Lane, South Walsham, Norwich, Norfolk NR13 6EA. Tel: 01603 270449.
Admission: £3 adults; £2.70 OAPs; £1 children. Entry to bird sanctuary £1. **Times**: 11am - dusk.

23-31 Oct
THE CARAVAN & OUTDOOR LEISURE SHOW
Earls Court Exhibition Centre, Warwick Road, London SW5.
Public show for the caravanner, motorcaravanner and outdoor enthusiast.
Things to see: Caravans, motorcaravans, tents, camping equipment, accessories, service companies, small boats, outdoor clothing and leisure wear.
Contact: Joanna Peck, P+O Events, Earls Court Exhibition Centre, Warwick Road, London SW5 9TA. Tel: 0171-370 8203.
Admission: TBA. **Times**: 10am - 6pm.

23 Oct-1 Nov
THE BRITISH INTERNATIONAL MOTOR SHOW
National Exhibition Centre, Birmingham.
Major motor show.
Things to see: Cars, commercial vehicles up to 3.5 tonnes, accessories and components, garage equipment, tyres, magazines and associations.
Contact: The Society of Motor Manufacturers and Traders Ltd, Forbes House, Halkin Street, London SW1X 7DS. Tel: 0171-235 7000. Tax: 0171-235 7112.
Admission: £10 adults; £5 children/OAPs. **Times**: 23rd - 31st: Oct 9.30am - 7pm. 1 Nov: 9.30am - 5.30pm.

24-25 Oct
BRITISH OPEN CHAMPIONSHIPS
River Dee, Llangollen, Clwyd, Wales.
National canoeing competition.
Things to see: Canoe slalom competitions in superb surroundings on a spectacular stretch of the River Dee.
Contact: Slalom Development Officer, BCU, Adbolton Lane, West Bridgford, Nottingham NG2 5AS. Tel: 01636 705363. Fax: 01636 701910.
Admission: N/A. **Times**: Racing takes place each day for most of the day.

24-25 Oct
FOUR SEASONS CRAFTS SHOW
Sandown Park, Esher, Surrey.
Craft fair.
Things to see: Quality crafts created by experts from all over the country. Halloween theme.

Dates can change, events can be cancelled – Please check with the organisers before setting out!

Contact: Four Seasons (Events Ltd), 23A Brockenhurst Rd, South Ascot, Berkshire SL5 9DJ. Tel: 01344 874787.
Admission: £2.50-£3.50 adults; £2-£2.50 OAPs; £1 children. **Times**: TBA.

24-25 Oct
AUTUMN COUNTRYSIDE CELEBRATION
Weald and Downland Open Air Museum, Singleton, Chichester, West Sussex.
Heavy horse and steam event.
Things to see: Steam threshing, ploughing with heavy horses, vintage tractors. Plus lots of country crafts.
Contact: C Zeuner, Weald and Downland Open Air Museum, Singleton, Chichester, West Sussex PO18 0EU. Tel: 01243 811348.
Admission: TBA. 1997 guide: £4.90 adults; £4.30 OAPs; £2.30 children; family ticket £12 (2 adults, 2 children). **Times**: 10.30am - 5pm.

25 Oct
BOAT JUMBLE
The Historic Dockyard, Chatham, Kent.
Boat jumble.
Things to see: Thousands of block and tackle bargains, from a shackle to a complete boat.
Contact: The Historic Dockyard, Chatham, Kent ME4 4TE. Tel: 01634 812551.
Admission: £2.50 adults; children free. **Times**: 10am - 4pm.

25 Oct
A STARLIGHT SPECIAL
National Tramway Museum, Crich, Matlock, Derbyshire.
Special event at the National Tramway Museum.
Things to see: The feel of cobbles underfoot, old-fashioned street lights, the clattering of hooves - an absorbing illusion through to an illuminated twilight. The Red House Carriage Museum joins us with its horse-drawn omnibus to help you time-travel.
Contact: Lesley Wyld, Marketing Manager, National Tramway Museum, Crich, Matlock, Derbyshire DE4 5DP. Tel: 01773 852565. Fax: 01773 852326.
Admission: £5.90 adults; £3 children; £5.10 OAPs; £16.20 family ticket. **Times**: TBA.

Dates can change, events can be cancelled – Please check with the organisers before setting out!

26 Oct-1 Nov
TREASURE TRAIL
National Tramway Museum, Crich, Matlock, Derbyshire.
Half-term fun for children.
Things to see: Different clues for different ages - the thrill of the chase and the chance of prizes.
Contact: Lesley Wyld, Marketing Manager, National Tramway Museum, Crich, Matlock, Derbyshire DE4 5DP. Tel: 01773 852565. Fax: 01773 852326.
Admission: £5.90 adults; £3 children; £5.10 OAPs; £16.20 family ticket. **Times**: 10am - 5.30pm.

26-30 Oct
HALF TERM FUN FOR CHILDREN
Leeds Castle, Maidstone, Kent.
Event designed for children.
Things to see: Learning and fun, Different activities. Further details TBA.
Contact: Leeds Castle, Maidstone, Kent ME17 1PL. Tel: 01622 765400.
Admission: TBA. **Times**: TBA.

30-31 Oct
PHOTOGRAPHERS' EVENINGS
Didcot Railway Centre, Didcot, Oxfordshire.
Steam trains in action at night.
Things to see: Great Western Railway steam locomotives in action and specially staged around the engine shed for night photography.

Contact: Jeanette Howse, Didcot Railway Centre, Didcot, Oxfordshire OX11 7NJ. Tel: 01235 817200.
Admission: TBA. **Times**: Fri: 4pm - 10pm; Sat: 10am - 10pm.

31 Oct
FIREWORKS FAIR
Beaulieu Abbey, Beaulieu, Brockenhurst, Hampshire.
The South's biggest and best fireworks display.
Things to see: Two bonfires, fireworks, vintage fairground rides to enjoy. Plus a special fireworks display especially designed for children.
Contact: Stephen Munn, Marketing Manager, Beaulieu Abbey, Beaulieu, Brockenhurst, Hampshire SO42 7ZN. Tel: 01590 612345.
Admission: TBA. **Times**: Gates open 5.30pm. Fireworks display for children at 6.30pm with the main event later in the evening.

31 Oct
GLENFIDDICH WORLD PIPING CHAMPIONSHIPS
Blair Castle, Pitlochry, Perthshire.
Annual International Piping Championships.
Things to see: Pipers and pipe bands.
Contact: Mrs L Maxwell. Tel: 01698 843 843.
Admission: TBA. **Times**: TBA.

31 Oct
HALLOWEEN CARNIVAL
River Foyle and Guildhall Square, Derry, N.Ireland.
Music and fireworks spectacular.
Things to see: Opening with spectacular River Foyle Musical Fireworks Display followed by live music from two stages, with a huge crowd in fancy dress.
Contact: Nuala McGee, Festivals Officer, Recreation & Leisure Department, Council Offices, 98 Strand Road, Derry BT48 7NN Tel: 01504 365151 ext 6668.
Admission: Free. **Times**: 7.30pm – 10pm.

31 Oct
HALLOWEEN AT THE HALL
Beningbrough Hall, Shipton, Beningbrough, York.
Halloween activities for children aged 3-12.
Things to see: Halloween activities followed by a Spooky Fancy Dress Competition. Bring your pumpkins!
Contact: The National Trust, Beningbrough Hall, Shipton, Beningbrough, York YO6 1DD. Tel: 01904 470666.
Admission: Normal admission prices apply. **Times**: From 2pm. Spooky Fancy Dress Competition is at 4.30pm.

31 Oct
TRADITIONAL BONFIRE CELEBRATIONS
The Seafront, Littlehampton, West Sussex.
Bonfire & fireworks display.
Things to see: Torchlight procession, giant bonfire and spectacular fireworks display.
Contact: Mr Richard Cooper, 46 Kent Rd, Littlehampton, West Sussex BN17 6LA. Tel: 01903 725149.
Admission: N/A. **Times**: TBA.

31 Oct-1 Nov
FIREWORKS SPECTACULAR
Alton Towers, Staffordshire.
Major firework display.
Things to see: Fireworks, music and lights combine together in a magnificent spectacle with Alton Towers as the backdrop.
Contact: Matt Ward, Assistant Press Officer, Alton Towers, Staffordshire ST10 4DB. Tel: 01538 703344.
Admission: Usual park admission charge. **Times**: At the end of the operating day. Approximately 6pm - 6.30pm.

November

1 Nov
RAC VETERAN CAR RUN
Serpentine Road, Hyde Park to Madeira Drive, Brighton.
Major veteran car run.
Things to see: 400 veteran cars, all built prior to 1905, driving from London to Brighton along the A23 and B2036, starting from Hyde Park. Many of the participants in period costume.
Contact: Colin Wilson, RAC Motor Sports Association Ltd, Riverside Park, Colnbrook, Slough, Berkshire SL3 OHG. Tel: 01753 618736.
Admission: N/A. **Times**: Starts from Hyde Park, 7.30am.

5 Nov*
DEVONPORT HIGH SCHOOL FOR BOYS BONFIRE & FIREWORK DISPLAY
DHS for Boys School, Paradise Road, Plymouth, Devon.
Fireworks display.
Things to see: Large bonfire and fireworks display.
Contact: Mr R H Faulkner, DHS for Boys School, Paradise Road, Plymouth, Devon PL1 5QP. Tel: 01752 564682/208787.
Admission: 1996 guide: £2.50 adults; £1.25 children/OAPs. **Times**: 6.45pm - 8.30pm approx.

5 Nov
GRAND BONFIRE & SPECTACULAR FIREWORKS
Bught Park, Inverness.
The Highland's largest bonfire and firework display.
Things to see: Bonfire and firework display set to a musical theme. Past themes include: "A Night at the Movies" & The Loch Ness Monster". Full supporting entertainment, fun fair, refreshments and torchlight procession.
Contact: Jon Hogan, Events and Promotions Officer, Highland Council, Town House, Inverness IV1 1JJ. Tel: 01463 724262.
Admission: Free. **Times**: TBA.

5 Nov
LEWES BONFIRE CELEBRATIONS
Lewes, East Sussex.
Fireworks display and procession.
Things to see: Large fireworks display plus torchlit street processions, spectacular costumes, brass, jazz, pipe and military bands, tableaux effigies, set pieces and fire pieces. Very crowded streets; if possible arrive early in order to find good vantage point.
Contact: Keith Austin, 25B Priory Street, Lewes, East Sussex. Tel: 01273 471516.
Admission: N/A. **Times**: 5.30pm - 12 midnight+.

5 Nov*
STOCKTON FIREWORK PARTY
Stockton Riverside, Cleveland.
Major fireworks display.
Things to see: Probably the biggest fireworks party in the north of England, with large fireworks display, local radio roadshow(s) and guest appearances of celebrities/artists.
Contact: Graham Reeves, Events Development Officer, Stockton-on-Tees Borough Council, PO Box 116, Gloucester House, 72 Church Road, Stockton-on-Tees TS18 1YB. Tel: 01642 393939 ext 3911.
Admission: N/A. **Times**: 6pm - 8.30pm.

5 Nov
BRIDGWATER GUY FAWKES CARNIVAL
Bridgwater, Somerset.
Europe's largest illuminated carnival procession.
Things to see: Illuminated procession with over 80 large floats 100ft long, 11ft wide, 17ft 6ins high, each one lit by thousands of light bulbs. 40+ walking entries. Parade culminates in massive squibbing display.
Contact: Publicity Officer: Mr C Hocking, 14 Castle Street, Bridgwater, Somerset TA6 3DB. Tel: 01278 429288. Also: D Croker, 49 Alfoxton Road, Bridgwater, Somerset TA6 7NN. Tel: 01278 421795.
Admission: N/A. **Times**: 6.45pm - 10.15pm. Squibbing 10.30pm approx.

6 Nov
BIG NIGHT OUT
Melford Hall Park, Long Melford, Sudbury, Suffolk.
Fireworks display and entertainment.
Things to see: Procession with marching bands and floats. Plus giant bonfire, large and small fair rides and firework display by Paines to be set off to music.
Contact: Sandy Basham, 26 Third Avenue, Glemsford, Sudbury, Suffolk CO10 7QJ. Tel: 01787 280941.
Admission: £3 adults; £1 children. **Times**: 7.30pm procession leaves Park Corner, Long Melford, walking to Melford Hall Park whan at approx 8pm bonfire lit with fireworks to follow.

6-8 Nov
FIREWORKS SPECTACULAR
Alton Towers, Staffordshire.
Major firework display.
Things to see: Fireworks, music and lights combine together in a magnificent spectacle with Alton Towers as the backdrop.
Contact: Matt Ward, Assistant Press Officer, Alton Towers, Staffordshire ST10 4DB. Tel: 01538 703344.
Admission: Usual park admission charge. **Times**: At the end of the operating day. Approximately 6pm - 6.30pm.

7 Nov*
RUSHMOOR BONFIRE & FIREWORK SPECTACULAR
Manor Park, Aldershot, Hants.
Major fireworks display and laser show.
Things to see: Fireworks and lighting of massive bonfire. Children's torchlight procession, Walls funfair and children's entertainers.
Contact: Phil Stoneman, Leisure Dept, Rushmoor Borough Council, Farnborough Road, Farnborough, Hants GU14 7JU. Tel: 01252 398760.
Admission: £3.50 adults (£3 in advance); children under 16 free. **Times**: Gates open: 5.30pm. Torchlight Procession: 6.45pm. Fireworks display: 7.30pm. Bonfire lit: 7.50pm.

7 Nov
FUN & FIREWORKS PARTY
Beale Park, Lower Basildon, Reading, Berkshire.
Fireworks Party.
Things to see: Massive bonfire, funfair, stalls, BBQ and other hot food, music, two bars and wonderful fireworks over the lake.
Contact: Beale Park, The Child-Beale Trust, Lower Basildon, Reading, Berkshire RG8 9NH. Tel: 0118 984 5172.
Admission: £3 adults; £2 children. **Times**: 6pm - 11pm.

7 Nov
LEEDS CASTLE GRAND FIREWORK SPECTACULAR
Leeds Castle, Maidstone, Kent.
Fireworks display.
Things to see: Spectacular displays of fireworks above a floodlit Leeds Castle. Spectacular and safe, the biggest display in the South East is reflected in the castle moat.
Contact: Leeds Castle, Maidstone, Kent ME17 1PL. Tel: 01622 765400.
Admission: Box office Tel: 01622 880008

for ticket availability and prices. **Times**: Gates open 5pm; display starts 7.30pm. Gates closed prior to display at 7pm.

7 Nov
LODDON VALLEY LIONS FIREWORK FIESTA
Wellington Country Park, Riseley, Reading, Berkshire.
Fireworks display and entertainments.
Things to see: Large fireworks display (£4,000 worth), floodlit woodland walks, steam train rides, fairground organs, band and other attractions. Arrive early to obtain best position on raised mound near cafeteria.
Contact: G J Wheeler, Lighting Showroom, Coronation Road, Basingstoke, Hants. Tel: 01256 322297.
Admission: £3 adults; £1.50 children. **Times**: Gates open 5.30pm. Fireworks programme commences 7.30pm approx.

7 Nov
ROYAL VICTORIA FIREWORK EXTRAVAGANZA
Royal Victoria Country Park, Netley Abbey, Southampton.
Major fireworks display.
Things to see: Very large 30-minute fireworks display plus bonfire and stalls.
Contact: The Park Centre, The Royal Victoria Country Park, Netley Abbey, Southampton SO31 5GA. Tel: 01703 455157.
Admission: TBA. Approx £3 per adult. **Times**: 7pm - 10pm.

7-8 Nov
DEVON COUNTY ANTIQUES FAIR
Westpoint Exhibition Centre, Clyst St Mary, Exeter, Devon.
Major antiques fair.
Things to see: Beautiful antiques and collectables among the estimated one million items on offer. 500 stands in one hall. Plus free lectures, seminars and exhibitions.
Contact: Val Dennis, Devon Counties Antiques Fairs, The Glebe House, Nymet Tracey, Crediton, Devon EX17 6DB. Tel: 01363 82571.
Admission: £3.50 adults; children free. **Times**: Sat: 10am - 5pm. Sun: 10am - 5pm.

8 Nov
WEYMOUTH NOVEMBER CELEBRATIONS
Weymouth Beach, Dorset.
Fireworks display.
Things to see: Major fireworks display and giant beach bonfire. Plus fairground and attractions.
Contact: Mr H G Bailey, Leisure & Entertainments General Manager, Pavilion Complex, The Esplanade, Weymouth, Dorset. Tel: 01305 772444.
Admission: Free. Contact the Weymouth Tourist Information Centre. **Times**: Contact the Weymouth Tourist Information Centre for event update and programme on 01305 785747.

13-15 Nov
FOUR SEASONS CRAFTS SHOW
Thorpe Park, Nr Chertsey, Surrey.
Craft fair.
Things to see: Quality crafts created by experts from all over the country. Dickensian theme.
Contact: Four Seasons (Events Ltd), 23A Brockenhurst Rd, South Ascot, Berkshire SL5 9DJ. Tel: 01344 874787.
Admission: £2.50-£3.50 adults; £2-£2.50 OAPs; £1 children. **Times**: TBA.

13-15 Nov*
MURPHY'S MEETING
Cheltenham Racecourse, Gloucestershire.
Top horse race meeting.
Things to see: Three days of top quality horse racing. The excitement of horse racing at the highest level, plus 60 trade stands, displays of hounds, birds of prey and terrier racing.
Contact: E W Gillespie, Cheltenham Racecourse, Prestbury Park, Cheltenham, Gloucestershire. Tel: 01242 513014.
Admission: £5 - £20. **Times**: 11am - 5pm.

14 Nov
PANGBOURNE SCULLS REGATTA
Beale Park, Lower Basildon, Reading, Berkshire.
Rowing Regatta.
Things to see: The UK's largest sculls regatta in the busy rowing calendar. Unbeatable views with informal atmosphere.
Contact: Beale Park, The Child-Beale Trust, Lower Basildon, Reading, Berkshire RG8 9NH. Tel: 0118 984 5172.
Admission: £2.50 adults; £1.50 children. **Times**: 10am - 5pm.

14 Nov
LORD MAYOR'S SHOW
From Guildhall to the Royal Courts of Justice, City of London.
Inaugural procession for London's new Lord Mayor.
Things to see: Colourful procession for London's new Lord Mayor through the streets of the City of London, with bands, floats and military parade. A spectacular aerial display of fireworks will be fired from a barge moored on the Thames. Route maps are available from mid-September from the City of London Information Centre, tel: 0171-332 1456. Arrive early for best vantage points.
Contact: Public Relations Office, Guildhall, London EC2P 5EJ. Tel: 0171-332 3099.
Admission: N/A **Times**: Procession starts approx 11am. Fireworks at 5pm.

16 Nov
WESTON SUPER MARE NOVEMBER CARNIVAL
Town Centre, Weston Super Mare, Somerset.
Illuminated carnival.
Things to see: Large illuminated carnival procession with approximately 100 floats and tableaux, costumes, etc.
Contact: Mr T Churton, 16 Ebdon Road, Worle, Weston Super Mare, Somerset BS22 9NA. Tel: 01934 510621.
Admission: Street collection. **Times**: 7.30pm - 10pm.

18 Nov
CHRISTMAS ILLUMINATIONS: "THE BIG SWITCH-ON"
Guildhall Square, Derry, N.Ireland.
Switch-on of the city's illuminations.
Things to see: Colourful Christmas illuminations, cartoon characters and celebrity guests, and arrival of Santa.
Contact: Nuala McGee, Festivals Officer, Recreation & Leisure Department, Council Offices, 98 Strand Road, Derry BT48 7NN Tel: 01504 365151 ext 6668.
Admission: Free. **Times**: Warm-up 7pm, switch-on at 7.30pm, fun continues to 9pm.

20-22 Nov
FOUR SEASONS CRAFTS SHOW
Transport Research Laboratory, Crowthorne, Berkshire.
Craft fair.
Things to see: Quality crafts created by experts from all over the country. Dickensian theme.
Contact: Four Seasons (Events Ltd), 23A Brockenhurst Rd, South Ascot, Berkshire SL5 9DJ. Tel: 01344 874787.
Admission: £2.50-£3.50 adults; £2-£2.50 OAPs; £1 children. **Times**: TBA.

21 Nov
AINTREE BECHER CHASE MEETING
Aintree Racecourse, Liverpool.
Major horse race meeting.
Things to see: Top level horse racing, including a race over the "National" fences.
Contact: The Racecourse Manager, Aintree Racecourse, Aintree, Liverpool L9 5AS. Tel: 0151-523 2600.
Admission: From £10. **Times**: Contact the racecourse.

Dates can change, events can be cancelled – Please check with the organisers before setting out!

21-22 Nov
NORTH WEST BIRD FAIR
The Wildfowl & Wetlands Trust, Martin Mere.
Special weekend for ornithologists.
Things to see: One of Britains biggest wildlife spectacles with hundreds of wild swans and thousands of geese from Iceland and Russia. Plus stalls and exhibits including bird holidays, books, telescopes, outdoor clothing and bird care products. Floodlit swan feeds at 3pm and 5pm each day.
Contact: Mrs E Beesley, Martin Mere, The Wildfowl & Wetlands Trust, Burscough, Ormskirk, Lancs L40 0TA. Tel: 01704 895181.
Admission: £4.50 adults; £3.50 OAPs; £2.75 children. Concessions for groups. **Times**: TBA.

22-23 Nov
NATIONAL PRIMESTOCK SHOW & SALE
Bingley Hall, County Showground, Stafford.
Specialist livestock event.
Things to see: Supreme champion cattle, sheep and carcasses having won one of the Top National Primestock shows. All under cover with special photographic area and special shopping section for ladies.
Contact: The Secretary, County Showground, Stafford ST18 0BD. Tel: 01785 258060.
Admission: Sun: £2.50. Mon: £4. **Times**: 9am - 6pm.

22-25 Nov
NETWORK Q RAC RALLY
Sections in England and Wales.
International motor rally.
Things to see: Britain's largest annual sporting event. High speed motor action mainly on gravel forest roads. Last round of the FIA World Rally Championship.
Contact: Colin Wilson, RAC Motor Sports Association, Motor Sports House, Riverside Park, Colnbrook, Slough, Berkshire SL3 0HG. Tel: 01753 681736.
Admission: Varies from location to location. **Times**: Starts from Cheltenham 7.25am, Sunday 23 Nov.

Dates can change, events can be cancelled –
Please check with the organisers before setting out!

27-29 Nov
FOUR SEASONS CRAFTS SHOW
The Fairfield, Kingston-upon-Thames, Surrey.
Craft fair.
Things to see: Quality crafts created by experts from all over the country. Dickensian theme.
Contact: Four Seasons (Events Ltd), 23A Brockenhurst Rd, South Ascot, Berkshire SL5 9DJ. Tel: 01344 874787.
Admission: £2.50-£3.50 adults; £2-£2.50 OAPs; £1 children. **Times**: TBA.

28 Nov
DEVON COUNTY ANTIQUES FAIR
Matford Centre in the Exeter Livestock Centre, Matford Park Rd, Marsh Barton, Exeter, Devon.
Antiques fair.
Things to see: Beautiful antiques and collectables among the many items on offer. 430 stands in all.
Contact: Val Dennis, Devon Counties Antiques Fairs, The Glebe House, Nymet Tracey, Crediton, Devon EX17 6DB. Tel: 01363 82571.
Admission: £2 adults; children free. **Times**: 10am - 5pm.

28-29 Nov*
VICTORIAN CHRISTMAS
Southend High Street, Essex.
Victorian Christmas.
Things to see: Dickensian market, carol singers, jugglers, jesters, Victorian costumed characters and much more.
Contact: Lisa Tidder, Special Events, Southend Borough Council, PO Box 6,

Southend-on-Sea SS2 6ER. Tel: 01702 215166.
Admission: N/A. **Times**: 11am - 4pm.

29-Nov-2 Dec
ROYAL SMITHFIELD SHOW
Earls Court Exhibition Centre, Warwick Rd, London SW5.
UK's premier farming business event.
Things to see: Farm machinery, cattle, sheep and a separate meat carcase exhibition.
Contact: P&O Events Ltd, Earls Court Exhibition Centre, Warwick Rd, London SW5 9TA. Tel: 0171-370 8226.
Admission: TBA. **Times**: 9am - 6pm.

December

3 Dec*
TRAFALGAR SQUARE CHRISTMAS TREE
Trafalgar Square, London.
Opening ceremony for the Trafalgar Square tree.
Things to see: The opening ceremony with the tree and carol singers at night, with the spectacular illuminated backdrop of the National Gallery and St Martin-in-the-Fields. Carol singing every evening up to Christmas Eve. Tree remains in place until 6 January.
Contact: Luella Barker, Department for Culture, Media & Sport, 3rd Floor, 2-4 Cockspur Street, London SW1Y 5DH. Tel: 0171-211 6393.
Admission: N/A. **Times**: Carol singing, 4pm - 10pm.

4 Dec*
RICHMOND VICTORIAN SHOPPING EVENING
Richmond, Surrey.
Annual Victorian themed event with stores open till 9.30pm.
Things to see: Carriage procession led by "Queen Victoria", "The Duke of Wellington" and civic dignitaries. Street entertainment, buskers, carol singers, charity stalls, mulled wine, mince pies, "best costumed visitors" competition etc. "Snow" is forecast!
Contact: Mrs Liz Carran, 5 Old Palace Terrace, The Green, Richmond, Surrey TW9 1NB. Further information from Richmond Chamber of Commerce. Tel: 0181-332 7722
Admission: Free. **Times**: 7.30pm carriage parade. Shops open until 9.30pm.

4-5 Dec
WINMAU WORLD MASTERS DARTS CHAMPIONSHIP
Paragon Hotel, Lillie Road, Earls Court, London SW6.
International darts championship.
Things to see: The world's top darts players, darts action, presentations, etc. 35 nations participate.
Contact: Olly Croft, British Darts Organisation, 2 Pages Lane, Muswell Hill, London N10 1PS. Tel: 0181-883 5544. Fax: 0181-883 0109.
Admission: Approx £8.50 to cover both days. **Times**: 4th: 12 noon - 9pm, 5th: 10.30am - 3pm.

4-9 Dec*
CLOTHES SHOW LIVE
NEC, Birmingham.
Fashion and beauty show.
Things to see: Fashion shows, makeovers, celebrities, beauty and hair demonstrations, etc.
Contact: H Steel, Barker Brown Ltd, 1st Floor, 32-36 Great Portland Street, London W1N 5AD. Tel: 0171-637 3313.
Admission: TBA. **Times**: Fri, Sat, Sun: 9am - 6.30pm. Mon - Wed: 9am - 6.30pm.

5-6 Dec
KIRKBY LONSDALE FATHER CHRISTMAS WEEKEND
Town centre, Kirkby Lonsdale, Cumbria.
Christmas event.
Things to see: Arrival of Father Christmas in a horse-drawn carriage, waving his wand to switch on the Christmas lights, then handing out presents to children (Saturday 5 Dec). Other activities on Sunday 6 Dec.

Contact: Tourist Information Centre, 24 Main Street, Kirkby Lonsdale, Cumbria.
Admission: N/A. **Times**: From 12pm onwards.

5-6 Dec
DICKENSIAN CHRISTMAS
High Street, Rochester.
Theme Christmas.
Things to see: The High Street undergoes a transformation to the Victorian era for the weekend, and provides an excellent opportunity to see Dickens characters come to life.
Contact: Visitor Information Centre, 95 High Street, Rochester, Kent. Tel: 01634 843666.
Admission: N/A **Times**: 10am - 6.30pm approx.

6 Dec
ENGINE MUSEUM OPEN DAY
Prickwillow Engine Museum, Main Street, Prickwillow, Nr Ely, Cambridgeshire. Special Christmas museum Open Day.
Things to see: Old drainage engines running, plus many other attractions. **Contact**: Joan Stacey, Prickwillow Engine Trust, Main Street, Prickwillow, Nr Ely, Cambridegshire CB7 4UN. Tel: 01353 688360.
Admission: £3 adults; £1.50 children; £2 OAPs; £7 family. **Times:** Engines run: 12 noon - 4pm; Museum open 11am - 4pm.

12 Dec
DEVON COUNTY ANTIQUES FAIR
Salisbury Leisure Centre, The Butts, Hulse Road, Salisbury, Wiltshire.
Antiques fair.
Things to see: Beautiful antiques and collectables among the many items on offer. 140 stands in one hall.
Contact: Val Dennis, Devon Counties Antiques Fairs, The Glebe House, Nymet Tracey, Crediton, Devon EX17 6DB. Tel: 01363 82571.
Admission: £1.50 adults; children free. **Times**: 10am - 5pm.

12-13 Dec
VICTORIAN CHRISTMAS
Weavers' Triangle Visitor Centre, 85 Manchester Road, Burnley, Lancs.
Recreation of Victorian Christmas.
Things to see: Traditional decorations, seasonal refreshments, music and Father Christmas (probably arriving by boat).
Contact: The Curator, Weavers' Triangle Visitor Centre, 85 Manchester Road, Burnley, Lancs BB11 1JZ. Tel: 01282 452403.
Admission: Free. **Times**: 2pm - 4pm.

17-21 Dec
OLYMPIA INTERNATIONAL SHOW JUMPING CHAMPIONSHIPS
Grand Hall, Olympia, London.
Showjumping with other events.
Things to see: The top indoor show jumping event with leading riders from the UK and around the world. Plus traditional family favourites such as the Shetland Pony Grand National, Dog Agility Stakes and other fun events, all culminating in a Christmas Finale. Also many trade stands.

Contact: Laura Heard. Tel: 0171-370 8206.
Admission: TBA. **Times**: Matinee performances at 1pm and performances end at 4.30pm. Evening performances begin at 7pm and end at 10.45pm. Doors open at 5.45pm for evening performances. Morning events also take place on certain days.

25 Dec
CHRISTMAS DAY BOY'S & MEN'S BA'
Streets of Kirkwall, Orkney.
Traditional street football.
Things to see: A centuries-old game of mass street football played between the Up-the-Gates (Uppies) and Down-the-Gates (Doonies). Goals are the site of an old castle and the waters of the harbour. Upwards of 200 men take part and each side attempts to take the ba' (ball) to its own goal. The ba' can be carried, kicked or smuggled – there are no rules and games can last for hours.
Contact: J D M Robertson, Shore Street, Kirkwall, Orkney. Tel: 01856 872961.
Admission: N/A **Times**: Boy's ba' 10.30am; Men's ba' 1pm.

26 Dec
KING GEORGE VI TRIPLEPRINT CHASE
Kempton Park Racecourse, Sunbury-on-Thames, Middlesex.
Major steeplechase meeting.
Things to see: Top class steeplechase and hurdle racing that attracts the best steeplechasers in the country as well as some of the best that France and Ireland have to offer. Plus the chance to see all the most famous faces of the racing industry.
Contact: Racing Department, Sandown Park Racecourse, Esher, Surrey KT10 9AJ. Tel: 01372 470047.
Admission: £25 members enclosure; £15 grandstand; £7 silver ring. **Times**: 12.45pm - 3.30pm approx.

26 Dec
TRADITIONAL MUMMERS PLAY & MORRIS DANCING
Stocks Hill, Moulton, Northampton.
Traditional entertainment.
Things to see: Traditional dance and drama involving morris and sword dancing, and a mummers play.
Contact: Barry Care, 8 Chater St, Moulton, Northampton. Tel: 01604 646818.
Admission: Free. **Times**: 11am - 12 noon.

26-27 Dec
BOXING DAY SPECIALS
Midland Railway Centre, Ripley, Derbyshire.
Christmas steam train event.
Things to see: Steam trains with plenty of winter steam effects, Santa's grotto and presents for the children, plus the museum, country park and animal park.
Contact: Alan Calladine, Midland Railway Centre, Butterley Station, Ripley, Derbyshire. Tel: 01773 747674.
Admission: TBA. **Times**: 11.15am - 3.40pm.

29 Dec-1 Jan
EDINBURGH HOGMANAY CELEBRATIONS
Various venues, Edinburgh.
Hogmanay festival.
Things to see: A festival of light and fire in the mid-winter with numerous events, both ticketed and free: Torchlight Procession, carnival, live music, Kids Hogmanay, fireworks, ceilidhs, classical concerts, sports events and much more, including the spectacular Street Party on the night of the 31 Dec.
Contact: Tourist Information Centre, 3 Princes Street, Edinburgh. Tel: 0131-557 1700.
Admission: Various. **Times**: Various.

31 Dec
BIGGAR NE'ERDAY BONFIRE
Main Street, Biggar, Lanarkshire.
Druid bonfire ritual.
Things to see: An ancient Druid custom

of lighting fires to encourage the sun to rise back up into the sky and bring back the long daylight hours. A torchlight procession followed by a huge bonfire which is lit in the middle of the town.
Contact: David Aitken, 24 Edinburgh Road, Biggar, Lanarkshire ML12 6AX. Tel: 01899 220661.
Admission: N/A. **Times**: Starts 9pm.

31 Dec
FLAMBEAUX PROCESSION
Drummond Street, Comrie, Perthshire.
Traditional torchlight procession.
Things to see: Torchlight procession "to ward off the evil spirits", with pipe band and fancy dress.
Contact: Crieff Tourist Information Centre, Town Hall, High Street, Crieff, Perthshire PH7 3HU. Tel: 01764 652578.
Admission: Free. **Times**: 11.30pm - 1am approx.

31 Dec
INVERNESS HIGHLAND HOGMANAY
Town Centre, Inverness.
Hogmanay festival.
Things to see: The "reel" Highland Hogmanay Street Party. Piping, traditional & celtic rock music combined with a firework crescendo. Pubs, hotels & restaurants joining in with music, food and drink. Family events, street entertainment over the new year period.
Contact: Jon Hogan, Events and Promotions Officer, Highland Council, Town House, Inverness IV1 1JJ. Tel: 01463 724262.
Admission: Free. **Times**: TBA.

31 Dec
NOS GALAN ROAD RACES
Mountain Ash, Rhondda Cynon Taff.
Traditional running event and ceremonies.
Things to see: Children's fancy dress fun run, men's and women's 5km races. Plus the appearance of celebrity "Mystery Runner" at St Gwynno's churchyard and Beacon in Mountain Ash. Presentation ceremonies and spectacular fireworks display finale.
Contact: Andrew Wilson, Rhondda Cynon Taff County Borough Council, The Town Hall, Mountain Ash CF45 4EU. Tel: 01443 472461.
Admission: N/A. **Times**: Races start at approximately 5.30pm.

Regional Index

Check this index for events of the year in your area. To find the full listing for any event, first consult the main Index on page 167

Channel Islands

Cumbria

East Anglia
Including Cambridgeshire, Essex, Norfolk & Suffolk

East Midlands
Including Derbyshire, Leicestershire, Lincolnshire, Northamptonshire & Nottinghamshire

Heart Of England
Including Gloucestershire, Herefordshire , Shropshire, Staffordshire, Warwickshire, West Midlands, Worcestershire & the Cotswolds

Sewing For Pleasure Show
Sheriff's Ride
Shrewsbury Carnival & Show
Shrewsbury Flower Show
Shropshire & West Midlands Show
Shrove Tuesday Football Game
Shrovetide Fair & Pancake Race
Staffordshire County Show
Stationary Engine Rally
Tetbury Woolsack Day
Three Counties Show
UK Masters
Vintage Sports Car Club Hillclimb
Walsall Illuminations
Wenlock Olympian Games
Yonex All England Open Badminton

Isle of Man

Easter Festival of Sport & Drama
International Football Festival
Isle of Man Open Darts Championships
Manx Grand Prix
Manx International Cycling Week
Manx International Car Rally
Manx National Rally
Peel Sports Festival
Southern 100 Motorcycle Races
TT Festival Fortnight

London & Middlesex

Alternative Fashion Week
Annual Grimaldi Service
Autumn Equinox Ceremony
Beating Retreat - The Massed Bands of the Household Division
Benson & Hedges Cup Final
Benson & Hedges Masters
Caravan & Outdoor Leisure Show
Charles I Commemoration
Chelsea Flower Show
Chinese New Year Celebrations
City of London Flower Show
Covent Garden May Fayre & Puppet Festival
Daily Mail Ideal Home Exhibition
Enfield Steam & Country Fair
England Versus South Africa
England Versus Sri Lanka
England Versus Wales
England Versus Ireland
FA Umbro Trophy
Four Seasons Crafts Show
Great British Beer Festival
Great Spitalfields Pancake Race
Hampton Court Palace International Flower Show
Head of the River Race
Historic Commercial Vehicle Society London To Brighton Run
Horse of the Year Show
Hyde Park Horsemen's Sunday
Independent Travellers World
International Ballroom Dance Championships
International Women's Day Show
Latin American Fiesta Da Cultura
London Classic Motor Show
London Harness Horse Parade
London International Boat Show
London International Mime Festival
London Marathon
London Parade
London To Brighton Bike Ride
London To Brighton Classic Car Run
Lord Mayor's Show
Middlesex County Show
Middlesex Seven-a-Side Finals
Midsummer Poetry Festival
Move It - Mime Festival
Nat West Trophy
Notting Hill Carnival
Olympia International Showjumping
Open Dance Festival
Oxford & Cambridge Boat Race
Paddington Performance Festival
Pearly Harvest Festival
Punch & Judy Open Air Festival
Putney Town Regatta
Road Racing & Superbike Show
Royal Gun Salutes
Royal Smithfield Show
Royal Tournament
Sea Cadet Corps Trafalgar Day Parade
Shakespeare in Spitalfields
Spitalfields Community Festival
Spitalfields Dog Show
Spitalfields Show
Spring Equinox Ceremony
Tetley Bitter Cup Final
Trafalgar Square Christmas Tree
Triangular Tournament Final
Trooping The Colour - The Colonel's Review
Trooping The Colour - The Major General's Review

The North
Including Cleveland, Co Durham, Northumberland & Tyne & Wear

The North West
Including Cheshire, Merseyside, Lancashire & Greater Manchester

Northern Ireland

The South
Including Hampshire, Dorset & the Isle of Wight

Royal Victoria Firework Extravaganza
Rushmoor Bonfire & Firework Spectacular
South of England Town Crier's Championship
Southampton Balloon & Flower Festival
Southampton International Boat Show
Spring Autojumble & Classic Car Show
Tank Museum Battle Day
Tolpuddle Rally
Tweseldown Club Point-to-Point Steeplechases
Ventnor Carnival Procession
Vintage Motorcycle Rally
Weymouth Carnival Day
Weymouth November Celebrations
Weymouth International Beach Kite Festival
Weymouth Oyster Festival

The South East
Including East Sussex, Kent, Surrey & West Sussex

Amberley Veteran Cycle Day
Annual Philippine Festival
Archery at Hever Castle
Arlington Grove Show
Arundel Festival
Arundel Festival Fringe
Autumn Countryside Celebration
Autumn Vintage Gathering
Battle Medieval Fair & Festival of Food
Bexley Show
Biggin Hill International Air Fair
Blantyre Park Show
Boat Jumble
Bognor Birdman - The Original
Brighton International Festival
British Nations Cup & Grand Prix
Broadstairs Dickens Festival
Bromley Pageant of Motoring
Caronjoy Horse Show
Cartier International Polo
Classic Car & Country Show
Cobweb Run
Sea Shanty Festival
Dickens Festival
Dickensian Christmas
Direct Line Insurance International Tennis Championships
Easter Weekend at Hever Castle
Egham Royal Show
Embassy World Professional Darts Championships
Enfield Festival of the Countryside
Epsom Summer Meeting
Eridge Horse Trials
Festival of Dover
Festival of English Food & Wine
Festival of Transport
Four Seasons Craft Show
Gardeners' Weekend
Glorious Goodwood
Half Term Fun For Children
Hastings Half Marathon
Hastings Traditional 'Jack In The Green'
Heavy Horse Day
Holiday on Ice
Jousting at Hever Castle
Kent County Show
King George VI Tripleprint Chase
Leeds Castle Balloon & Vintage Car Fiesta
Leeds Castle Celebration of Easter
Leeds Castle Grand Firework Spectacular
Lewes Bonfire Celebrations
Littlehampton Regatta
London to Brighton Bike Ride
London to Brighton Classic Car Run
London to Southend Classic Car Run
Historic Commercial Vehicle Society London To Brighton Run
Mad Hatter's Tea Party
Mallard Royle Horse & Pony Show
May Day Music & Dance
Merrie England Weekend
Model Railway Exhibition
New Year's Day Treasure Trail
Norman Rochester
Old Ship Royal Escape Race
Open Air Concerts at Leeds Castle
Parham Steam Rally & Family Show
Patchwork & Quilting Exhibition
Penshurst Place Classic Motor Show
Pioneer Motorcycle Run
RAC Veteran Car Run
Ramsgate Victorian Street Fair
Richmond May Fair
Richmond Victorian Shopping Evening
Road Bike Show
Rochester Sweeps Festival
Roman Festival For Schools
Sedan Chair Race
Shepway Airshow
South East Garden Festival
South of England Horse Trials
Steam Special & Victorian Fair
Summer Heavy Horse Spectacular
Surrey County Show

Beale Model Boat Trade Show
Benson & Hedges Celebrity Pro-Am
Benson & Hedges International Open
Blenheim International Horse Trials
Braemore House Classic Car Show
British Craft Show
British Rhythmic Gymnastics
Bucks County Show
Burford Dragon Procession
Chiltern Riding Club Show
Chilterns Craft Show
Combe Mill in Steam
De Havilland Moth Club Fly In
Eagle Horse Show
Easter Lambs
Easter Steamings
Festival of Gardening at Midsummer
Four Seasons Crafts Show
Fun & Fireworks Party
Henley Royal Regatta
Herts County Show
Hocktide at Hungerford
Hurley Regatta
Knebworth Classic Car Show
Leighton Buzzard Railway Autumn
Steam Up
Leighton Buzzard Railway Model Mania
Leighton Buzzard Railway
Teddy Bears' Outing
Loddon Valley Lions Firework Fiesta
Luton Carnival
Luton Festival of Transport
Luton Hoo Classic Car Show
Luton Junior Tennis Tournament
Luton Show
Marlow Amateur Regatta
Medieval Craft Show
Newbury Garden & Leisure Show
Newbury & Royal County
of Berkshire Show
Newbury Steam Funtasia
Old Berks Hunt Point-to-Point
Oxford University Point-to-Point
Oxonian Cycling Club Cyclo Cross Races
Pangbourne Sculls Regatta
Photographers' Evenings
Reading Half Marathon
River Thames Flower Show
Royal Ascot
Royal Windsor Horse Show
Spring Holiday Steamdays
Steam Threshing
Taplow Horse Show
Thame Show
Thomas the Tank Engine
Wargrave & Shiplake Regatta
Woodcote Rally

Wales

Anglesey County Show
Barmouth to Fort William Three Peaks
Yacht Race
British Open Championship
British Landyacht Championship Series
Caldicot Carnival
Capel Bangor Agricultural Show
Cardigan Bay Regatta
Chepstow Castle 1648
Denbigh Flower Show
Hay Festival
Ian Rush International Soccer Tournament
Leukaemia Research Fund Vintage
Car Rally
Llandrindod Wells Victorian Festival
Llangollen International Music
Eisteddfod
Man Versus Horse Versus Bike Marathon
Mid Wales Festival of Transport
Monmouth Conservative Association
Annual Charity Raft Race
National Championship Series
Nos Galan Road Races
Royal Welsh Show
United Counties Show
Usk Show
Wales Versus Scotland
Wales Versus France
Welsh Festival of Dressage
Welsh NSPCC It's A Knockout
Championships
Welsh National Sheepdog Trials
World Bog Snorkelling Championships

The West Country
Including Cornwall, Devon, Somerset, Wiltshire & the Isles of Scilly

Adventure Sports Special
American Independence Day Displays
American Indian Weekend
Atlantic Alone
Avocet Cruises
Badminton Horse Trials
Bath Annual Spring Flower Show
Bicton Horse Trials
Bridgwater Guy Fawkes Carnival
Bristol Balloon Fiesta Nightglow

Yorkshire & Humberside

National Basketball Cup Finals
Nidderdale Show
Nostell Priory Country Fair
Otley Show
Rainbow Craft Fair
Ripley Show
Sowerby Bridge Rushbearing Festival
Spring Plant Fair
Teddy Bears' Picnic
Three Peaks Race
Vintage Weekend In Hebden Bridge
Wensleydale Show
West Indian Carnival
Whitby Folk Week
World Coal Carrying Championship
York City Council Busking Festival

Index